ONLINE INNOVATION
PRACTICAL METHODS, TECHNIQUES AND TOOLS TO KICK-START YOU 100% ONLINE

BIS Publishers
Borneostraat 80-A
1094 CP Amsterdam
The Netherlands
T +31 (0)20 515 02 30
bis@bispublishers.com
www.bispublishers.com

ISBN 978 90 6369 621 4

ONLINE INNOVATION

PRACTICAL METHODS, TECHNIQUES AND TOOLS TO KICK-START YOU 100% ONLINE

GIJS VAN WULFEN

BIS PUBLISHERS

CONTENTS

ONLINE INNOVATION

If you would have asked me at the beginning of 2020 whether you could effectively innovate 100% online, I would have said, 'NO WAY'! And now I know I was so wrong. Yes, you can innovate your organisation 100% online. You can devise new products, services, experiences, processes, and business models without any doubt. Since 2020 we, and many others with us, have proven this in practice.

Of course, it was quite a struggle to bring our FORTH innovation methodology 100% online, after its being employed as a 'best practice' for initiating innovation offline for 15 years. We made all the beginner mistakes ourselves. We copied the methodology one-on-one from offline to online with eight-hour workshops a day, which was utterly boring. We experimented with online tools, which in those days, could not handle 25 people brain dumping their ideas simultaneously on the digital collaboration board. Everyone's screen froze, and we had to break away from the online brainstorm. And most of us were untrained in handling those online tools, so each time, the plenary session had to be stopped to explain again 'how to vote', for example, on the digital collaboration board. We had a steep learning curve and managed to work out an inspiring online process for the FORTH innovation method, which delivers great results when working remotely.

For almost all organisations, the transition to remote work in 2020 and 2021 was a restrictive work-from-home one that they hadn't been planning to do. They didn't have the communication or collaboration policies, the online tools, nor a working-online culture in place. All at a time when innovation was needed more than ever to deal with completely new market circumstances. As we saw people struggle, making the common mistakes we did too, we decided to write this practical book to guide people to become great online innovators.

ONLINE INNOVATION inspires you with effective online collaboration tools, techniques, methods, and rules to kick-start yourself to innovate your work and your organisation completely online. That's why this is a practical 'HOW-INNOVATE-ONLINE' book. After describing ten common pitfalls, we share some great tools and techniques that work in practice. We discuss the 'Achilles' heel' of innovating online and present you ten methodologies you can use for online innovation in a hands-on way. The Lightning Decision Jam, the Design Sprint, and the FORTH innovation method will be highlighted, and we work out a hybrid version of this methodology. At the end of the book, you find a systematic description of twenty-five tools and ten methods to get a clear overview at a glance to help you pick the right ones for your online innovation journey.

We hope that this book is a support for you as a consultant, coach, facilitator, manager, or student in the field of design (thinking) and innovation. We are sure that innovating online is here to stay. We see a huge increase in hybrid innovation projects, combining offline and online workshops – using all the online advantages while being personally engaged offline.

Next, there are a few people I'd like to thank specifically: my excellent online-skilled co-authors Maria Vittoria Colucci, Andrew Constable, Florian Hameister, and Rody Vonk, without whom I could never have published this book; designer Frederik de Wal for co-creating another book with me in a wonderful style; text editor John Loughlin; and publisher Bionda Dias for her support making ONLINE INNOVATION a reality.

Let's innovate online!

Gijs van Wulfen

CONTENTS

CHAPTER 1

ONLINE INNOVATION IS MORE RELEVANT THAN EVER

New communication – collaborative tools have changed the way we think about working remotely. More and more organisations now embrace working from home, or from anywhere, and have facilitated their employees doing so. For some people, it has even become a lifestyle. They have become digital working nomads, living their dream. They work in coffee shops or co-working spaces where they rely on their wireless internet devices to do their work whenever they want. With the onset of the Covid-19 pandemic at the end of January, 2020, working remotely from home became a necessity for all instead of a nice option for few.

THE RISE OF WORKING ONLINE

For almost all organisations, the transition to remote work in 2020 was a restrictive one that they hadn't been planning to do. So, most employees were not ready for it. They didn't have the communication, the collaboration policies, or the tools. And a lot of organisations had neither a culture-of-working-online in place.

It was one big improvisation when countries went into lockdown in spring 2020. Companies started to adapt in record time to become productive in their new work-online reality. And some of them found their teams and businesses benefiting so much from the new remote setup that they started to consider remote work as an opportunity in a growing digital economy. Before the Covid-19 pandemic, it was predicted that by 2025, an estimated 70% of the workforce would be working remotely at least five days a month[1]. That percentage will probably be much higher as organisations embrace working online.

A great example is Facebook. As you can read here, Mark Zuckerberg wants Facebook to be the most forward-leaning company on remote work at their scale in ten years.

CHART: WE ARE GOING TO BE THE MOST FORWARD-LEANING COMPANY IN REMOTE WORK.

Facebook CEO Mark Zuckerberg said on May 21st, 2020, that the social media giant will start allowing many of its 50,000 employees and recruits to work from home permanently, adding to a small but growing number of tech companies that have embraced decentralized work during the coronavirus pandemic.

'We are going to be the most forward-leaning company on remote work at our scale, with a thoughtful and responsible plan for how to do this,' Zuckerberg said in an interview. 'We're going to do it in a measured way over time.'

Within the next five to ten years, Zuckerberg anticipates that about 50% of Facebook's workforce will work remotely. That would mean a significant shift in the concentration of personnel that could radically alter how the company operates, as well as have an impact on the San Francisco Bay Area. That process will start with 'aggressively opening up remote hiring' – first in the United States, then elsewhere – beyond the urban hubs where Facebook has offices. 'It doesn't seem that good to constrain hiring to people who live around offices,' Zuckerberg said.

Facebook will also let existing employees apply to work remotely. Those who have demonstrated good

performance and can work remotely may then be allowed to do so permanently. Facebook has already told the vast majority of staff that they can work from home through the end of this year.

Source: https://www.nbcnews.com/tech/tech-news/mark-zuckerberg-half-facebook-may-work-remotely-2030-n1212081

THE MINDSET OF PEOPLE ON WORKING ONLINE CHANGED

Working online has been seen by some people as advantageous over commuting to the office every day. A report from 2019 among 2,500 remote workers reveals the most significant benefits remote workers see in working online[2]. Having a flexible schedule and being able to work from any location are by far the main benefits.

Another study surveyed more than 4,000 people working remotely during the pandemic to determine what they think of working at home[3]. It reveals that both productivity and the work-life balance improved during the pandemic: '**Fifty-one per cent of survey respondents indicate that they have been more productive working from home during Covid-19**, and 95% of respondents say productivity has been higher or the same while working remotely. And though there are many reasons why performance has improved (despite the stresses of the pandemic), some of the **top reasons respondents gave for their increased productivity include**:

- ▶ Fewer interruptions (68%).
- ▶ More focused time (63%).
- ▶ Quieter work environment (68%).
- ▶ More comfortable workplace (66%).
- ▶ Avoiding office politics (55%).

According to the researchers, 'this improved productivity may help explain why **61% of workers review remote work more positively** and why 50% also say their employer views remote work favourably now. However, 37% of respondents said that they miss "nothing" about the office, and only 4% would prefer to return to the traditional office full-time.'

Isn't that amazing. Only 4% prefer the traditional office full-time. People's mindset changed, as you can also conclude from the quotes of other research presented here by Remoters. net[4]. What about you? Did you change your mindset on working remotely during the pandemic?

CHART: HOW DO EMPLOYEES EXPERIENCE THE SWITCH TO REMOTE WORK?

Keith, E-commerce and SEO specialist, says:
'Overall, the switch to remote work has been fantastic for me. The freedom has been great. The biggest challenge for me is more pandemic related. I need to grab lunch or a coffee with a friend once in a while. That was the only uniquely positive aspect of being in an office.'

David Iwanow, Search and Traffic Lead at Danone, says:
'Went from one to two days a week remote to 5 days a week remote.... I haven't been into the office in ten months but have found my productivity has improved as I'm able to focus on bigger projects [and am] less distracted. The reduced time lost to travel to/from work has allowed more family time with discussions with my manager post-Covid [sic] it will return to one to two days a week in the office, but that might be April/May based on current infection numbers and vaccine rollout plans.'

Reji Yates, Founder at B-DigitalUK, says:
'The switch was good. Obviously, I had to work out a set-up for me to work properly but so far, amazing. It definitely has changed my remote working perception! I think it's brilliant now. I would only consider remote working now ... I absolutely will keep it after Covid.'

Areej AbuAli, Founder Tech SEO Women and In-House SEO Manager, says:
'It was better than expected. I hired, on-boarded, and trained team members fully remotely, and it worked really well. On a personal basis, it's given me so much *time* back and helped me save lots of money.'

Chris Green, Head of Marketing Innovation at Footprint Digital, says:
'The switch was relatively easy. We already worked 100% on the cloud and had Slack & Meet. When went from WFH lite to full-remote overnight. Nine-plus months later, I'm missing an office setup. Wherever you are, don't underestimate the importance of being comfortable when working.'

Source: https://remoters.net/remote-work-trends-future-insights/

Of course, it's not all good news. Despite a booming favourable mindset on working remotely, people still struggle with some aspects of it. When asked, 'What's your biggest struggle with working remotely?' to 2,500 remote workers, they said that unplugging after work, loneliness, and collaborating and/or communication were their biggest dislikes about working online.

THE MINDSET OF COMPANIES ON WORKING ONLINE CHANGED TOO

There has been much debate among organisations about working from home and whether or not it's a productivity boost or productivity drain. Study after study into remote work has made clear that remote workers are more productive than their office-bound counterparts. A nearly two-year study in 2015 by Stanford professor Nicholas Bloom at Ctrip, China's largest travel agency with 16,000 employees, showed an amazing productivity boost among the remote workers equivalent to a full day's work[5]. There were several reasons for this productivity boost. First, they were not late for the office. Second, they were not leaving early multiple times a week. And third, they found working remotely less distracting and were able to concentrate more easily at home.

We experienced that asynchronous communication was an essential factor in team productivity when we did our first experiments bringing the proven FORTH innovation method[6] 100% online. The offline synchronous way of working with lots of meetings with many people makes it difficult to make meaningful progress because you are tied up in meetings all the time with everyone together. Working online asynchronously has the great advantage that you can work on something 24/7 on moments you chose yourself while not being distracted.

Not only did the mindset of employees, or independent professionals like us, change concerning working remotely. No, also the mindset of employers and their CEOs altered positively. Have a look at the eight quotes of CEOs from a PwC survey of 669 CEOs worldwide during the summer of 2020 that show how they drastically changed their mindset on working remotely, resulting in great enthusiasm[7].

'We have changed the ways we work, from styles we thought were inviolate to radically different structures and processes. This is supported through the greater use of digital and technological solutions and adopting a more flexible and trusting mentality.'
Engineering and construction CEO, UK.

'The pandemic has radically improved customer and employee interest in, and adoption of, digital tools.'
Communications CEO, US.

'The organisation has had to pivot very quickly to working digitally, and we fully intend to build on that to transform how we work in the future.'
Technology CEO, UK.

'People are moving towards business process digitisation and becoming comfortable with online payments and online transactions. There is a great opportunity for companies and governments to take advantage of digitisation.'
Technology CEO, Sri Lanka.

'The new normal of being able to conduct trade without travelling, without personal meetings, and to engage with stakeholders just as effectively has opened a new avenue for massive cost reductions and higher productivity. The need to strengthen the supply chain locally and be self-dependent is also an opportunity to differentiate.'
— Consumer goods CEO, India.

'Working remotely has forced us to embrace technology. That technology has taught us that we can be as efficient as, and in some cases more efficient than, before and has provided us with the opportunity to consider [adding] team members who may not be local to our business.'
Asset and wealth management CEO, Canada.

'We will spend less time and effort in travelling and introduce dual pricing. Pricing based on remote delivery is a better value for customers and gives staff a better quality of life. We will honour city salaries and allow people to work from wherever they want. The in-person presence will only be required on an infrequent basis.'
Business services CEO, Ireland.

'Trust in our employees is at an all-time high. Working from home will become the norm, not the exception, and now we trust our employees to perform without constant supervision.'
Oil and gas CEO, Canada.

Source: https://www.pwc.com/gx/en/ceo-agenda/ceo-panel-survey-emerge-stronger.pdf.

REMOTE COLLABORATION IS HERE TO STAY

The same PwC survey of 669 CEOs shows that 78% agree that remote collaboration will remain[8]. This is confirmed by a Gartner survey of company leaders (also summer 2020) in which 80% of the CEOs plan to allow employees to work remotely at least part of the time after the pandemic, and 47% will enable employees to work from home full-time[9].

As both employees and companies are optimistic about working remotely, there's only one conclusion possible: remote collaboration is here to stay.

MORE ONLINE TOOLS ARE AVAILABLE AND THEY ARE GETTING BETTER

The present remote working mega boost would not have been possible without the rapid development of information and communication technologies that have changed our methods of communicating and sharing information. Traditional departments and teams now frequently give way to virtual teams, working intensely with online working tools. These new digital tools have made interactions between geographically dispersed people so much easier.

Collaboration is an essential ingredient for creating. This applies to any discipline of professionals ranging from engineers, to marketers, designers, artists, researchers, and developers. Whether you're working in your office, studio, or home, you need efficient and effective online tools for discovering new insights, sharing ideas, testing them, and transforming concepts in reality. More and more online tools spring up every year while existing ones continually improve their features and functionality.

There are now thousands of digital tools available to effectively work 100% online in teams. They vary from online collaboration platforms like Miro and Mural; video conferencing tools, like Zoom or Butter; tools for workshop preparation and instruction, among which are SessionLab or Loon; tools for prototyping and testing, like Marvel, and Toonly; and tools to make your online workshops more interactive, like Mentimeter and Tscheck.in. In Appendix 1 you find 25 online tools to innovate remotely.

As you know so well, Zoom is a video conferencing platform that allows people to meet face-to-face virtually. Originally it was meant for enterprises and universities. Now Zoom connects everybody. Zoom is a big story in the technology world, with over *300 million daily meeting participants connecting during the pandemic.*

Zoom was founded by Eric Yuan. He is a former corporate vice president for Cisco Webex. He had a vision from his college days that technology would one day allow mobile, easy-to-use video calls for people to stay connected. And this became his obsession.

He left Cisco in April, 2011. And he took with him 40 engineers to start his new company. In September, 2012, Zoom launched a beta version that could host conferences with up to 15 video participants. And after two years of Beta testing and fixing issues, the Zoom videoconferencing platform was launched in January 2013.

Zoom grew very fast. It reached a million users within a few months of its launch, ten million in a year and 40 million by February, 2015. In 2017, four years after the platform's launch, Zoom was valued at $1 billion, making it what is called a 'unicorn' company. The fast growth, ease of use, and Zoom's reliability were contributing to this significant achievement.

Why did Zoom become a success among users? Traditionally, video conferencing platforms were mainly targeted at the business-to-business market and very expensive. Zoom offered customers a 3-in-1 package of video conferencing, mobility, and web meetings all for $9.99. Zoom was also the first platform that offered mobile screen sharing within video conferences. Zoom even gave users free 40-minute meetings for up to 100 people! That offer is how we often start using it. And a great asset of the platform is that it also works with slow, saturated internet.

During the pandemic, Zoom boomed with *more than 300 million daily meeting participants*. It was the perfect product for meeting virtually with co-workers, classmates, friends, and loved ones during a pandemic. People needed a platform to reach out to each other, and there was one that stood out: Zoom.

Also, we professional online innovation facilitators love Zoom. Without a great videoconferencing platform, our online innovation projects would be impossible, and this book would have never been written. The killer feature for us is the break out rooms for collaboration in smaller teams.

Sources: https://www.forbes.com/sites/jonmarkman/2020/10/26/zoom-enters-perilous-new-growth-phase/?sh=36022c75e1e0, https://en.wikipedia.org/wiki/Zoom_Video_Communications, https://www.theaugust.com/featured/zoom-sucess-story-eric-yuan-immigrant-billionaire/

THE PANDEMIC HAS A HUGE IMPACT ON THE WORLD ECONOMY

The IMF estimated that the global economy shrunk by 4.4% in 2020[10]. This makes the great lockdown the worst recession since the great depression of 1930 and far worse than the global financial crisis of 2009. The Covid-19 pandemic caused a crisis like no other with a significant impact on people's lives, livelihoods, and the economic perspective for companies and organisations.

The pandemic created a clear distinction between economic winners and losers, as you can see here[11]. We will pick out a few sectors to give you some examples. The housing market was hot in 2020, as people were looking for larger spaces for at-home work and schooling. As we all were at home, the video game industry boomed, too, because it allowed players to pass the time alone while still interacting with their friends. Gaming consoles were sold out, and gaming platforms like Facebook Gaming and Twitch experienced record growth. Amazon and other online retailers worldwide were among the biggest winners because people got very cautious about leaving their homes. The big technology companies are also amongst the winners, like Apple, Alphabet, Amazon, Microsoft, Netflix, and Zoom, since staying at home caused us to connect 100% online. We all needed hardware as digital services. Online creators benefitted, too, as views on digital platforms like YouTube accelerated as we stayed home watching videos on meditation, cooking, and working out.

There are a lot of losers, too, unfortunately. Going on vacation wasn't an option anymore during the pandemic, making the travel and hospitality market collapse. When video conference calls are working just fine for so many of us in business, the question is if business travel will ever recover. Shopping malls and non-food retailers also got in big trouble; many had

Winners and Losers of the Covid-19 pandemic	
Winners	Losers
Housing	Travel and hospitality
Cannabis	Oil
Solar	Banks
Bitcoin	Airlines
Videogames	Malls
Big Retail	Automakers
Big Tech	Manufacturing
Creators	Movie Theatres
Streaming	

Source: https://edition.cnn.com/2020/12/30/business/winners-losers-2020-business/index.html

to close as people turned massively to online shopping. Aircraft manufacturers like Boeing and Airbus were hit by the downturn in air travel as their customers delayed or cancelled aircraft purchases. Airports had a dramatic year because global air passenger traffic dropped by 60% in 2020[12]. And UNESCO reports that 'In the film industry, it is estimated that ten million jobs will be lost in 2020, while one-third of art galleries are estimated to have reduced their staff by half during the crisis. A six-month closure could cost the music industry more than $10 billion in lost sponsorships, while the global publishing market is expected to shrink by 7.5% due to the crisis caused by the pandemic[13].'

Both from a personal and a business perspective, the world was turned upside down during the pandemic. After the initial crisis management, the question became how people, organisations, and companies might create a great future again.

RESILIENCE AND INNOVATION ARE MORE RELEVANT THAN EVER NOW

Resilience is the ability to recover quickly from difficulties. That's the mantra today for many organisations and companies: be resilient to play to win again. They will need to rethink and innovate with great scrutiny in order to create a successful future, because doing more of the same with fewer people often is not an option. Operational excellence, doing better things, or doing the same things in a better way won't help businesses like airports, hotels, theatres, cruise companies, or high street retailers, will it? In this worldwide digitalisation, boom innovation is now more relevant than ever for all organisations. Do you have to re-invent your business too?

Before moving on, let's clarify what we mean by innovation, since the term has been defined in so many ways over the past several decades. In our view,

'An innovation is a feasible valuable offering, such as a product, service, process, or experience with a viable business model that is perceived as new and is adopted by customers.'

Let me exemplify the keywords in this definition:

Feasible. Feasibility is a precondition for a new product, service, process, or experience to be launched. If it's not feasible, it's just a dream. Although dreams are a great source of inspiration, they will not provide continuity to your organisation.

Valuable. Your customers have to change their present behaviour. They will only adopt your innovation when it brings value to them. Most often, it's a solution for a customer pain point. In other cases, your innovation might even be fulfilling a long-cherished wish. It has to be relevant to them. The other perspective here is that your innovation should have value for your organisation. It might be financial, like generating additional revenues and EBITDA (earnings before interest and taxes). It might also be strategical by being a way to step into a new market or target a new customer group. Innovation has to add significant value for you and your customers; otherwise, it's not worth the effort, right?

Offering. We like to see innovation in broader terms than mere product innovation. That's why we use the word 'offering', which was coined by Larry Keeley in his book *Ten Types of Innovation*. An offering can be any form of a product, service, process, or experience. As early as 1934, the famous economist Schumpeter proposed a broad definition of innovation as he distinguished among new products, new methods of production, new markets, new supply sources, and new ways of organizing enterprises[14].

Viable Business Model. Every organisation needs to secure its future, especially now. That's why innovation should provide a viable business model which contributes to the goals of the organisation. This applies to companies, non-profit organisations, and even governmental organisations.

Perceived as new. Innovation comes from the Latin word *innovat*, which means to renew or alter. The combination of *in* and *novare* suggests 'to come up with something entirely new.'[15] The question is...new for whom? New for you? New for your company? New for your market? New for the world? These days, everybody tends to label everything as 'NEW'. In our view, it's only new when the customer perceives a product, service, process, or experience as new.

Adopted. Innovation is only successful when adopted by customers, users, clients, or whatever you may call them. Adoption distinguishes the tops from the flops and is one of the biggest challenges for every innovator. So, add clear value so it will be adopted!

PICKING THE RIGHT MOMENT TO INNOVATE: NOW

Not innovating is no longer an option for an organisation that wants to be in good shape after the Covid-19 pandemic.

In practice, we see organisations approach innovation in two different ways: those who want to innovate and those who need to innovate. We call those who want to innovate the active innovators and the ones who need to innovate the passive innovators. As you can see in the chart, their roles are defined by the moments they innovate their business. Every company, business unit, or product has its lifecycle of introduction, growth, maturity, and decline. Active innovators who want to innovate give innovation priority at the end of the growth stage. Before they reach maturity, they want to innovate, often for several reasons simultaneously:

- ▸ To keep their revenue stream growing
- ▸ To maintain an innovative mindset
- ▸ To boost internal entrepreneurship (intrapreneurship)
- ▸ To address changing needs and wants of customers
- ▸ To lead in technology
- ▸ To expand their business by new business models, distribution channels, and customer groups
- ▸ To stay an attractive employer on the market for talent
- ▸ To anticipate new governmental regulations or market liberalization

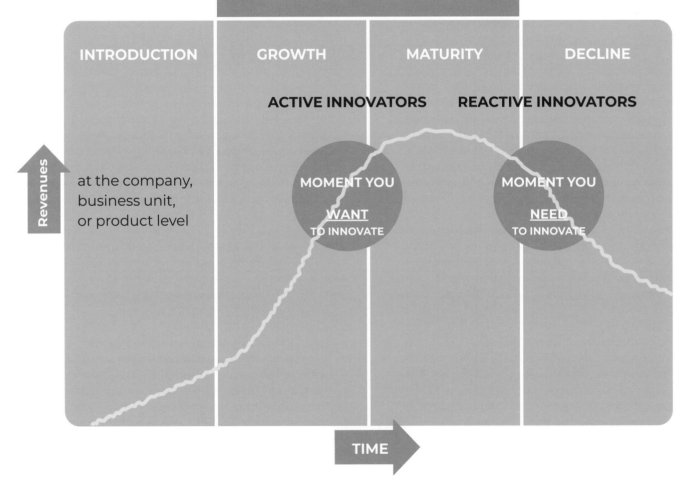

TWO INNOVATION SWEET SPOTS

INTRODUCTION	GROWTH	MATURITY	DECLINE

ACTIVE INNOVATORS

REACTIVE INNOVATORS

at the company,
business unit,
or product level

Revenues

MOMENT YOU

WANT

TO INNOVATE

MOMENT YOU

NEED

TO INNOVATE

TIME

Reactive innovators, on the contrary, wait. They wait until they get hit by a crisis, their markets saturate or get disrupted by new technologies and/or business models. The Covid-19 pandemic crisis hit all of us overnight. It required an immediate response to save companies from going under. They reorganized their work, went digital, and laid-off people in the short term. Reactive innovators need to prioritise innovation to stop revenues and profits from falling and to build a new future for their organisation.

Both types of innovators have their challenges. The good news for active innovators is that there are plenty of resources available when the company is doing well. Their challenge is to cope with a lack of urgency at the operational level of the organisation: 'Why should we innovate? We're damn busy and doing great!' We guess that most of the winners in the pandemic crisis belong to this category. The primary goal of ZOOM was to handle their growth; though of course, being in tech, they cannot neglect to stay innovative at all times.

The good news for the reactive innovators is that there is currently a great urgency at the operational level of the organisation to solve problems, because there have often been collective layoffs due to the business slow-down or even business-stop. Their challenge is compounded by both a lack of resources and a lack of time, since they will have to move quickly with significant impact.

Are you an active innovator or a reactive one? And what about your organisation? The central question is not if you should innovate. It's HOW you can start and lead innovation the best way. That's why we have written this book because the Covid-19 pandemic has also drastically changed the way we can innovate and has created new digital opportunities, which we will explore with you.

INNOVATING 100% ONLINE INSTEAD OF OFFLINE

One day in March, 2020, overnight, all our offline workshops helping organisations innovate their portfolios were cancelled and postponed until further notice. For us, doing nothing was also not an option. We, as innovators, had to innovate, too. And that's precisely what we did. We are all facilitators of the FORTH innovation methodology, a framework that has been used worldwide to jumpstart innovation for nearly two decades (www.forth-innovation.com). FORTH is a scientifically proven method to ideate new products, services, processes, experiences, and business models. It combines business thinking and design thinking. Based on a structured roadmap, appealing new concepts are developed, worked out in business cases, and ultimately accepted by all involved in five steps. An in-person FORTH innovation journey contains 15 workshops with a multidisciplinary team of 10 to 15 people in 15 weeks.

We digitalised our innovation methodology in April and May 2020, experimenting ourselves with different online communication practices and collaboration platforms in collaboration with 25 innovation facilitators from all over the world. And we made all the beginner's mistakes ourselves, which we describe in the next chapter. We had a steep learning curve, even though – as it is for so many experts – we had a considerable knowledge base. We still remember so well how, when we were all online for our brainstorming session, ready to share all our out-side-the-box ideas with 20 or more people, suddenly Mural stopped functioning correctly, which was the unexpected end of our session at what should have been the most creative moment of our online journey. It was all learning by doing. Since then, we experimented 100% online with a lot of innovation methods, techniques, and tools and our major discovery is that online innovation works a little differently than offline innovation. The devil is in the details, as they say.

Based on our practical experience, we guide you on your online innovation journey in this book. We share practical information on the best online innovation tools in chapter 3, 10 online innovation techniques in chapter 4, 10 rules for innovation in chapter 6 and 10 online innovation methods in chapters 7-10. In chapter 5 will present the Achilles heel of working online and share tips on how to compensate for this.

In chapter 11, we share with you our vision on hybrid innovation and discuss the best of both worlds. In the two appendices at the end, you will find overviews of 25 online tools for innovation and 10 innovation methods summarised in two pages each. Before we go into the details, let's define online innovation first, and discuss why we should consider starting innovation online anyway.

SEVEN ARGUMENTS TO START INNOVATING ONLINE

Online innovation is an innovation process that is facilitated 100% online. It has become relevant for when you have to work remotely, as during Covid-19 restrictions. To facilitate workshops 100% online to innovate is the only option. Organising offline workshops during a pandemic runs the risk of being postponed...and postponed.... An online innovation process, during which everybody works from home or frankly anywhere, is not vulnerable to these risks and is a certain to proceed toward the progress you need for your organisation or your client.

Besides this obvious reason, we experienced in our online work at least seven other arguments for why you should consider starting to use online methods, techniques, and tools to innovate.

1. **EASY TO APPLY.** When you work together with others from all over the country, continent, or even across the world, innovating 100% online is an easy way to create together.

2. **SAVING TIME AND MONEY.** Working online saves everyone both travel time and costs as people can stay home or anywhere else with a good internet connection.

3. **ALWAYS OPEN, 24/7.** Online innovation gives you the advantage of working asynchronously, which means that everyone can work online at their preferred moment, as the online workshop collaboration boards are open 24/7.

4. **EVERYONE GETS A FAIR CHANCE.** When you innovate online in a structured way with, for example, the together-alone technique or silent voting procedures, introverts have an equal chance to co-create valuable content both with influencing opinions and decisions as do extroverts.

5. **EASY TO SHARE.** Sharing inspiration and information in digital formats like videos, jpegs, or documents during innovation projects is very easy on online whiteboard collaboration platforms like Miro, Mural, or Trello.

6. **YOU BENEFIT AS AN EMPLOYER.** The freedom offered to employees to work wherever they want with flexible hours is an excellent motivation for people who can't stand regular office life. A new generation is growing up as digital nomads.

7. **IT WORKS.** Argument one through six would be worthless if innovating online wasn't effective. But it is; our practice delineates this. We put the proven offline FORTH innovation method online. After some initial growing pains, it proved to be as effective as offline workshops in most aspects, which we will cover later.

Ultimately, the mindset of people and the organisation about working online changed, and the tools to work remote got better. And now, you too can innovate online very effectively. So, innovate online and take advantage of these seven benefits.

In the next chapter, we will start with ten common mistakes when starting innovation online (which we also made ourselves). Let's innovate 100% ONLINE!

[1] https://www.vox.com/recode/2019/10/9/20885699/remote-work-from-anywhere-change-coworking-office-real-estate.
[2] https://buffer.com/state-of-remote-work-2019
[3] https://www.flexjobs.com/blog/post/survey-productivity-balance-improve-during-pandemic-remote-work/
[4] https://remoters.net/remote-work-trends-future-insights/
[5] (https://www.inc.com/scott-mautz/a-2-year-stanford-study-shows-astonishing-productivity-boost-of-working-from-home.html
[6] https://www.forth-innovation.com/
[7] https://www.pwc.com/gx/en/ceo-agenda/ceo-panel-survey-emerge-stronger.pdf
[8] https://www.pwc.com/gx/en/ceo-agenda/ceo-panel-survey-emerge-stronger.pdf
[9] https://www.hrdive.com/news/gartner-over-80-of-company-leaders-plan-to-permit-remote-work-after-pande/581744/
[10] https://www.businesstoday.in/current/world/covid-19-pandemic-hamstrung-global-economy-in-2020-imf-estimates-44-contraction/story/426598.html
[11] https://edition.cnn.com/2020/12/30/business/winners-losers-2020-business/index.html
[12] https://www.aviation24.be/airlines/global-air-passenger-traffic-to-drop-by-60-to-1-8-billion-in-2020/
[13] https://en.unesco.org/news/covid-19-hits-culture-sector-even-harder-expected-warns-unesco
[14] Dave Richards, *The Sevens Sins of Innovation*, Palgrave Macmillan, London, 2014, p.14.
[15] Max McKeown, *The Innovation Book*, Pearson, Harlow, United Kingdom, 2014, p. xxix.

KEY MESSAGES FROM THIS CHAPTER

▸ **Sparked by the pandemic, a shift from offline to online happened worldwide.**

▸ **The mindset of people and organisation on working online changed.**

▸ **Online tools for collaboration and communication improved user experience.**

▸ **Resilience and innovation are more relevant than ever now.**

▸ **Online innovation has different dynamics to offline.**

▸ **Innovating online gives you seven advantages.**

CONTENTS

CHAPTER 2

TEN COMMON PITFALLS WHEN STARTING INNOVATION ONLINE

Running an online workshop or project can be challenging. A useful workshop is highly collaborative with well thought-out processes and a set of tools that aid this process. Online workshops require various techniques to help the transfer of in-person sessions to the online world. But moving your sessions online can come with pitfalls, which, unless mitigated, will ruin your session and hinder the development of an organisation's innovation culture.

As this book discusses, we have to ensure that we are prepared for such pitfalls and do not become ensnared in those that have ruined many a good innovation project. Here we'll explore the challenges of running online workshops that you should consider when planning and delivering your online innovation sessions.

The pitfalls cover many facets of online work, from ensuring the innovation team participants know how to use the workshop tools, managing the technical considerations, and managing the rules of engagement within the online session. These points have been taken from our own experience of running hundreds of workshops with clients online. We aim to make these short points actionable to develop an online innovation culture in your organisation.

We will start with the most critical consideration of having a bad internet connection. Without an internet connection, your workshop will not launch, and the rest of the points are useless.

PITFALL 1
BAD INTERNET LIMITS PARTICIPATION

We all know the importance of a good and reliable internet connection. It plays a vital role in all our activities in online workshops. Every electronic device uses an internet connection – from computers to mobile phones. As long as the internet connection is reliable, so may we be. However, a bad internet connection can affect your productivity and cause you to experience many unwanted problems.

A regular and constant high-speed internet connection is required if you want to run and attend online workshops comfortably. There are two types of connections that you can choose: Wired and Wireless. Although both of them guarantee an uninterrupted and speedy transfer of data, I would recommend using a wired connection wherever possible. For example, a wireless connection can be thought of like radio waves, which drop up and down between devices. These drop-off points can cause your connection to drop out, leading to problems using Zoom and Miro tools. Therefore, always try to physically connect your PC/Mac to the router to help with your connection. This leads us to bandwidth.

Low bandwidth means slow and unpredictable uploads and downloads that might bring a delay in the video or audio stream. An adequate bandwidth means uninterrupted service and allows the user to connect to multiple participants simultaneously. There are many ways to reduce the bandwidth constraints during your session. First, stop the camera feed when you are not speaking or engaging in the session. Video is a significant draw on your connection's bandwidth resources, and although not ideal, we should stop the video connection.

Second, when you aren't talking, mute your audio connection; audio also uses valuable resources that may hinder your workshop. If you find that your connection falters, a simple trick is to switch off the audio and use a dial-in connection such as a conference call to communicate via telephone. Although this could be classed as not ideal, it is a vital backup device to use should low bandwidth affect your connection.

And third, close all applications when running your session. Other applications use memory and processing power, which affects how your system engages with your workshop tools. Always only have open the tools required for your workshop to allow a more reliable experience for all.

We experienced these bandwidth problems first-hand when we ran workshops at the start of the Covid-19 pandemic. They created problems with the workshop's in-person experience. We had to reschedule an extra workshop session, which complicated the project timelines and led to many headaches. Therefore, we recommend that you always be prepared to adjust how you run sessions and the tools you use to mitigate the use of poor internet connections.

This leads us to the next pitfall for a facilitator, relying 100% on tools that may not work all the time.

PITFALL 2
RELYING 100% ON TOOLS THAT
MAY NOT WORK ALL THE TIME

We have all been there: you start a workshop, and something happens to your video conferencing tool or your digital whiteboard stops working. So, what do you do if this happens?

Most facilitators understand the importance of having a backup plan when online tools fail. But what few people realise is that if you are not prepared to use another solution, your customers will have no choice but to go elsewhere for their needs. Many people make the mistake of assuming they can 'workaround' problems that arise by 'preparation'.

The truth is, if you rely 100% on a single set of tools, you will find one day that your preparation is not sufficient, and your customers have other options to meet their aims. However, if you had taken the time to prepare and learn additional tools, then you can turn the situation around and ensure that the online workshop runs seamlessly.

When you fail to have a backup plan in place, you are putting your session and innovation project at risk. No matter how big or small the problem is, if you do not take the time to back up and prepare for the failures that can arise, you are setting yourself up for failure.

Some examples of good practices are:

Video conferencing
Although we have named Zoom as our preferred choice, you, as a good facilitator, should be aware of other solutions to meet your workshop needs. Google Meet allows innovation project team members and customers to chat over video and text. As it is integrated into Google, this becomes a seamless task and can be used across different platforms. Other platforms that you might consider are Butter, through which you can apply techniques outlined in this book to engage, facilitate, and chat with your workshop participants.

Digital whiteboards
Our two preferred choices for digital whiteboards are Miro and Mural. Both have some great features and should be

utilised when running an online session. One pro-tip is to ensure that you have digital whiteboards set up in both platforms to allow you to switch between them seamlessly should a problem arise. As we will discuss in the tools section, each has positives and negatives, and which platform you choose should match the client's objectives and requirements for the workshop.

As Benjamin Franklin said, failure to prepare is preparing to fail[2], so ensure that you are skilled across the different platforms required when running online workshops. A workshop must aid the creative process by equipping the participants with the tools that meet the requirements. These include requirements such as effective communication, ways to display ideas, and ways to visualise insights. So, as we have discussed, ensure that you can cover these areas using a multi-tool approach to get your workshops off to the best start and prepare for the worst that can happen in your sessions.

PITFALL 3
TRYING TO COPY IN-PERSON TO ONLINE

Several practitioners have attempted to move in-person workshops to the online format in a cookie-cutter approach. This includes aspects such as the length of the sessions and an assumption that all participants are comfortable in their new environment and ask questions if they are stuck during the process.

First, we recommend that we should keep online sessions to below three or four hours per session. Sitting in front of a screen is exhausting, and it can be tough to stay focused for anything longer than this. These sessions should include breaks and areas for conversations that are not part of the formal process. Another pro-tip is to use the natural break-points in your workshop to split the sessions up and continue either later in the day or carry these over to another session.

When working in an in-person workshop, there are opportunities throughout the day to chat and to connect with your fellow participants. The informal conversations help build rapport and help generate a more inclusive environment, making people more engaged and comfortable at voicing their opinions during the workshop. But a common mistake we have seen assumes that this will happen in an online session, which is a significant pitfall to overcome. As facilitators, we need to create these moments proactively to promote sharing ideas with strangers in the session. So, before we start the formal workshop, it's essential to get everyone comfortable and start working as a team.

One way to do this is to create a virtual watercooler, where the participants can hang out and get to know each other and connect outside the session. These online watercoolers help the team to get comfortable communicating across digital channels when they haven't met before. It also allows team members to understand each other's expertise and fit into the workshop's upcoming process.

Holding these sessions before a workshop can help you as the facilitator to identify different communication styles and conflicts which can be mitigated before the session to allow for a more productive session. A virtual watercooler can be a specific place (like Slack, Wonder, or even a break out room in Zoom). We have successfully run a weekly virtual coffee shop format in previous innovation projects promoting this practice. As long as it connects your team and familiarises them with one another before meetings happen, it will help lay the foundation for successful online sessions.

Finally, remember that in an in-person meeting, you can read body language, so ensure that when you are facilitating a session, you review each participant's cameras to ensure that they understand the process and do not need any help. You should also explain the exercises using precise language to mitigate the lack of body language and build a common understanding.

PITFALL 4
PARTICIPANTS DON'T KNOW
HOW TO USE THE TOOLS

An important element of ensuring a productive online workshop is that participants understand how to use the tools and understand what the process will look like once the session starts.

We always suggest that this should be part of the onboarding session with the participants to ensure that they have both the technical capacity to use the tools and that the tools are set up correctly. As a facilitator, you do not want to find out on the first morning of the workshop that the participants are unsure of how to use a certain tool or were not expecting elements within the process[1].

We always give the participants a tour of the digital whiteboards and use the video conferencing software that we will use in our sessions to allow them to get used to basic functions such as using break out rooms, muting and unmuting, and sharing their screen, etc. When giving the participants a whiteboard tour, let them play around on it by asking them to complete a small exercise you've designed. This could be something simple: filling in post-it notes of their details, enumerating their aims of the workshop, or finding an image that reflects how they are feeling. Getting them to use the whiteboard is much better than you as a facilitator giving a presentation because they will learn more quickly by actually being active. The most important aspect is that they learn how to navigate the workspace, so keep what you show them to a minimum and be sure not to confuse them with advanced options[1].

You need to ask the participants to check that their communication tools are set up correctly and if their webcams and microphones are working properly. This can unearth issues such as user privileges stopping them from accessing these functions. If this is the case, they should consult with their IT team in advance of the workshop, and as a facilitator, you should follow up to ensure the problem has been resolved.

An important thing to remember is that it's likely that the team may not have participated in an online innovation session before. Therefore, it is good practice before you facilitate the workshop to run them through the innovation process and tools you will be using in each element. This will allow them to become more familiar with the tools, the process, and how they fit together.

You want to portray that that workshop is not an online meeting, but that it will be fun, collaborative, and challenging for all involved. Stating this can sometimes change the participants' mindset before the session because they understand what to expect and that they need to be ready to contribute. If you ensure that you onboard the participants in this manner, you will find that the workshop is a lot smoother, exercises will be faster, and you can keep the sessions shorter.

PITFALL 5
YOU DON'T HAVE THE RIGHT SETUP

Numerous tools can be used to run an online workshop. The digital space can be confusing to participants, so you will need to ensure participants are prepared as discussed above. If you are running the session, I would strongly suggest that you invest in two screens because this helps to ensure that you can see the digital boards and all the participants. We use one screen for the board and the other for the participants. This allows you to read the room better, check if someone looks confused or distracted, or is having technical problems. We would also suggest getting a timer since you will need this to keep the time of the exercises in the workshop to ensure you can fit everything planned.

As we suggest in this book, you can use specific tools for different types of actions that you wish to apply. When running an innovation project, we would suggest the following tools[1].

Digital whiteboard
The whiteboard will become the session's focal point, so we need to ensure we take the time to prepare this for the workshop. You can create ad hoc, beautiful templates, but if you are new to running a workshop, you should use one of the templates we discuss in this book.

If you do create your own board, we recommend that you create a separate frame for each exercise and for each part of the workshop to aid the participants' visual appearance and understanding. Not only does this allow you to structure your workshop clearly, but it also allows the participants to feel a sense of accomplishment as they move through the frames.

Digital whiteboards, like Miro, include several important features that you will likely find useful in your workshops when brainstorming ideas, for example voting for preferred options and grouping post-it notes to see patterns. They are the workshop's heart and soul, so you want to spend time ensuring your board is right for your workshop.

Video conferencing
If you are running the sessions, you want to see all the session participants allow you quickly to recognise any issues that might interfere in the session. As discussed, we would use one screen for this feature and another for the whiteboard. Zoom is a great choice of video conferencing software and is freely available, although it's important to state that for running workshops, you would need to upgrade your licence to premium due to the 40-minute limit per session. You can use other tools such as Google Meet, which is free, although they do not have certain facilities, such as break out rooms, that can help your sessions.

Overall, investing in these tools will be beneficial to you and your sessions, and we strongly advise that this is something that you pursue.

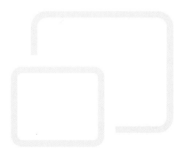

PITFALL 6
NO CLEAR RULES OF ENGAGEMENT

Sparked by the Covid-19 pandemic, organisations face growing pressure to maximise productivity by using online workshops to develop innovation.

Many companies are experimenting with various online workshops, which are becoming standard. Yet, many companies are practising online workshops without applying the correct engagement rules or applying the etiquette required to manage a successful innovation workshop.

The etiquette factors can be viewed from two different angles. First, as a facilitator, you should always ensure that you have a set agenda for the workshop and that the participants have been fully prepared for the session. This will stop questions at the start of the session, leading to delays that will affect the timing of your workshop. The facilitator should also state what is expected of each person in the session. This is important because it will set the tone for the workshop and everyone will understand how to complete certain tasks.

An example of this would be arriving on time for the meeting and committing to the session. This means that participants do not multi-task or drop the session for another meeting. Multi-tasking is a big problem with online workshops because everyone is remote and can view other screens on their PC with a click of a mouse. A pro-tip is that if you see the screen flicker on the participant's screen, they will be multi-tasking and it's advisable to bring them back into the session by asking how they are getting on.

An online meeting should follow the same engagement and etiquette as an in-person session. In an in-person session, you wouldn't be answering emails, replying to calls, or checking the internet, so ensure that the participants adhere to the rules. All cameras should be on unless there are issues with the internet, in which case it is then fine to switch off to reduce the bandwidth, and all microphones should be on mute until they wish to speak. This will stop unwanted background noise from polluting the workshop environment.

There are no official rules for online meeting etiquette, just a set of general guidelines. If someone is non-professional, the facilitator should pick up on this and address it one-to-one. If you find that the lack of etiquette doesn't improve, you may need to speak to the project leader or sponsor to address it and remove the person from the session.

The last thing to mention in online meeting etiquette is courtesy. You must maintain a good attitude during business meetings, no matter who is involved. You want to be polite and friendly, but you also need to be professional. By holding workshops using this online etiquette guide, you can have a successful meeting and stay out of trouble.

PITFALL 7
BEING UNAWARE OF THE
TOOLS AVAILABLE

The importance of being aware of the tools available for online innovation workshops is one of the most important things you can do to help stay ahead of the curve, bring new ideas, and make the sessions more enjoyable. You may know lots of different methods and techniques for in-person workshops, but how do you find the best tools for your needs in the future? Well, you have made a great start buying this book. As you explore the chapters, you will be introduced to these tools and what they can be used for. You have probably read many books or articles on online innovation and become familiar with some of the well-known tools such as Zoom, Miro, and others, so why should you know more?

So why should we be aware of the available tools?
If you are reading this book, we would suggest you are an innovator, and this goes to the heart of why you should look into other tools. Innovation involves continually looking at your toolkit, processes, and procedures to see what improvements can be made to keep you, your organisation, and your clients ahead of the game. Innovative businesses often have strong management and well-trained and motivated employees. These businesses maintain a culture of innovation, continually looking at every aspect of the practice – not just its products and services – and asking the question, 'How can it be done better?' Innovation can come in the form of small changes to your existing workshops or form a completely new type of workshop, such as moving in-person to online. The innovation idea may come from internal sources such as a product development team or be inspired by external forces such as customer requests or developments in related technologies.

Some tips for becoming aware of the available tools

Become an investigator
First, you should always try to find out as much as possible about any tool you are considering. Write down your main activities in the workshop and rate the tools on a scale of one to ten. If you find that you rank tools below five, try to understand why this is and write it down.

This reflective activity is one of the best practices that you should not overlook and is the core of becoming

a master of online innovation workshops. Once you understand why they may not be working for you, it will make sourcing the new tools much easier and targeted for your needs. This approach is similar to that of any good researcher; you need to understand 'why' you want to change the tool or try another tool before you can test what you have before you. You can then enter the keywords of what you are trying to achieve into a search engine of your choice and the relevant options will be displayed at the top.

Use the information available
Appendix 1 presents you a list of the top 25 online innovation tools for you to review, try, and identify what is new and improved in the market. Information is very cheap now; more and more sources publish their content online free of charge to allow you to make a more educated guess of what you require. Use channels such as Youtube, which is now the world's second-largest search engine, to watch introductions, how-tos, and other types of product videos, which will help you visually test the tool to make a more educated choice.

Use social media and peers
The third aspect of becoming aware of the tools is to engage with your peers via social media. All the main tools are presented on social channels and promote product updates and free webinars. Another aspect of social media that is important is to find peers in the innovation space that may have used the tools you are looking to use. You can easily find these people by asking a question online to start a conversation. This example of social proof is important to allow you to feel confident in your choice of tool.

Test the tools
since most tools offer a free option or trial, just download them and try them out. In our online innovation journey, we tried hundreds of tools to get this list down to the 25 that you will find in Appendix 1. So, go out and play with them, discuss them with your peers, and run informal sessions on them to see if they meet your needs. You wouldn't buy a car without test driving it, and the same should be said for any online tool. Just because one person says it is great doesn't mean it suits you, so test it.

Finally, being patient is essential and one of the best practices for learning and understanding new tools online. Treat learning each tool like a challenge. That way, you'll have a greater chance of remembering essential concepts, which will help you retain the critical aspects better in the long run.

Following these tips is an excellent way to make sure you get the most out of any online tool, and they will allow you to become aware of the different tools available. Using these best practices as a reference, you can avoid getting frustrated with learning online tools. This will help you run a better online workshop, become a better facilitator, and deliver better results for your business or yourself.

PITFALL 8
NO UNDERSTANDING OF
CULTURAL DIFFERENCES

Holding online workshops in different cultures is a challenge to many innovators and facilitators. The simple reason for this is that many practices and traditions vary across cultures. For instance, some people from one country may not want to show their face on the camera due to religious beliefs. Thus, it can be challenging to hold online workshops with people whose practices and traditions do not match, and we must plan for this.

Holding online workshops in different cultures can be challenging, but it can also be made much easier through careful planning and research. First of all, you need to identify the main differences between the cultures you are trying to accommodate. For instance, you need to determine if the workshop participants are reserved or outspoken, emotional or measured. There is an excellent book on this topic by Erin Meyer, a professor at INSEAD and The Culture Maps author[4]. She presents the differences clearly of what to be aware of when any facilitator or innovator works worldwide.

Also, think about the environment where the workshop takes place. Determine if the participants are at their best meeting virtually within their office or at home. Again, this can affect how they communicate in the session due to pressures to conform. Once you have determined these differences, create protocols and establish norms so that your colleagues understand how the workshop will run to stop any unwelcomed surprises during the sessions.

When there are several different cultures represented in the workshop environment and when you know the differences between these cultures, you also need to determine how these cultures can add to your workshop by bringing new viewpoints and perspectives that will aid the creative process.

The next thing you will want to consider is how formal or informal each person's business culture is. For instance, businesses with a very traditional culture tend to be more formal when it comes to business meetings and workshops.

Simultaneously, companies with a more informal culture are much less formal, so be aware of this . A word of caution: don't force the dynamic of the online workshop when working across cultures. For example, it can be disrespectful to challenge a publicly more senior manager or person in Japanese culture. In contrast, in particular Latin cultures, they tend to be much more forthcoming in feedback and public signs of disagreement. When you onboard participants into the workshop, try to understand these cultural elements and encourage people to provide feedback in different ways.

Another example of the cultural differences is obviated by the hand gestures[3] used during workshops. There are tools such as Zoom that allow participants to state they wish to speak and encourage this, although this may not always be used. For example, raising your hand to talk in western cultures is accepted, whereas, in certain middle eastern countries, this is disrespectful.

The last consideration to make is the level of trust that each party needs to work with others. Different cultures expect different levels of trust, but some participants will try to put everyone on the same level. This is good because everyone has similar goals and visions, and you can all work together towards achieving those goals. However, this doesn't always work out the way people would want to. Therefore, it takes time to build trust by not overlooking the importance of team bonding, which encourages colleagues to get to know each other outside the workshop so that cultural differences won't obscure collaboration.

PITFALL 9
NO CLEAR GOAL OR AGENDA
FOR THE SESSION

Having no clear goal of the workshop is a significant pitfall for both in-person and online workshops. Don't be distracted by the word 'goal'. By the time you finish this section, you will have learned how important it is to have a clearly defined goal for your online workshop. You may also know how important it is to stay focused on that goal and stay committed to the process so that you will end up somewhere. So, let's get started.

The first thing you want to do when setting up your online workshop is writing down your goals, your plans, and the steps you want to take to reach those goals. This will help you set up your workshop with an objective in mind. If you don't know what those specific project goals are, start discussing this with the project sponsor or decision-maker and don't run the online workshop until this has been decided. Once you understand the innovation project goals, make sure to include a clear and concise description of what you want to accomplish for your online workshop. Also, make sure it is your goal to focus on what others need to achieve in the session.

Setting up an online workshop is about starting with a clear goal in mind. It is about making a step-by-step action plan to get to where you want to go. Without a clearly defined goal statement, you might end up anywhere.

> *If you don't know where you are going, any road will get you there.*
> — *Lewis Carroll, Alice in Wonderland* [5]

That's why it's essential to have a clearly defined goal statement for your workshop. So, before you begin your workshop, read your goal statement to everyone involved.

If you already have goals for your online workshop, you must set the details. The first step is to sit down and write out your goals. Be clear about what you hope to achieve. Include your estimated time to reach each goal and what you wish to accomplish at the end of the workshop. Having your written goals helps you focus during the workshop for yourself and all participants involved.

You will be amazed at how much clarity you will experience when you follow through with your workshop's written goals. Once you have your goals, set an action plan to meet them. As you work towards meeting your workshop goals, you will end up where you want to be and have a much more productive session that benefits the project and the participants involved.

Last, ensure that you have a detailed agenda of the online session. Some tools, such as SessionLab, see Appendix 1, will help you structure your thoughts and timing. Ensure that your agenda covers what's going to happen, the learning outcomes you are trying to reach, their timing, and how to connect to the online workshop to ensure that everyone's time is used the most productively. Like any aspect of an online or in-person workshop, it's important to plan to build confidence in the process, enabling better buy-in for all involved during the process.

PITFALL 10
THE WRONG PEOPLE IN THE INNOVATION TEAM OR WORKSHOP

The best way to ensure that an innovative activity occurs is by inviting the right people into the workshop. It is essential to ask the right questions and have the right tools and methodologies to work with individuals to help them implement ideas properly. An online innovation workshop should be set up with a few specific goals to take action than to make improvements. To set actionable goals, it is important to consider the skills of each of the individuals invited and their areas of expertise. Who is invited to the workshop can depend on the type of innovation project or workshop you are running, but this will help you understand various areas to look out for .

When you are leading a workshop as an external facilitator, it is essential to know the organisation. The more information generated about the organisation, the more useful the information you can use in the workshop and overall project.

Once you know about the organisation, it is essential to know what type of innovators they are. While some workshop members may be promising innovators in one particular field, it does not mean that the entire group can be innovative. An excellent way to find out this type of information is to ask the decision-maker or project sponsor, or to meet various team members outside of the office. For example, someone who has a lot of technical experience and who is an excellent problem-solver might make a good team member, as long as everyone else in the team also has a good spread of knowledge and skills to contribute to the workshop.

You should invite other groups of participants from research and development, those who work in sales and marketing, and those who work in operations. Of course, all of these groups have different needs for the information that they present. It is essential to know who to invite to an innovation workshop based on these preferences.

Once you have identified the participants, you should ask to speak to them one-on-one to get to know them and brief them about the online workshops aims and the process that will be followed. If all goes well, you will find that your workshop has a diverse group with a set of skills and knowledge that can contribute to the overall process and meet the organisation's objectives.

Other people to consider inviting are

Someone who can see opportunities
Being able to remove the blinders and see beyond the obvious is vital. So, make sure that you consider this when building your team.

Someone who can draw
Innovation workshops include elements of a visual process. This is the same online as offline, and although not essential, it's good to have someone who can draw diagrams and concepts. This will help to communicate ideas, concepts, and prototypes as you go through the process of innovation.

Someone who challenges the status quo
As co-author Gijs Van Wulfen states, it is always good to invite the naysayers to the online workshops. Challenging the status quo is at the core of innovation; bringing someone into the session who will ask those awkward questions can promote much more enriching conversations.

Someone who is outside the organisation
Getting an outside perspective can help the company. An outsider will see the situation from a different perspective, be honest, and challenge conventional thinking.

Look at your strategic partners to find the right person and make sure you don't get someone who will agree with you to keep a good business relationship. It is very valuable to have partners who will be honest with you, even if what they have to say is not what you want to hear!

Of course, many factors go into an innovation team, and can depend on the methodology used. But by following the points made in this chapter, you will be in a much better position to start innovating online in the right direction.

In the next chapter, we will introduce you to the best online innovation tools: online collaboration platforms, video conferencing tools, tools for preparation and instruction, tools for prototyping and testing, and tools to make online workshops interactive.

[1] AJ & Smart. (2020). The Ultimate Guide to Remote Design Sprints. Retriever from https://ajsmart.com/remotedesignsprints
[2] https://www.businessinsider.com/7-must-read-life-lessons-from-benjamin-franklin-2011
[3] Bright Side. (2020). 15 Hand Gestures That Have Different Meanings Overseas
Retriever from https://brightside.me/wonder-places/15-hand-gestures-that-have-different-meanings-overseas-769110/
[4] https://erinmeyer.com/books/the-culture-map/
[5] https://www.goodreads.com/quotes/642816-if-you-don-t-know-where-you-are-going-any-road

KEY MESSAGES FROM THIS CHAPTER

▷ **Pitfall 1**   **Bad Internet, which limits the participants from taking part**

▷ **Pitfall 2**   **Relying 100% on tools that may not work all the time**

▷ **Pitfall 3**   **Trying to copy in-person methods Online**

▷ **Pitfall 4**   **Participants don't know how to use the tools**

▷ **Pitfall 5**   **You don't have the right setup**

▷ **Pitfall 6**   **No clear rules of engagement**

▷ **Pitfall 7**   **Being unaware of the tools available**

▷ **Pitfall 8**   **No understanding of cultural differences**

▷ **Pitfall 9**   **No clear goal or agenda for the session**

▷ **Pitfall 10**   **The wrong people in the innovation team or workshop**

CONTENTS

CHAPTER 3

THE BEST ONLINE INNOVATION TOOLS

Innovation is not just about having a clear process; it is just as much about sharing ideas, sparking new ways of thinking, and interacting with each other. Most of us are familiar with in-person workshops where, if they are facilitated well, most of these elements are present. This is different when collaborating online to get the best results from a team and keep everyone engaged. Therefore, it is essential to use a well-thought selection of online tools. Besides a videoconferencing tool, you will also need, for example, tools for online collaboration and making your workshop interactive.

For online innovation, there are many great tools for different activities like online collaboration, video-conferencing, prototyping, planning and creating workshops, brainstorming, communication, and much more.

In Appendix 1 you will find an overview of 25 tools, each with a brief description of what the tool is, why to use it, to which innovation methods and techniques described in this book the tool fits, the killer feature, when to avoid it, and more. For this chapter, we have selected ten of our favourite tools from that list to describe them more extensively for you.

We have divided the tools into five categories:
Online collaboration
Videoconferencing
Preparation and Instruction
Prototyping and Testing
Making workshops interactive

In the chart, you see the 25 tools divided into five categories. The ten highlighted tools are the ones described in this chapter.

CHART: 25 ONLINE INNOVATION TOOLS

Online collaboration	Video conferencing	Preparation and Instruction	Prototyping and Testing	Making workshops interactive
miro	zoom	SessionLab	Marvel	Mentimeter
MURAL	Microsoft Teams	Boardle	toonly	TSCHECK.IN
Trello	butter	loom	Speechelo	Kahoot!
padlet	Jitsi Meet	calendly	Canva	
slack	wonder		Google Forms	
Howspace	Google Meet			
klaxoon				

So how do you select the tools for your online innovation project? We advise you to use a combination of an online whiteboard tool for collaboration and a videoconferencing tool for communication. In the videoconferencing tool, you explain the process steps and the tools, and you create break out rooms to work in smaller teams. While in break out rooms, participants can collaborate live together on a digital whiteboard. This gives them an experience close to being in the same room together.

Other tools we introduce are for preparation and instruction. They are very helpful to make sure your workshops run smoothly. Since in innovation, you need to prototype and test ideas, we have selected some tools for that. And, last but not least, we describe tools to make your workshop interactive and more engaging, something to pay attention to when innovating online.

Five general tips using online tools for innovation

Tip 1: Combine a videoconferencing tool and a whiteboard tool
We recommend always use a combination of a videoconference tool (like Zoom or Butter) for communication and a whiteboard tool (like Miro or Mural) for collaboration. We have found this to be a very valuable combination since you then make use of each tool's strength. There are videoconferencing tools with whiteboard functions, but they are far less useful than those in tools that focus only on that.

Tip 2: Test the technology
Do take into account that using the combination of a videoconference tool and a whiteboard tool may eat up more bandwidth of participants, which could cause connection issues. Always do a tech onboarding workshop before your actual workshop or meeting. This means you ask all participants to join a scheduled workshop – before your actual workshop – in which you do a test run with the tools you plan to use. Any issues that may occur can be tackled, or you can change your selection of tools. If a participant has bandwidth issues, you can ask them to disable video for (parts of) the workshop, for example.

Tip 3: Check for new features, updates and free versions
While being aware of the fact that over time new tools will appear and existing ones will develop and will be extended with new or improved features, we think it is necessary to give an overview of the tools we use – and for what activities and purposes – at the time of writing of this book. We recommend always checking if the tools have free versions available (many do) and what the restrictions are. Since these may change over time, check for the latest options. There may be limits in the duration of use in a workshop while you have access to all the features. For example, with Zoom, the limit is 40 minutes. In other cases, you have access to limited features.

Tip 4: Master the tools
The tools that we have selected are relatively easy to use. Of course, it will depend on how skilled you are in using digital tools, but basically, anyone that can use a computer properly should be able to use the tools mentioned in this chapter. Do make sure that if you are a first-time user of a tool to educate yourself properly before facilitating a workshop. There are

many instructional videos available, either on the website of the tool itself or on Youtube. Do check these out to train yourself. You can schedule a test workshop with friends or colleagues to try out the tools before your actual workshop.

Tip 5: Collaborate with a tech-savvy person
If you feel insecure about using new tools or having a hard time learning them, ask a tech-savvy co-facilitator, friend, student, or colleague to help you out. You can request this person to explore the tools you want to use and educate you about the key features. You can also invite a tech-savvy person to support you as a co-facilitator in a workshop. This will take the pressure off of yourself so you can focus on the process.

ONLINE COLLABORATION PLATFORMS

In in-person innovation workshops, facilitators use all kinds of tangible materials and tools for collaboration. Think of post-it notes, markers for writing and drawing, brown paper to put on the wall on which participants can put their post-its and other relevant content, poster-sized templates to be used in the different steps of an innovation process, whiteboards, digital screens, and so on. With the progression of a workshop or project, the room in which the team works will fill with all kinds of ideas. You want to capture all that content so that you can go back to it in the next workshop or when working on a longer project. It is not always possible to leave it all in the room since you may have run a workshop in an external, rented venue, or you have to tidy up the office space or meeting room for the next users. You will then probably end up photographing everything that's on the wall, rolling up brown papers and flip charts and storing it all somewhere for later use. Or you find yourself typing out all the handwritten text to digest the input or to share it with the participants, colleagues, decision-makers, or your client.

For online innovation, there are some great tools that make your life so much easier. Tools like Miro and Mural are cloud-based whiteboard tools with many great features that – if combined with the right videoconferencing tools – facilitate online collaboration very well. And all the content is directly available in a digital format and accessible for everyone (if they have the rights) whenever they require access, even outside of workshops.

 **miro**

MIRO – WWW.MIRO.COM

Miro is a cloud-based online infinite whiteboard tool that allows innovation teams to collect all their input digitally. You can go from ideation to execution on an infinite canvas. It's scalable, includes many pre-built templates, and works cross-device. While working simultaneously, everyone can see directly what others are contributing. Since innovation is about developing new insights and creating new solutions together, Miro is a great tool for collaboration when innovating online.

With Miro, you can do just about anything you would want to do when facilitating an in-person workshop. All the ideas that you would put on brown paper, white-boards, or the wall, you can put on this digital whiteboard – digital sticky notes, images, text, pdfs of templates you would typically print out – can be placed on a digital backdrop. But there is more. You can upload videos to play within Miro or paste a link to a Youtube video. Have a pdf file you want people to see? Just upload it, and with one click, you make all pages in the file visible on the white-board!

And there is more. When using sticky notes, you can adjust the size, the colour, and the font. Did your board get a bit messy? No worries! Just select all your post-its, resize them, and, when you drag them, they will all be nicely aligned in columns and rows. Do you want to know

how many post-its have been written by your team? Just select the items on your board, filter for post-its and voila! This saves you a lot of counting.

To keep your work organised, you can use frames. By putting all the items you need in a specific step of your process like templates, explanatory text, images et cetera in one frame these will all stay together. For example, when you create a frame for each process step, all participants can easily find the content they need. When you give all your frames the right name, in the available frame index, you can quickly find the content you are looking for, and with one click, you will be brought to the specific frame.

Screenshot from a Miro board

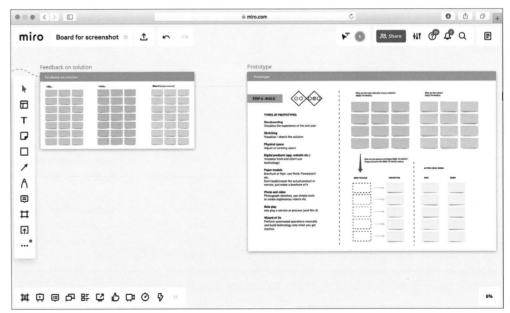

ONLINE INNOVATION

Another great feature is the voting option. If you are including decision-making in your process, allowing your team to vote is advisable. It is quick, democratic, and you will instantly have insights into what your team prioritises. When you initiate voting, participants of the workshop can vote by simply clicking on the post-its (or other objects of your choice).

Many more functions make Miro more than a suitable tool to use for online innovation. It fits a variety of techniques and ways of working that make online innovation successful. We already mentioned the voting option. To avoid becoming mired in discussions, this is a very useful function. Using a tool like Miro is great for combining synchronous and asynchronous work. This means you can collaborate online in scheduled workshops, but also even when workshops are not being run, the whole team has access to the Miro board, which allows them to contribute individually whenever it suits them. You are not dependent on being in the physical room where all the content is; it's all digitally available in the cloud.

The bulk mode is a great feature to allow participants to write ideas without being distracted by what others are writing. And the other way around: nobody sees what you are writing until you are done. This is an excellent fit with the technique of working together-alone, where you combine individual work with group work.
 Since you can put anything on a Miro board, it is excellent to use it for a Lightning Demo, a technique described in greater detail in the next chapter. But basically, in a Lightning Demo, participants put inspiration they found by doing (desk) research – examples of innovations from a wide range of industries – on the whiteboard as a source for inspiration for an ideation session. Do you want to visualise an idea? No problem! Just draw it on a piece of paper, scan it, and upload it to Miro.

Besides the great features, Miro also has a library of templates ready to use for your processes. Scroll through the many examples, select your favourite, and with a click, it is on your board. Do you want to personalise the template? No problem! Just change and add as many things as you like. To learn more about Miro, check out: Miroverse – accessible from within Miro – where you can find proven workflows, projects, and frameworks within the Miro community.

MURAL – WWW.MURAL.COM

Mural is a cloud-based digital collaboration whiteboard where you can go from ideation to execution on a big canvas. To help you set up your workshops, it includes more than a hundred pre-built templates. To allow anyone to contribute and collaborate anytime, anywhere, it works cross-device.

The great thing about a tool like Mural is that it enables teams to work remotely, both synchronously and asynchronously. So, for example, if you work for a multinational with offices around the world, everyone can contribute during scheduled online workshops as well as in between workshops at any individual's convenience. Of course, there are many advantages of working with a team in-person – think of real personal interaction and social talk that helps for team building – but working remotely has some great positive aspects, too. You don't have to arrange a global team to travel to one place, pay for expenses like hotels and meals, and face challenges like taking people out of their busy day jobs for a couple of days. A tool like Mural (or Miro) is the perfect online spot for innovation processes with all their different stages that need space for insights, creativity, and focus.

Mural is a very easy to use tool with a great number of functions, for example, the digital post-its. These are as simple to use as real ones. Just click on your favourite colour in the menu, and off you go! Start typing, and your contribution appears on the whiteboard right away. And you can see live what your team members are writing.

Since you may end up with a lot of content on your Mural board, there are two features that help you find the content you are looking for: the find feature by which you can type in a word you know is somewhere on the board and be directed right to it; and to organise your content, you can create so-called outlines. These are areas you can select and give a

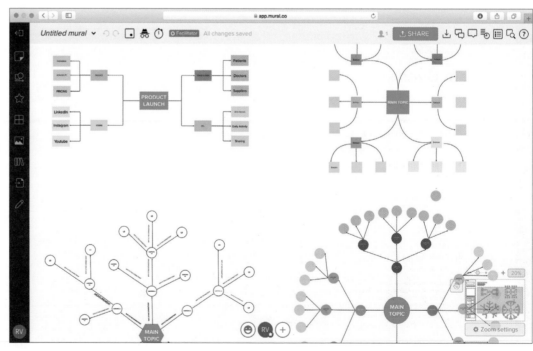

name to that will appear in an index of outlines. Just click on the name of the outline, and you will be taken to that specific part on the board.

Do you want to get insights into your participants' opinions? Just start a voting session with a few clicks. This is great for anonymous voting since participants can't see each other's votes until the voting session ends. This means they will not be distracted, nor will they be biased in their voting.

Furthermore, to empower facilitators, Mural offers some so-called facilitator superpowers. These include a timer to stay on schedule when running timeboxed workshops,

summoning all participants to the area on the Mural board you want them to look at, so you don't need to waste time 'cat herding'. And there is the option to designate other people as co-facilitators, which gives them extra functionalities to host a workshop together with you.

For speeding up the preparation of a workshop, Mural has a library with more than a hundred templates ready to use. Choose a template from one of the categories such as design thinking and innovation, instruction and facilitation, or any other and off you go!

There is much more to Mural. And both Miro and Mural keep adding and improving features and functionality. There will always be differences in the tools, and you may find one fitting your way of working better than the other. Or you might prefer the graphic design of the different elements of one of the tools over the other. It is a matter of trying them both out and deciding which you prefer. As our German co-author Florian Hameister says, 'Mural or Miro is like choosing between a BMW and a Mercedes. They are both top car brands; it's just a matter of style.'

Page 44 and 45
Screenshots from a Mural board

HOW COMMUNICATION TOOL SLACK WAS BORN OUT OF A FAILING VIDEO GAME

*I*nnovation is about experimenting and being prepared to pivot. When you are doing new things, you don't know beforehand where you will end up. And by taking action, you will gain new insights that will help you decide what your next steps should be. On your journey, you may encounter not only barriers but also unexpected new opportunities. This could mean that it is better to say goodbye to that idea you fell in love with and pivot to an unexpected, better opportunity that presents itself. Slack founder Stewart Butterfield and his team set out to create something new and original for the massively multiplayer online role-playing game (MMORPG) market. As it turns out, they revolutionised how we communicate at work instead.

Slack was born out of a gaming company called Tiny Speck. Butterfield and his team didn't intentionally set out to create a SaaS (Software as a Service) product for the workplace. They built a tool for themselves. It was created out of necessity and allowed the company to pivot from a confused gaming product to a Popular, profitable productivity tool.

Video game developers might not seem like the most logical group to make a sticky, engaging communications tool for today's workplace, but Tiny Speck's gaming expertise provided a significant competitive advantage. Butterfield and his team already knew how to make repetitive tasks fun and engaging, as this is the core of the MMORPG gameplay experience. This is a genre of role-playing games in which many players interact with each other over the Internet. Making work-based communication fun and engaging would be the secret sauce that made Slack so wildly successful.

The development team building their game Glitch consisted of just four people in New York, San Francisco, and Vancouver. To overcome the challenges of communicating across multiple time zones, Butterfield and his team used Internet Relay Chat (better known as IRC). This online chat tool was enormously popular in the late 1980s and early 1990s. IRC served Glitch's developers well – for a while. Before long, however, Butterfield and his team felt IRC was no longer up to the task. They needed something more. That's when they decided to start building their own communications tool.

Butterfield had no plans to develop Tiny Speck's internal chat tool as a commercial product. Instead, the team kept tweaking and improving its nascent communications tool as they worked on their game. New functionality was added on an ad-hoc basis.

Meanwhile, Glitch didn't attract enough new players. Its design and features could not cope with what players of the MMORPG genre were attracted to. Besides that, the game was based on Adobe Flash, which once was the industry standard but has since fallen out of favour. Although Glitch would, in the end, fail as a game, it ended up producing an incredibly valuable application: the communication tool that the Tiny Speck team used for their offices. Tiny Speck pivoted from Glitch to the development of this cloud-based, collaborative chat platform designed to make conversations easier between team members, which would be named Slack.

However, while Tiny Speck was using Slack internally for several months, the team using it still consisted of just a handful of people. To keep improving the product, Tiny Speck needed more users. Butterfield and his team started asking around and calling in favours from friends at other companies. They listened to the feedback of the early adopters carefully, tweaking and refining the product as they went.

Many start-ups focus all their energy on growing as rapidly as possible. By contrast, Slack focused on growing steadily. Each time the company received new feedback on Slack, they would address or implement changes based on that feedback, but they also invited more large teams to try the product. The company practised active listening to continue to address customer needs as they occurred. Slack today has many features that the team implemented due to a commitment to reading and analysing end-user feedback. This iterative approach to development helped Tiny Speck build a reliable product based on how people were actually using it and progressively expand its user base.

Slack and its founder have a fascinating history that goes through a lot of twist and turns. This communication platform is a must-have service for millions of organisations, and the company's responsiveness to applying customer feedback to its product development fuels the growth of its avid fanbase.

Butterfield may not have achieved his dream of creating a successful online game, but revolutionising team communications is a great consolation prize.

SLACK – WWW.SLACK.COM

Resources: https://blog.lemonadestand.org/an-in-depth-history-of-slack-and-its-overnight-success/
https://usefyi.com/slack-history/

VIDEOCONFERENCING TOOLS

During the Covid-19 pandemic, most of us had no choice but to familiarise ourselves with videoconferencing. Many meetings and workshops that generally would have taken place in-person now had to be done online. We simply had no choice. The good thing is that there are quite some great tools for videoconferencing. In Chapter 1, you read about the rapid growth of Zoom.

For collaborating online, having the ability to use video and see participants in workshops is very important. We appreciate that due to circumstances like limited bandwidth or cultural restrictions, using video is not always possible. But encourage everyone to turn their camera's on if they can. It makes collaborating online less impersonal!

The available tools for videoconferencing have their strengths and differences. For online innovation, you want to look for those that suit the way you want to deliver your workshops. For example, it is advisable to split bigger groups into smaller teams for more effective collaboration. In face-to-face workshops, you would give each team a separate workspace. When collaborating online, find a tool with virtual break out rooms that can be managed easily.

We have picked two tools that we think are easy for you to work with and have the functions needed for online innovation workshops: Zoom and Butter.

zoom

ZOOM – WWW.ZOOM.US

Zoom is a cloud-based videoconferencing tool that allows you to set up virtual video and audio conferencing. It has a quite easy to understand interface, which makes it very user-friendly. It is one of the tools used by many people and organisations since the start of the Covid-19 pandemic. The name has even become a verb in itself: let's Zoom!

There are many very useful features in Zoom for running online innovation workshops. First of all, the gallery view allows you to see up to 49 people on your (desktop) screen at once. This is great because being able to see participants helps to make your workshops more 'human'. Not all videoconferencing tools allow you to see this many people, so this is a significant advantage of Zoom.

Since discussions on innovation in a large group often lead nowhere, working in smaller groups is highly recommended. The break out room functionality in Zoom is great to tap into this. With a click of a button or two, the workshop host can send participants to break out rooms. These can be set up during the workshop or beforehand. Or people can be assigned randomly. The facilitator (when having host rights in Zoom) can quickly jump in and out of break out rooms to guide the different teams in each step of the process. Need to get everyone back in the plenary room? Just close the break out rooms, and everyone will be sent back to the main workshop. This makes an online workshop very efficient since in in-person workshops can be challenging to get everyone together.

To explain a theory, a process step, or to show slides, there is the share screen functionality. You can choose to share a specific window (for example, your PowerPoint window or a browser tab). It is also possible to share a particular section of your screen. If you want to play a video, no problem. Just make sure you have selected the box to share your computer sound and start your video. Do you want to play music before your workshop or on breaks? Just find your favourite playlist on your music streaming service, go to the advanced sharing options in Zoom, and share your music. These sharing options work quite smoothly in Zoom, which is not necessarily the case in other videoconferencing tools.

It can be challenging to have conversations in a video conference. Sometimes people start to talk while their microphone is muted. As a facilitator, think about when you want people to contribute by word of mouth and when it can be in writing. There is a chat feature in Zoom for people to type what they want to say. Especially with larger groups, this can be very effective. When you want to have spoken conversations, always ask everyone to mute themselves to avoid disturbing background noise. As a host in Zoom, you can mute people by clicking on the allocated button in the participant list.

Besides using the chat function for interactivity, there is also the option to do a poll. Simply create questions with this built-in feature to engage your audience. This is extra important in online workshops due to the lack of normal human interaction in in-person workshops (like those spontaneous conversations at the coffee machine).

One of the challenges when working remotely can be finding a quiet working area that doesn't show the laundry you just did at home. That is where the virtual background feature comes in handy! Just select a virtual background, and only you and the chosen virtual background are visible for participants. Don't bother about tidying up when running late for a workshop; find this feature, and you are good to go!

Have you never used Zoom before and want to try it out? No problem! You can use the tool for free. The only restriction is that you are on a time limit: after 40 minutes, your workshop will be ended automatically. If it is no trouble for your audience to join again, then you will be fine. Of course, you are better off with a paid account to not frustrate your participants. But at least with the free version, you can try out Zoom before buying.

Screenshot from a Zoom meeting

THE BEST ONLINE INNOVATION TOOLS

 **butter**

With Butter you can run smooth and interactive virtual workshops. It is an all-in-one platform built with all the tools you need to host interactive workshops, training workshops and live courses. Although it has similar features to other videoconferencing tools like Zoom, it is more than just that. Butter implements other aspects of hosting a successful workshop, such as a poll feature and a timed agenda with a countdown to let participants know when the time is up. The laser focus of Butter is on running online workshops smoothly. Besides this focus, it stands out from other tools because of its fresh design.

In an online workshop, it is essential to manage conversations well. This is quite different to being in an in-person workshop. Most of us have been in online meetings where everyone wants to participate in a conversation, but only one person can talk at a time. To help manage this, Butter has the speaker queue function. So instead of a raise your hand feature where you only see who wants to say something, a queue appears where you can see who has risen their hands first. This way, everyone gets heard and always knows who's up next.

The built-in agenda is also a great feature. You can create agendas before your workshop and timebox each point. While in your meeting, the agenda is visible, which allows everyone to see how much time there is left for a topic which helps to maintain focus. You can also adapt your agenda while in your meeting, which allows flexibility.

As mentioned before, Butter aims to make online workshops work smoothly. To that end, another helpful feature is Miro integration. This online whiteboard tool can be used directly from within Butter, so no need to have a separate browser window open. Just click on the Miro icon, find the board you want to use – or create one from scratch – and off you go!

Putting your participants in smaller teams to allow them to collaborate is also possible. Just create different break out rooms and assign participants by dragging their names to the right room. It is easy to check in on your groups by hopping between rooms or peeking in! Do you need to send a message to all the break out rooms at once? Then simply broadcast your message to all rooms.

Just as described in the section on Zoom, Butter allows for using different techniques for online innovation. You can use the chat function to add extra interactivity to your workshop when spoken word is less handy: for example, when you want quick responses from everyone in bigger groups. You can also consider using the poll feature for that. Also, the working together-alone technique can be used in Butter. Ask everyone to contribute in silence by muting themselves. This way, every participant can add to the workshop without being disturbed by others.

Butter doesn't need an install on your computer. You can use it with a browser, which makes it easily accessible for almost everyone. Consider, though, that there is a limit to the number of participants for a workshop (200). And only a maximum of 20 participants can use video. These limits may change over time, so we recommend always to check the latest options.

Screenshot from a Butter meeting

3. TOOLS FOR PREPARATION AND INSTRUCTION

When facilitating online workshops during your innovation process, having a structured workshop agenda is very important since you are less flexible than when facilitating in-person workshops. This also requires giving participants clear instructions since, in remote workshops, you want them to collaborate as efficiently as possible.

For these reasons, we will explain SessionLab, which is a great tool to help you prepare your workshops easily. When you don't just want to rely on live explanation during your workshop, use Loom to make explanatory videos that will help your team to clearly understand what is expected from them.

To run any workshop successfully, there are three important things: preparation, preparation, and preparation! Plan and prepare the activities you are going to do, the breaks, and any materials and templates. For online workshops, this also means setting up your virtual digital whiteboards in Miro or Mural.

Preparation is especially important in online workshops. You are less flexible since you want to make your workshops shorter than in-person workshops to keep everybody engaged. So, you may find yourself being on a tighter schedule. By having prepared your workshop well, you make sure you don't run out of time. Having a well-prepared agenda doesn't mean it is set in stone. The better prepared, the easier it is to move around, add or skip activities. SessionLab comes in very handy here since it keeps track of your workshop timing. As soon as you take out an activity, your overall timing is adjusted automatically.

In SessionLab, you can create the agenda for your workshop by the minute. It is an online workshop planning platform that allows you to break your content into chunks and outline a workshop, organising it into various time blocks. Every block in the agenda represents a different module or activity in your workshop. In each block, you can add instructions on how to run the specific activity, make an overview of materials you need, and add attachments. In preparing your workshop, you can collaborate on SessionLab with co-facilitators.

To create your agenda, drag and drop exercises and modules in a workshop plan. The tool offers an inspiring library of activities to integrate into your workshop when you need inspiration. You can search hundreds of exercises, filter by the number of participants, duration, and topics, and add exercises that fit your workshop plan. Create a workshop plan from scratch or browse the library to see if there is a ready-made workshop agenda you can use to adjust to your needs. Are there any activities that you are sure you are not going to use in your workshop? Simply drag them into the parking lot. This way, you have your carefully prepared activities at hand to put in your agenda later or even while you are running your

workshop. Are you running a workshop with a co-facilitator or colleague? No problem! You can collaborate on your preparation in SessionLab. You all can change things or add comments and more.

Do you want to save your session plan in another format? Simply export it to a PDF or Word file. You can also duplicate your plan if you want to use it as your starting point to create another workshop.

Screenshot from a SessionLab workshop agenda

THE BEST ONLINE INNOVATION TOOLS

LOOM – WWW.LOOM.COM

If there is a message you want to get across in a quick, clear, and easy way, Loom is the perfect video-tool for you. With Loom, you can simultaneously record your camera, microphone, and desktop to create instantly shareable videos. With this tool, it takes less time than it would to type an email. Use it to explain the features of the online tools you want to use for your innovation project. Record your explanation while showing what you do on screen. Use it while explaining a template you have put on a digital whiteboard (for example, in Miro or Mural), so your team can work on it asynchronously. For anything you want to explain, you can use Loom.

Loom makes any message personal since you can record your face while showing on the screen what you are doing. From this perspective, using this tool makes online innovation a bit more human; Loom adds a personal connection. If you prefer not to be in the picture, you can choose to record your screen only. There is also an option to record your camera only.

Want to take a breath while recording? Simply pause your recording and continue whenever you are ready. In the pro-version, you can also draw on the screen if you want to highlight something.

Once you are done recording, your video will appear in your library on your Loom account. You can then trim your video if needed, add comments, and download or copy the video's link to share it on social media. If you are not happy with the result, you can delete your recording directly.

Because of its simplicity and ease of use, Loom is a useful tool for online innovation workshops. You can create a video for every step in your innovation journey, explaining tasks to instruct participants. Do you want to give your participants instructions before a workshop about the tools and platforms you will use in your online workshop? Why not provide them with a guided tour, recorded in Loom. This way, you guide users to quickly find their way to navigate around a platform. You are notified once someone views your video, and recipients can add comments. You can also embed a Loom video thumbnail in an email instead of a link, which encourages people to open it.

Of course, you can use your creativity and think beyond using Loom for creating instructional videos. Why not create a video to explain your prototype so you can test it with your target audience? Especially in the early stages of an innovation process, where you want to create low fidelity prototypes to get feedback quickly, Loom is a very helpful tool.

Making videos is not something everyone feels comfortable with. But in this era of Youtube and other video platforms, people are used to simple, short, and quickly made videos that are not spotless. Don't go for perfection; focus on a clear explanation. Don't worry if there is an 'uuhh' in your instruction video. People don't expect a perfect-for-cinema result. They expect a human to help them on their way.

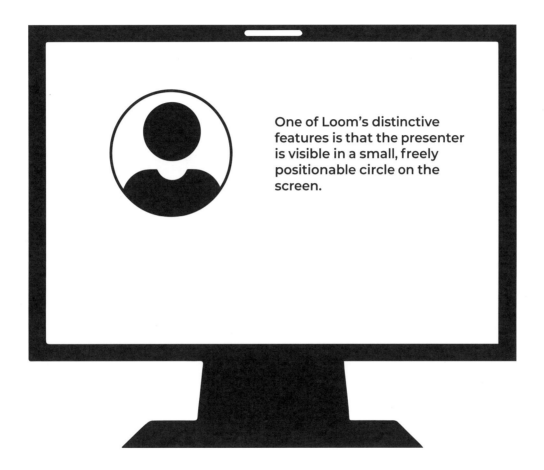

One of Loom's distinctive features is that the presenter is visible in a small, freely positionable circle on the screen.

4. TOOLS FOR PROTOTYPING AND TESTING

When you are innovating, you are doing new things or things in a new way. This means the risks are high since you are doing something you have not done before. So how do you know if the solution you came up with will work? It is not good to start building a high-quality end solution right away because hardly any idea survives without criticism from first contact with the target audience!

By building a prototype and testing your new concept with your target audience, you will learn what can be improved. Keep in mind that a prototype is not a scaled-down model of your end solution. You want to focus on the core elements to test assumptions. This means keeping it small in both execution as well as in the parts of your solution you are going to prototype and test.

To help you build your prototypes quickly, there are a lot of tools out there. Of course, it depends on what you need to prototype which of those tools are the most suitable. To inspire you and to give you some ideas, we have picked two tools as examples. The first is Marvel, with which you can build first drafts of apps and websites, and develop and improve them step by step. The other tool is Toonly, an animated explainer video tool to get your story across in an engaging way.

In Chapter 7, we will discuss online innovation methods. One of these methods is Pretotyping: a method to quickly and economically validate whether your idea is worth pursuing in your innovation process. The word Pretotype is a neologism that indicates the realisation of a fake product-service you want to realise that simulates (pretends) and precedes the real one.

WWW.MARVELAPP.COM

Marvel helps you to turn any sketch or image into an interactive prototype for an app or website. It has everything you need to bring ideas to life and transform how you create digital products with your team. So instead of presenting static designs, use easy to create interactive prototypes to communicate ideas better.

To build your realistic prototypes, you don't need to write any software code. In just minutes, you can make your ideas interactive by just uploading images or photographing your sketches, adding hotspots, and creating hyperlinks. Bringing

your ideas to life like this is the fastest way to go! You simply don't want to allocate a lot of time and budget to something that has not proved to work yet, do you?

One of the best features is that you can easily share your prototype in seconds via email or social media to get early feedback from your target audience, customers, and stakeholders to test your assumptions.

It may be hard for some people to start building something almost from scratch. They even may have an 'I can't draw' attitude. Providing them with hands-on, easy-to-use tools will help them overcome any barrier. Also, using some templates as a starting point can help. There are some available in Marvel. Another way to trigger inspiration is to let people take a close look at their favourite apps on their smartphone and copy and morph features, designs, and layouts. Or do a Google search for 'GUI elements' (Graphical User Interface) to give yourself a head start. UI Stencils can also be a great help. Just put your pencil in and start creating your screen designs!

Marvel is an easy, simple app with a very steep learning curve! It is a great tool to visualise app ideas literally within minutes and start the conversation when testing with possible customers, which comes in handy in any innovation method where you want to create quick prototypes to test with users and get feedback.

TOONLY

Prototyping is being creative in clearly explaining your solution, so people understand it and so that you may therefore receive feedback to improve your concept. A great way to tell your story is by creating animated videos. This way, you create easily digestible content that is enjoyable to watch. With an animated explainer video, you can communicate abstract subjects very easily.

Toonly is an animated explainer video creator that you can use to create simple videos to provide information on your solution and how that solution works. It is great for creating an engaging video about the user experience once your solution has been realised. It helps your target audience understand the idea better so they can provide you with valuable feedback.

The tool is easy to use. You can choose a background for your video and click and drag characters onto it. Click your mouse to animate them, and off you go! There is a massive library with tons of characters, props, and backgrounds. The images are all custom drawn, not stock. To make your life even more comfortable, Toonly offers pre-made scenes combining a background, characters, and props into one complete package.

To finish off your video, you can record a voice-over, upload a professional one, or use audio exported from other software. You can also drag and drop background royalty-free music to create the right mood in your video.

A tool like this is great in any process where you need to prototype your solution. And especially when you are innovating online with remote teams, creating an animated video makes it very easy to spread your ideas across teams or to show it to decision-makers and people you want to test it, too. You can easily send it – for example, accompanied by a feedback form – to many people at the same time to get a lot of feedback in a short period.

Another way to use this tool is to explain tasks or to instruct participants authentically and engagingly, which Is helpful when you want to combine synchronous and asynchronous work in your process.

5. TOOLS TO MAKE WORKSHOPS INTERACTIVE

Keeping participants engaged during a workshop is challenging when collaborating online. Everybody is working remotely and on their own. There are no spontaneous conversations between participants. When the workshop ends, everyone is back in their own (private) bubble after one click of a button. No small talk, no unexpected, engaging personal conversations. Therefore, it is extra important to make online workshops engaging and interactive, which we discuss more extensively in Chapter 5.

There are multiple ways to foster interaction in an online workshop. You can use the chat function in a videoconferencing tool or simply use spoken word. Besides that, many tools allow everyone to contribute, based on your workshop's content, or to trigger those personal stories you miss out on when working remotely.

In this chapter, we describe Mentimeter, a tool for creating interactive quizzes, polls, and Q&As, and Tscheck.in which is a very simple tool to start conversations on a personal level.

Mentimeter

MENTIMETER

Quizzes, polls, and Q&As are great ways to engage participants whether you are in a remote, in-person, or hybrid workshop. Mentimeter is a cloud-based tool that allows you to interact with your audience. Very quickly, you can get feedback and input from everyone. Since being online feels more distant than being in the same physical room, adding interactivity to online workshops is especially important to keep your audience engaged.

Mentimeter enables you to turn workshops into interactive experiences that are fun for both you and your participants. You can create word clouds based on your participants' input, ask a quick multiple-choice question to let your audience vote, or energise the entire (virtual) room with a quiz competition!

By using this tool, you can interact with your target audience in real-time. Participants can give their input using a mobile phone or any other device connected to the Internet. You get unbiased results visualised in a way that encourages reflection and sparks discussion. It is easy to use, enabling you to turn your audience's opinions into real-time tangible and actionable data. With Mentimeter you can easily boost your workshops, and it helps you become a better-skilled facilitator by giving more engaging workshops.

To give you a head start, in Mentimeter you will find pre-designed templates to make your slides look professional with just one click. And to inspire you, there are all kinds of example slides available for different purposes like evaluation, check-in, and icebreakers. And there are many different ways to visualise participants' input, like open-ended questions, word clouds, Q&A, and pie-charts, doughnut-charts, and spider-charts.

Besides the engagement you create with your participants by asking them to interact and to share their ideas and answers, the outcomes of your polls or quizzes can also be great conversation starters. Especially in online workshops, this is important due to the lack of direct interpersonal contact.

One of the features in Mentimeter is creating word clouds.

ONLINE INNOVATION

Adding a personal touch to your online workshops is very important. To engage people on a personal level, it comes in handy to use conversation starters. It is not for nothing that there are brands out there that print triggering questions on their products to challenge the reader to start a conversation based on an unexpected topic.

In all its simpleness, the online tool Tscheck.in does exactly that: it randomly shows questions on your screen that can be used as conversation starters at the beginning or the end of your workshops. Simply choose the 'tscheck in' or 'tscheck out' option depending on what you prefer.

In an online workshop, you can go to the website and share your screen with the participants. Ask a person to answer the question shown. You can ask that person to identify the next person who can answer the same question or click 'shuffle', and a new question will appear for that person to answer.

Besides using this tool at the beginning or the end of an online workshop, you can, of course, also use it as an energiser during a workshop, for example, right after a coffee break. It will break the formality, and it helps everyone to be off topic for a moment. This makes them more creative in what they are working on: if you give people a short, simple task for which they have to focus on something different, their creativity will be piqued.

Screenshot from Tscheck.in

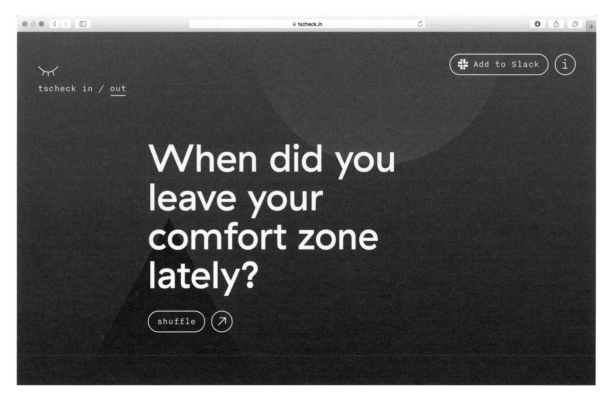

There is nothing more to this tool. It works as easily as that! But this simplicity makes it a powerful instrument to make connections on a more personal level, besides the more formal content of your workshop. It can even trigger new connections and conversations between participants outside your online workshops.

Tscheck in question examples:
Which habit do you want to break?
For what in your life do you feel especially grateful?
Which is your least favourite fruit?
What is the best gap in your CV?

Tscheck out example questions:
What made you laugh today?
To make tomorrow more optimistic, I will...
What is your favourite dinner?
What is the first thing you are going to do after work?

Now you are familiar with the best digital innovation tools for online innovation workshops; we will present you in the next chapters ten online innovation techniques to get the most out of your innovation journeys.

KEY MESSAGES FROM THIS CHAPTER

▸ **There is more to online innovation than just scheduling videoconference calls with a team. With the right tools, you can make your workshops much more engaging and effective.**

▸ **Use a videoconferencing tool like Zoom or Butter combined with a digital whiteboard tool like Miro or Mural for online collaboration.**

▸ **Add interactivity like polls or quizzes to your workshops with a tool like Mentimeter.**

▸ **To make your workshops even more personal, use Tscheck.in, which randomly generates check-in and check-out questions to connect your participants.**

▸ **Besides tools to use in workshops, there are very helpful online tools to instruct participants asynchronously (in between workshops, for example) and even quickly build prototypes of your solution for testing purposes.**

▸ **Always check for the latest features and updates of the tools to see pricing plans and free versions. In many cases, there is a free version available – with all or at least many of the functionalities – that you can use for a limited time, which allows you to check if the tool is for you.**

CONTENTS

CHAPTER 4

ONLINE INNOVATION TECHNIQUES

In the previous chapter, we showed you ten tools we use frequently and found very helpful in facilitating online innovation workshops. But a fool with a tool is still a fool. That's the reason why we present you ten techniques in this chapter to help you prepare and facilitate your online innovation workshops better, and to prevent you from falling into the pitfalls of Chapter 2. They also help to minimise (some of) the Achilles' heels of online innovation we will discuss in the next chapter.

We group the ten online techniques in three categories: designing engaging workshops, facilitating interactive workshops, and communication and feedback.
In designing engaging workshops, we show you what it means to make a Virtual Room Design, how making videos helps you, and what combining synchronous and asynchronous work means. In the second category, we describe how the techniques like together-alone, anonymous voting, the Bulk mode, Break Out Rooms, and Lightning Demos can help you to facilitate more interactive workshops. In communication and feedback, we have a look at the possibilities of online surveys and how the chat function can be used.

1. Virtual Room Design
In the offline world, a good workshop differs from an excellent workshop when the setting fits the purpose of the workshop; for innovation workshops, very spatial open rooms with lots of light function well to inspire people, as do crazy ones, like in a windmill or an art gallery. Nice music, a good light setting, and a great smell all add to the experience. The more senses are stimulated, the more someone becomes immersed, and the more intense the workshop will be.

Online, the experience is completely different. We do not see what our participants see. The gallery view of videoconferencing looks different on an 11-inch screen or a big 30-inch desktop screen. The sound quality and volume differ between old laptop speakers or good quality Bose headphones. You get inspired differently if you are sitting in front of your PC and looking at a beautiful lake and green hills or looking at your laundry in your bedroom.

Using online collaboration platforms and videoconference tools, it is possible to create at least a decent experience for your participants. We experimented with videoconferencing tools. We tried funny, serious, and spacious virtual backgrounds, which are nice for a specific activity or energiser. Still, in general, they are more disturbing, especially when parts of you or the participants disappear. With Butter or Wonder.me, it is possible to create a different feeling than Zoom or MS Teams' straightforward style. Butter has a fresh, playful, and colourful design. Wonder.me is also a bit more stylish. You can make a background picture to be your 'room', and because you can move around, it feels more open.

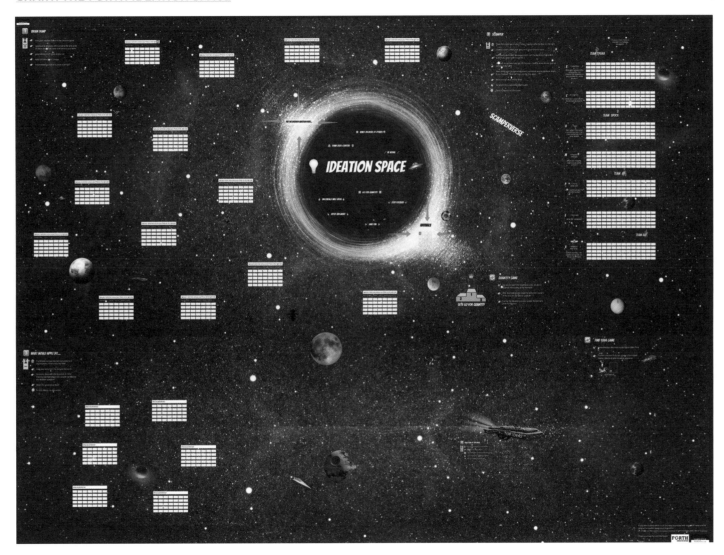

ONLINE INNOVATION TECHNIQUES

The best experiences we have had designing whiteboards with the online collaboration platforms are with Miro, Mural, or Klaxoon . With them it is possible to embed pictures, gifs, and videos and to design a room the way you as a facilitator like to have it, from using the colours and branding of your organisation to specific themes for the workshop. Everything is possible. For the idea generation phase of the FORTH innovation method, we designed a board that looks like you are in space. We created it so people would feel no limits, feel free to ideate without restrictions in an 'ideation space'.

The next level of experiences is AR/VR -Environments. We will discuss them in Chapter 11 on hybrid innovation. Watch their development closely as AR/VR will have a real breakthrough in the coming years in professional facilitation.

2. Making videos

The shift to online and more asynchronous work made it necessary to rethink how we present tasks or results. When someone does not understand the task or what was given, maybe because of a bad internet connection, because he was disturbed by something next to his screen, or if the issue was just badly explained by the facilitator, two things can happen. The participant is honest and asks if the facilitator can repeat what she just said. The other option is that he says nothing and will not do the task properly. Both are unacceptable for strictly timed and outcome-focused workshops.

'A picture says a thousand words'; A video does it even better. We have very good experiences with videos we make to explain tasks and to show examples, to instruct people online. Video offers a tremendous help when people perform asynchronous tasks, because if the message is not clear, the result will be an extended email ping-pong. With a video, we take our time and make short, entertaining videos to explain the tasks and give the participants an example directly, where

they then have to do the task. We get a lot of positive response for it.

The other action for which we use videos is to make the participants record a video of their results, their presentation, or their prototype. That helps to reduce time spent during presentations, raises their quality, and makes them more entertaining. We also reduce our online time with it. We shift these tasks to occur before workshops, if possible, so people can work on their presentations when they prefer and to provide considered feedback to start solving right away. With special tools presented in Chapter 3, like Loom or with video-conference tools like Zoom or MS Teams, you can record your videos. Making a presentation could also make sense using Toonly to create tool-making animated videos that sum up the findings.

TIP
When you make a video for assignments, focus on what the participants should do, not on your 'face'. Guide them visually through the process with an example. Make the video short (less than three minutes) and entertaining.

3. Combine synchronous and asynchronous work

One of the main advantages of working online in teams is that you can perform both asynchronous and synchronous work. What does that mean?

For parts of our innovation journeys, we meet in workshops. We are with all participants together in a videoconference, for example, and work in groups or individually, meaning we are all synchronous, working at the same moment on the same online whiteboard. Asynchronous means that the whole team works online in groups or as individuals, but not at the same time. We give them a time frame (most days) to do specific tasks on their own. Whenever they do it within this time slot does not matter.

We learned that it is even more relevant for participants to know why they are in this workshop and that it has to be relevant for them. How does that look in practice? We use it, for example, for our ideation sessions in the phase Raise Ideas of the FORTH innovation method (see Chapter 10). A few days before the actual ideation session, we already send our participants the prepared ideation whiteboard, with personal idea spaces and the ideation question. The participants are still in the Observe and Learn phase of the FORTH-journey and most of them already have many ideas in mind. So, they feel pretty happy to be able to put their ideas down on a board.

What is the advantage of working this way? Well, first of all, we save time in the workshop itself. Because we do not need to do the so-called braindump anymore. The participants shaped their ideas before the workshop asynchronously. It helps the participants write all ideas down when it suits them best, which results in both more and better ideas. Seeing all the ideas of all the others upfront results in two behaviours that benefit the innovation expedition. A competition on 'who has the most ideas?' and people getting inspired by all others' ideas. It puts them in a creative mood that helps get more ideas and more innovative ideas.

We also use asynchronous work after the ideation session. We end our workshop after presenting the ideas of the last idea generation technique. To initiate the converging phase selecting top ideas, we give the participants 24-48 hours to make their decisions. This has the advantage that the participants work when it suits them best, when they are alone and focused. This can be done with the technique of anonymous voting. In Miro, it is possible to set voting without disturbing the process on the boards.

We also use the technique Lightning Demos asynchronously if it fits timewise. Then participants can do their research alone and just do the presentation in the workshop itself.

> **TIP**
> We have the experience that the ratio of asynchronous and synchronous work always depends on the participants' commitment and engagement. In the FORTH innovation method, for example, we have in the beginning only a small amount of asynchronous work. We increase it over the progress of the process. In the last phase, Homecoming, the most work is done asynchronously. In the end, you have so much engagement and commitment that people always deliver.

ASYNCHRONOUS: YOU GET A CERTAIN TASK, WHICH HAS TO BE DONE BY A DEFINED DUE DATE. INDIVIDUALS OR GROUPS WORK ON THE TASK ON THEIR SCHEDULE

SYNCHRONOUS

SYNCHRONOUS: WORKSHOP/MEETING VIA A VIDEOCONFERENCING TOOL; EVERYBODY IS VIRTUALLY PRESENT, SIMULTANEOUSLY AND IN ONE SPOT

FACILITATING INTERACTIVE WORKSHOPS

4. Working Together-Alone

It often happens that teams have endless discussions about possible solutions while generating ideas. With the technique together-alone originated in the Design Sprint, you can solve this issue because participants get their own space and time to write down their thoughts before discussing them in the group. One of the main problems is that individual people cannot speak out or that team members influence one another due to hierarchy or other group dynamics, and certain great ideas get lost. To reduce these negative effects on the outcome, you can also use break out rooms to make smaller groups, which are hindered less by group dynamics or hierarchy.

How does it work?

Together-alone works best with collaborative digital whiteboards like Mural, Miro, or Klaxoon, because everybody can work within them simultaneously on the same task, and the results are visual in one spot. In the beginning, the facilitator explains and shows the assignment. If there are uncertainties, questions can be answered, so all participants have a clear and shared understanding of the assignment. The whole exercise is timeboxed. This means that you, as a facilitator, set a time for the exercise, so everybody knows how much time is available for the task. The difficulty is to find the right time frame. It always needs to be a little on the short side, so people do not get too relaxed or start doing something else.

Now everybody starts working on the same task, but alone. When using digital whiteboards, there are two options. Either they should generate thoughts and ideas totally by

ONLINE INNOVATION

A L O N E

ALONE: EVERYBODY WORKS ALONE IN SILENCE

TOGETHER

TOGETHER: EVERYBODY WORKS AT THE SAME TIME ON THE SAME TASK

themselves in a personal ideation space or using the private mode in MURAL or the Bulk mode in Miro.

Or they can see what the others are writing and build on the thoughts and ideas. Most important is that the ideas are written or drawn – made visible – so nothing gets lost, and each idea stands for itself without explaining, leaving little room for misinterpretations. We use together-alone for almost all exercises. Because we realise that online, when people go into break out rooms, they easily drift into talking, chatting, and discussing instead of creating. Together-alone helps speed up our processes and increase the engagement of the participants.

5. Anonymous voting

Making decisions is the most important and most challenging part of workshops, especially when talking about innovation. When it comes to decision making, people in western cultures start to discuss because everybody wants to be heard. That has two major disadvantages. On the one hand, the whole process needs a lot of time, frustrating everyone. On the other hand, the decision may be significantly biased by the hierarchy in the organisation, and extroverts dominate the conversation.

With anonymous voting, which you can use on the digital whiteboards Mural and Miro, you can solve this issue. With anonymous voting, you get a fast, clear, and unbiased picture of the opinions of the participants. It can be used as a decision or can be used to make the deciders help to decide.

How does it work?

As a facilitator, we open up a voting session. We give it a name and define the number of votes each participant gets. When we are using Mural, we start voting right away. The voting will pop up for all participants and everyone can vote directly. We can see who voted already. This makes it easy to see when it is time to close the voting. The results pop up directly after the closing, ranked by the number of votes received. We also see how many people voted on it, which is helpful if you have a tie. When using Miro, you have more options. You can define how long the voting will be open and on what exactly you can vote (which sticky-notes, or text, or pictures). That makes it possible to make voting asynchronous without limiting the activities on the board.

In our online innovation practice, together-alone and anonymous voting are a perfect combination to go forward quickly and with purpose.

> **TIP**
> **It is also possible to do limited anonymous voting with the poll functions of video conference tools like Zoom and Butter.**

When we work with another digital whiteboard without voting function, we use simple circles for an 'anonymous' dot voting.

6. Bulk mode

Generating ideas on digital whiteboards hinders some people's creativity because they have to also focus on the technical part of how to create a sticky note and write or draw on it. So, ideas or thoughts might get lost. For this case, the online collaboration whiteboard Miro has the so-called Bulk mode. We have good experiences with it. Participants use it when they want to focus and do not want to get distracted by others or worry about selecting a digital note to write on. When you start Bulk mode, the whole screen goes grey. Only in the centre of the screen you see something: a line, 'type in bulk add notes'. Here, you can type in your ideas. By pushing 'enter', you start your next idea without leaving this modus.

The Bulk mode can be used for two things. One is allowing people to focus, not getting distracted by the activity of others on the board. When using other whiteboards like Mural or Klaxoon, which do not have Bulk mode, we try to make it easy for participants and already have empty sticky-notes prepared. They just need to double-click, start writing and not worry about making their own sticky-note. The second use is when you want people to share problems: thoughts that should remain anonymous. If you are using Mural, you can use the private mode. Then your participants can only see what they are writing. The texts of the others are hidden.

> **TIP**
> **If you do not use Bulk mode or another digital white-board, you could tell your participants to open an empty word document or spreadsheet and start writing ideas there. Each idea has to be separated with the 'enter' button in the word document. For Mural, you need to copy everything and paste it into the board. Then for each idea, a sticky note will be generated. For Miro, it has to be in a spreadsheet format to work in this way.**

7. Break out rooms

In online meetings with Zoom, MS Teams, Butter, and many others, it is only possible that one person speaks at a time; otherwise, nobody can understand anything. To keep the workshops engaging as much as possible, participants need to communicate and share their thoughts verbally. For this, you can use so-called break out rooms (BOR). They are online-meetings separate from the main meeting room, providing the advantage that you can send participants into these rooms and get them back whenever you want. This is very important because some participants are already waiting in the plenum, and others are still in the BORs.

BORs are very useful in creating smaller teams, which helps introverts speak up more quickly since it is harder for them to do that in bigger groups. In our experience, BORs should not exceed five people. With more than five people in a room, attention goes down. Only a few will engage in the activity, while others will be passive and drift off. BORs are extremely valuable for getting to know each other in the beginning. Putting people in pairs into rooms for five minutes helps immensely to increase the mood and engagement. Because everybody is able to talk and has a direct personal connection, they are also helpful when group work is needed, and people need to communicate. Until now, Zoom has the best BOR feature. It is very simple to use and has many possibilities like random or manual placing, or participants can choose themselves.

As well as in Zoom, you can pre-set break out rooms in Butter before the actual meeting. The advantage of Butter is that you can set up more than one BOR setting in advance. That means you can create different BOR settings (four groups selected/five groups shuffle, etc.). During the workshop, you can also pre-assign the participants to different settings. That saves a lot of valuable workshop time, makes it easy for the facilitator, and feels smoother for the participants.

Tools like Wonder.me use a different approach. Every participant can move around in a virtual space and decide with whom he wants to have a video chat. Facilitators can broadcast so everybody, no matter where they are, can listen.

Here, break out rooms are generated and closed by the participants themselves naturally. This means you have much less control as a facilitator. This can be a disadvantage if you need to get a team to work towards their specific objectives.

When MS Teams did not have break out rooms, we used different channels as BORs. That initially seemed to be a good idea but proved to be a big failure. We had instructed the participants to come back after a certain time. But the discussion in the BORS was so intense that they lost time. Visiting all BORs and asking the participants to come back took almost ten minutes before everybody was back in the plenary workshop. And ten minutes is a lot of time in a tight and structured online workshop.

8. Lightning Demo
Lightning demo is an exercise coming from the Design Sprint. The idea behind this is to inspire the team to take off their blinders and stimulate thinking beyond their organisation or industry. It has two steps: research and presentation of the findings.

We start with research, when we ask all participants to come up with three products or services that might inspire us. They get about 25 minutes to search the internet. When using online collaboration tools like Miro or Mural, they can drag and drop the board's information. It can be anything, a website, a pdf, a video, or just text. We encourage our participants to research both inside their own company and sector, and also outside their industry. Other industries might be using great solutions already, and we do not want to reinvent the wheel. The participants need to write a sticky note with the 'big idea' behind each inspirational idea found.

Next, they present the findings. Each participant presents her inspiration with a time limit of three minutes for each finding.

We recommend that the presenter shares the screen while demonstrating her findings one-by-one. When all findings are presented, you have a colourful, inspiring whiteboard on Miro or Mural with their key points as a source of inspiration for the ideation phase.

TIP
Do this asynchronously. We, for example, try to finish the last problem space workshop with the problem statement and the 'how might we' question (HMW). Then we give the task to prepare lightning demos as preparation for the ideation workshop.

COMMUNICATION AND FEEDBACK

9. Chat function
The chat function in videoconferencing tools – it is simple, it is powerful, and everybody knows it. You can use it in five different ways.

1. **One-on-one communication.** It allows the facilitator and the participants to contact each other directly so messages can be exchanged without disturbing others. It is a little bit like the chit-chat of two people during offline workshops when they sit next to each other. Or we like to use it to give a tip or a comment to participants individually that others should not see. The only problem we experience is that the chat messages will mostly not be noticed right away, which kills the direct messaging.
2. **Additional communication.** Gijs van wulfen always says that if you want to explain something, use three ways to make sure everybody gets it: *tell, write, and show*. Here the chat function can help to explain an exercise or task.

3. **Short feedback.** Use the chat for quick feedback when you do not want to disturb the whole group's process by speech. It is also possible to use the chat as a simple voting tool when participants write within the tool their choice.
4. **For Interactions.** Chat can also be used for warm-up games, presenting your findings, and for Q&A.
5. **Share files and links.** If you want to share a file with participants or want them to go to a specific URL (for your digital whiteboard), you can share it in the chat.

> **TIP**
> In Zoom, you can also (auto)save the chat, so you have it also available after the session, which can be very useful if you want to be able to read the input of the participants later.

> **TIP**
> When you use a setup that has more than one chat possibility . For example, Miro and Zoom clarify what chat you will use and which should not be used.

10. Survey

We use surveys as well as polls. For online Innovation processes, we use them differently. Polls we use to get immediate feedback, mostly with multiple predefined choices. We use it to engage our participants in the workshop itself. Surveys we mostly use to gain insights and feedback for ideas from customers.

Polls
With Polls, you get quick, unbiased results visualised in a way that encourages reflection and sparks discussion. We use them a lot for a short check-in or check-out, feedback, or collecting insights during the workshop. Polls correlate closely to the anonymous voting technique because most polls are unknown and work the same way. Tools like Zoom, Butter, Howspace, and Klaxoon have polls already integrated so you do not need an additional tool. Kahoot and Mentimeter are poll tools that make workshops more engaging and fun. Kahoot has integrations with MS Teams, Zoom, and Slack. Miro and Mural have the already mentioned anonymous voting function. With them, you can create polls right on the collaboration boards. We also have good experiences with the poll function of Butter; it is easy to make, quite flexible, and looks good. Howspace even has AI-support to help you interpret the results correctly. For us, polls get fast results.

Surveys
We use surveys to get quantitative insights from participants or customers, or we ask for feedback on ideas or the outcomes of workshops. While polls make the most sense when used during workshops, surveys are done most often asynchronously so people can answer the questions in their own time. For surveys, we use Google forms or other survey tools (like Typeform). One specific example when we use it is concept testing in the Test Ideas phase of the FORTH innovation method. We do a short survey for each of the 10 to 15 developed concepts. The survey consists of the written concept with all relevant information, five rating questions and two questions where customers share their likes and dislikes about the concept. The survey is both long enough to get enough valid data as well as short enough that customers fill it out.

POLL   VS   SURVEY

POLL	SURVEY
% DON'T NEED DETAILED RESPONSES	NEED DETAILED AND EXTENSIVE FEEDBACK ☑
% NEED IMMEDIATE FEEDBACK	HAVE MANY QUESTIONS TO ASK ☑
% ONLY ONE QUESTION TO ASK	NEED TO GATHER PERSONAL INFORMATION ☑
% NO TIME FOR ANALYSIS	REQUIRE TEXT COMMENTS ☑

source: www.questionpro.com/polls/poll-vs-survey.html

TIP
Switching tools online takes time and has a certain risk that it does not work straight away. Depending on your participants' online skill set, your process and your timing, consider whether the additional value of bringing in another (poll) tool is higher than the risks.

Working online is different than in-person. We presented you great tools in Chapter 3, and ten useful techniques to employ them in this chapter. There is, of course, an Achilles' heel in innovating online, which we present in the next chapter, which discusses critical points we experienced during our online innovation projects.

KEY MESSAGES FROM THIS CHAPTER

▸ **Online innovation is not worse or better than in-person innovation. It is different, and you can facilitate awesome workshops with these techniques.**

▸ **Designing your virtual room and using video to explain it is the key to making your workshops customer-focused and clear.**

▸ **A fool with a tool is still a fool. Using the right techniques with these tools make a difference.**

▸ **Use polls to get fast insights for yourself as facilitator, and for the participants.**

▸ **Use break out rooms wisely to make your innovation workshop more engaging.**

▸ **Working together-alone is the key feature for making online workshops fast, engaging, and effective.**

CONTENTS

CHAPTER 5

THE ACHILLES HEEL OF WORKING ONLINE

Working online tires you out, right? The same is true for us, too. And that's not the only challenge confronting us as online facilitators of innovation. There are practical issues, perception issues, and human issues that lead to lower engagement. This chapter discusses the Achilles' heel of working online and what to do about it.

PRACTICAL ONLINE ISSUES

First of all, we have technical issues. You also experience that participants, maybe even you, with bad internet, have dodgy connections and frozen screens and make endless efforts to log in again. And while the online workshop continues, you start to feel helpless and sometimes hopeless, which is not the most productive mindset for a creative workshop. Sometimes it just sucks!

When you work with a team across different time zones, it's quite challenging to pick the right time slot for your workshops. We operate a lot with worldwide teams with people from Silicon Valley, Europe, and Asia Pacific, for example. When you start at 17.00 Central European Time, it's 08.00 in the morning on the USA's West Coast and exactly midnight in Malaysia. The Americans are ready, but the European participants are out of energy and you see the participants from Malaysia fall asleep behind their screens.

PERCEPTION ISSUES OF ONLINE WORK

In Non-Covid-19 times we have a choice of doing workshops online or in-person. There might be a perception in the company culture that online is less important. People would come together physically for strategic workshops, yet for less important subjects, online workshops are enough. If this is the case, you might experience as a facilitator or project leader that the participants' motivation to be present and to participate actively in the online workshop is not very high. Especially with screens turned off, they might be doing other things instead of participating actively.

HUMAN ISSUES WHILE WORKING ONLINE

Online video calls can't compare with physical interaction. We miss emotional moments like patting someone on the shoulder because you're happy to meet him or her, winking to someone to make contact or laughing out loud together about the same (bad) joke. But, on Zoom, everyone except the speaker is muted. No back-patting. No winking. And no big laughs together.

On a computer screen, facial expressions are very hard-to-read. You only see each other's façade, a lot of times with a virtual background, to hide the mess at home, or the children playing in the background. In real conversations, you get non-verbal cues that are helpful, because body language is important in showing emotions. But in a Zoom call, you are just talking to a screen. And you have no clue if it resonates with the others in the call. Do they understand it? Should you pause or perhaps slow down? Or, on the contrary, should you speed up? You just can't tell ...

The conversation flow online is much slower than when 'live' since we have to unmute first before we can speak. We think that 'you have to unmute' is the most said sentence online. All these factors together – the lack of interpersonal dynamics – is bound to lead to more miscommunication between people.

Due to the lack of personal connection, you run the risk that, especially in innovation teams where people have never met personally, you stay strangers to each other during the whole online project, as you never truly meet.

DISTRACTIONS AT HOME

You might have a problem focusing on your work at the office by always being disturbed by your colleagues. That's why for very important workshops everyone leaves their offices to a great quiet venue somewhere in the woods, near the seaside, or in the middle of nowhere. So in in-person workshops, when the participants put their cell phones in silence, you can control and minimize the distractions for participants as workshop facilitator.

That has completely changed since we all (had to) work from home online. When the cat jumps on your lap, the washing machine beeps that the laundry is done, or your doorbell rings, you are seriously distracted and often log out mentally from the online process. This happens more than we like. You will recognize the majority of the 50 distractions while working online at home that we mention in the following chart. Online it's hard to stay immersed in a workshop in a physical environment beyond your control.

CHART: 50 DISTRACTIONS WHILE WORKING ONLINE FROM HOME

1. My cat jumps on my lap.
2. The doorbell rings.
3. My washing machine beeps that the laundry is done.
4. My kid is hungry.
5. Participants in the call are not muted.
6. My dog starts barking.
7. My cursor is stuck in this ^!@%&^ tool.
8. My favourite series on Netflix starts now.
9. My kids come out of school.
10. My neighbours are shouting at each other (again).
11. It started snowing. Wow...
12. My mother calls.
13. My screen freezes.
14. I can't find the link to the Miro board anymore.
15. The lawnmower of the neighbour is making considerable noise.
16. My children need my computer for schoolwork.
17. The electricity has stopped.
18. I get blinded by the setting sun.
19. Oh, I forgot to put out the garbage.
20. MS Teams crashes mid-meeting.
21. There are construction noises outside.
22. My cell phone rings.
23. I have bad computer sound.
24. My pizza gets delivered.
25. No... I lost connection (again).
26. My girlfriend is WhatsApping me (continuously).
27. I need some time to prepare for my next call.
28. My neighbour's son has his percussion hour.
29. The session runs late, and I have to pick up the kids.
30. Our CEO is shouting she can't type on Mural anymore.
31. Muted participants talking.
32. My laptop is out of battery.
33. Other participants are sitting in the dark.
34. The kids of the neighbours upstairs are yelling.
35. Tesco is bringing the groceries.
36. I need to finish this memo now during the session.
37. Jehovah witnesses at my front door.
38. My son can't find his soccer shoes.
39. A non-muted participant has a barking dog.
40. The facilitator talks all the time while I need to think.
41. A courier called to say that I can pick up my parcel.
42. I'm seeing WhatsApping jokes with other participants.
43. I can't find the Miro link to this new board.
44. I need to cook a meal in the meantime.
45. My mother calls again.
46. I am (or others are) playing around with virtual backgrounds.
47. I hear police sirens: what's going on out there?
48. My kid kisses me goodbye.
49. I'm getting new emails continuously.
50. Just now, my washing machine transitioned to a spin cycle.

Source: online brainstorm with 20 participants of the training as a certified online facilitator of the FORTH innovation method from the USA, Canada, Costa Rica, Ireland, UK, Netherlands, Italy, South Africa, Malaysia, and the Kingdom of Saudi Arabia, February 2021.

ONLINE WORK DRAINS OUR ENERGY

Zoom or Microsoft Teams tires you out. Online work requires more focus than a face-to-face chat, as you can read in the interview with Gianpiero Petriglieri, an associate professor at Insead, and Marissa Shuffler, an associate professor at Clemson University. 'Our minds are together when our bodies feel we're not. That dissonance, which causes people to have conflicting feelings, is exhausting.'

In our experience, being in an online workshop for an hour feels the same as being in an offline workshop for two hours. When we started to bring the FORTH innovation method online in April/May 2020, we just copied the methodology, which resulted in eight-hour workshops with Zoom and Trello at the start. Besides the fact that it was boring, it was extremely tiring. As you will read later in Chapter 10, we brought back the workshops' length to a maximum of three or four hours, as we were completely knackered otherwise.

THE REASON ZOOM CALLS DRAIN YOUR ENERGY.

But what, exactly, is tiring us out? In this section, we like to quote an interview BBC Worklife had with Gianpiero Petriglieri, an associate professor at Insead, who explores sustainable learning and development in the workplace, and Marissa Shuffler, an associate professor at Clemson University, who studies workplace wellbeing and teamwork effectiveness.

Is video chat harder? What's different compared to face-to-face communication?
Being on a video call requires more focus than a face-to-face chat, says Petriglieri. Video chats mean we need to work harder to process non-verbal cues like facial expressions, the tone and pitch of the voice, and body language; paying more attention to these consumes a lot of energy. 'Our minds are together when our bodies feel we're not. That dissonance, which causes people to have conflicting feelings, is exhausting. You cannot relax into the conversation naturally,' he says.

Silence is another challenge, he adds. 'Silence creates a natural rhythm in a real-life conversation. However, when it happens in a video call, you become anxious about technology.' It also makes people uncomfortable.

An added factor, says Shuffler, is that if we are physically on camera, we are very aware of being watched. 'When you're on a video conference, you know everybody's looking at you; you are on stage, so there comes the social pressure and feeling like you need to perform. Being performative is nerve-wracking and more stressful.' It's also very hard for people not to look at their face if they can see it on screen or be conscious of how they behave in front of the camera. 'Most of our social roles happen in different places, but now the context has collapsed', says Petriglieri. 'Imagine if you go to a bar, and in the same bar you talk with your professors, meet your parents, or date someone, isn't it weird? That's what we're doing now... We are confined in our own space, in the context of a very anxiety-provoking crisis, and our only space for interaction is a computer window.'

Shuffler says a lack of downtime after we've fulfilled work and family commitments may be another factor in our tiredness. Some of us may be putting higher expectations on ourselves due to worries over the economy, furloughs, and job losses. 'There's also that heightened sense of "I need to be performing at my top level in a situation." Some of us are kind of over-performing to secure our jobs.'

Big group calls can feel particularly performative, Petriglieri warns. People like watching television because you can allow your mind to wander – but a large video call 'is like you're watching television and television is watching you'. Large group chats can also feel depersonalizing, he adds, because your power as an individual is diminished. And despite the branding, it may not feel like leisure time. 'It doesn't matter whether you call it a virtual happy hour; it's a meeting because mostly we are used to using these tools for work.'

So how can we alleviate Zoom fatigue?
Both experts suggest limiting video calls to those who are necessary. Turning on the camera should be optional, and in general, there should be more under-standing that cameras do not always have to be on throughout each meeting. Having your screen off to the side, instead of straight ahead, could also help your concentration, particularly in group meetings, says Petriglieri. It makes you feel like you're in an adjoining room, so it may be less tiring.

In some cases, it's worth considering if video chats are the most efficient option. Shuffler suggests that shared files with clear notes can be a better option than avoiding information overload when working. She also suggests taking time during meetings to catch up before diving into business. 'Spend some time to check into people's wellbeing', she urges. 'It's

a way to reconnect us with the world, and to maintain trust and reduce fatigue and concern.'

Building transition periods between video meetings can also help us refresh – try stretching, have a drink, or do a bit of exercise, our experts say. Boundaries and transitions are important; we need to create buffers that allow us to put one identity aside and then go to another as we move between work and private personas.
And maybe, says Petriglieri, if you want to reach out, go old-school. 'Write a letter to someone instead of meeting them on Zoom. Tell them you care about them.'

Source: April 2020. www.bbc.com/worklife/article/20200421-why-zoom-video-chats-are-so-exhausting

LOW SERENDIPITY

In innovation and creativity, the phenomenon of serendipity is well known. It's when someone accidentally finds something great. Our innovation projects benefit from seren-dipity, and we try to stimulate it by adding an Observe and Learn phase in our methodologies. Random encounters trigger serendipity. It's sparked by unexpected new inspira-tion, which triggers new ideas. On our in-person innovation journeys, these moments of serendipity are triggered by spontaneous meetings, which can happen at any moment during workshops: at breaks at the coffee machine or later at night in the bar. Unfortunately, you miss these moments during online workshops. So online, there's less serendipity from interactions by chance because personal interaction is minimal, or even absent.

All reasons mentioned above – the practical online issues, the lower status of online work, the lack of personal connection, the distractions at home, the energy drain of video conferencing, and the low chance of serendipity – lower engagement from participants during online workshops compared to in-person workshops at a special venue.

More bad news is that from our perspective, as innovation workshop facilitators, online workshops are in practice much harder to facilitate than in-person workshops for several reasons. As an online facilitator, you experience the same problems as the participants in connecting because you, too miss their facial expressions and body language. As facilitators, this is even more important when we are guiding the online innovation process. Getting a personal connection is essential for us facilitators to connect to each of the participants, to get a feel if there's a buy-in for the direction taken in the project, and to support the outcomes produced.

Getting personally connected to participants is so hard, especially when you are facilitating with, for example, the Microsoft Teams video conferencing tool. At the moment we wrote this book, you could only see nine people simultaneously, while the group we worked with was double that size. So, we could only see half the group, which is madness, of course. On the other hand, when using Zoom, for example, where you can see every participant when using Gallery View, you see the many videos of participants in such tiny dimensions that it becomes very hard to see facial expressions.

To be brief: the engagement of the group online is often minimal, while the online facilitator's job is much more demanding, because the online technology has to be managed at the same time, too.

THE ACHILLES' HEEL OF WORKING ONLINE

Although online workshops have many advantages, as you read in Chapter 4, the Achilles' heel for us as online guides is being able to create and experience a 'group flow'. You know these moments, too: where there's a high energy wave of excitement in your team, building upon each other's ideas leading to a familiar group feeling of creating something special.

While we have facilitated very successful online innovation workshops generating 1256 ideas with the FORTH innovation methodology 100% online, we never sensed this common group feeling as it's so hard to show and feel personal emotions behind a screen. Was the online workshop less successful? In a rational sense, No. But after the workshop, when we switched off Microsoft Teams and logged out of Miro, I was alone ... at home, which felt like a cold shower. In in-person workshops, we would have had a drink together to celebrate our success, and we would feel the high energy level and enthusiasm of everyone else. And we would see excited participants, all proud about the milestone reached. You miss the pat on the shoulder of your leader or the kind words, 'Well done, mate' from your colleague.

In online workshops 'RATIONALITY RULES', which is not bad, as results are great, too. You just miss those magical moments of feeling connected as a team.

HOW TO CREATE MAGICAL MOMENTS IN AN ONLINE PROJECT

So, we need to compensate for 'rationality rules'. And that's why we also focus on creating magical emotional moments for online teams. From the perspective of Jens Emrich von Kajdacsy, leadership and team coach, magical moments create togetherness. As online facilitators and project leaders, we should try to develop special team moments to facilitate the experiencing of togetherness in a team even while we are working remotely. This emotion emerges when something unexpected happens and surprises the people – when they learn as a team and create insights or ideas for a sustainable change that fuels togetherness. And moments when people feel proud to be part of a team or something bigger are typical magical moments.

CHART: HOW TO CREATE MAGICAL TEAM-MOMENTS ONLINE?

Sure, online experiences are not in-person. But this is no reason for not being able to create curiosity and relationships in the online world. The first question is, 'What makes a moment a magical moment?' My perspective on this is

TOGETHERNESS.
- These are moments that we experience together in a team. When something unexpected happens, and it surprises the team.
- To learn as a team and create insights for a sustainable change.
- Being proud to be part of a team or something more significant.

First TIP
THE PRESENT
Send your participants a little gift beforehand by the postman. This builds a physical bridge to and between the teammates in the online world.

The magical moment created...

Everyone loves to receive presents, especially when they are unexpected. It creates a really surprising opening moment when you unbox a package together online.

Second TIP
THE ONBOARDING
Preparation is essential for every event, especially in the online environment. Create a separate onboarding process before your online workshop to explain the process, platforms, and techniques. Let the participants introduce themselves, ask for their roles, and describe their superpower and passion. Above all, build a virtual playground area where they can try the new stuff. Mail your invitation and use the target platform you will facilitate your innovation journey on. And don't forget to check if everybody received it well.

The magical moment created...

With the onboarding process, you already escort your participants to the lobby of your workshop room. They will be prepared to start the workshop on a common level, to create outcomes and insights from the first moment on. Your participants will feel *safe and secure* because all of them have a shared jump base to start from.

Third TIP
THE PURPOSE

People want to know why they should do what they've been asked to do. Many of the teams in the online world prefer to wait for an in-person meeting because they are sick of online video conferences with long durations, without enabling video or voice because of performance issues, just watching a shared presentation. It's boring. They miss interaction and inspiring facilitation.

When you create online workshops, tell your participants why they should be part of it. Integrate them already in the concept process and make clear why you need them for this special journey. And don't forget to ask the team about their perspective on a higher purpose to understand their goals and targets to reach.

How to do it?

Connect your invitation to a workshop ALWAYS with goals you want to reach, and with a strong background, a particular purpose you can formulate by using words or a picture with a clear message.

Think about questions to ask in the onboarding process, team introduction, or the team's expectations, which triggers a possible 'why'. So, ask why we should do something instead of what we should do and connect these questions to current situations in the real world. For example, 'If you are thinking of the pandemic and its impact, why should we change the model of collaboration in the team?'

Let me remark on one point: Talking about what we are doing triggers the rational part of our brain. But when talking about why we are doing what we do, we trigger the limbic system and the emotional part of us.

By asking 'Why', you can already address your team's limbic system in the workshop from the start.

The magical moment created...

When you trigger the purpose by asking WHY it creates a special momentum within the team, it connects the people on a deeper and visionary sense to their goals and gives a great boost to reaching those goals together.

Fourth TIP
THE VALUE SYSTEM

Invite the team to create and rely on a shared value system. Talking about values and principles, explaining each to everyone's meaning is a strong element for understanding each other, how people act or react in a certain way, and for feeling safe. It permits the whole team to be themselves. Don't forget to let everybody confirm the common values you make together online.

How to do this?

In a team session, ask the team members to think about their values and principles, which are important. Timebox it with 15 minutes and let them write down the results for themselves.

In the next step, ask everyone which value they want to add to a team's common value system. It should be the most important one for them, and they should be given time to explain why it is their favourite.

They should use a formulation like, 'I want to add the value ____, because ____!"

Then ask the others if they understood the meaning and the context of the stated value and if they agree to integrate it into their value system. If so, ask how to formulate the value or the expression that describes the value at its best and write it on a flipchart or a whiteboard.

When all values are documented on the board, ask the team how to name it, which title they want to use, and ask for a consequence of the value system that the team or a team member will break. The consequence should come out of the team and be written on the board with the values before.

The picture of the whiteboard can be integrated as a background to the virtual team room.

The magical moment created...

Creating a common value system builds a trustful room, self-confidence, and an open atmosphere where people can be authentic and honest and speak directly from their souls. Be prepared to find new potential in your team when formerly calm people raise their voices.

Fifth TIP
EMOTIONS

A workshop in the online world is a special space that you may create and design with care. It demands your cognitive abilities on a high level, so you have to consider integrating a variety of different impulses – triggering the conscious and unconscious minds, and, indeed, emotions. We have five senses we can engage in when addressing our emotions to support an effective learning environment.

Include different tastes and smells to expand the user-experience. Use strong visual language like pictures and colours to create a familiar space for your customers. Decorate your room, your background, and yourself by carrying hats or clothing that fits your event topics. Tell a story; I mean, everyone likes stories that have a message. And music is a fantastic medium to transport feelings and flood a room with special kinds of energy.

The point is that it is already difficult enough to recognize and react to emotions in-person; all the more we should focus on this point in the online environment. And remember, our senses often lead to emotions, so why not engage all our senses in a workshop to support an effective learning climate?

The magical moment created...

The emotional state of workshop participants is a great determinator for their insights and the workshop's outcomes. Our senses trigger our limbic system, which is the home of our emotions, so this means we can create emotional moments by using them. Moments of sorrow and rage, fear and joy. And this leads to a deeper connection between you and the participants – it leads to real personal growth. If you get to this point, you will realize the true meaning of being a team.

 Above all, you will recognize a special flow within the team. That's the moment when the team discovers its soul and rides its team-wave.

Guest author: Jens Emrich von Kajdacsy, Team and Leadership coach [www.jensemrich.de]

In the next chapter 'Ten rules for online innovation', we will guide you further in facilitating innovation online, helping you deal with the challenges that online work creates for facilitators, project leaders, and online project teams. We will also support you in creating magical moments 'to motivate the elephant', as you will understand in a moment.

KEY MESSAGES FROM THIS CHAPTER

▸ **Online video conferencing can't compare with in-person interaction as it drains your energy.**

▸ **Practical online issues, the lower status of online work, the lack of personal connection and the distractions at home all hinder you.**

▸ **Serendipity has a lower chance to occur online than offline.**

▸ **All leads to lower engagement from the participants during online workshops. We compared offline workshops at a special venue.**

▸ **The Achilles' heel of online workshops can create and experience a 'group flow'.**

▸ **You need to create magical emotional moments, especially in an online project.**

CONTENTS

CHAPTER 6

TEN RULES FOR ONLINE INNOVATION

Working remotely, you encounter advantages and pitfalls. Some people love working online for its freedom, flexibility, and productivity, while others hate it because they miss social interaction, struggle with new tools, and become exhausted by the virtual experience.

To be sure, moving from in-person to online workshops is one of those dramatic shifts that you only experience every once in a while. The two primary questions are:

What do you need to help people change the way they do things?
How can you be more effective when starting online innovation?

CONSIDER BOTH THE RATIONAL AND THE EMOTIONAL SIDE

We like to use the metaphor that appeared in *Switch*[1], a book about change:
Imagine a person riding a six-ton elephant who wants to lead it to a lovely lake. He manages to guide it thanks to his intention, abilities, and strong control. Indeed, the elephant walks reliably, up to a certain point. After a while, he is tired and does not know how much further he has to walk and whether he will get there before nightfall. Moreover, a series of tree trunks on the path make it necessary for him to exert a tremendous effort to proceed; in short, he no longer wants to continue. So, even if you've never ridden an elephant, you can still imagine how things will end if the elephant doesn't want to move. Now let's find out who these two characters are: the rider is our rational mind, the one that expresses willpower, makes plans, defines actions for change, analyses data, and makes conclusions, while the elephant is the emotional mind, the one that maintains energy, intuition, enthusiasm, fear, sadness, and all our other emotions.

This story tells us that there are three conditions to facilitate any change:
Motivate the elephant: engage the emotional part so that it puts all its energy into motion and works alongside us.
Direct the rider: indicate the direction and support the rational element to take action.
Shape the path: remove obstacles from the environment.

Why do we love this metaphor? Going online needs a shift in mindset. We have suddenly found ourselves to be beginners again despite our long experience. The perimeter, and therefore, the circumstances are entirely diverse.

RULES MAKE THE JOURNEY SIMPLE

The ten rules we describe in this chapter will help you engage the emotional side online, set a clear direction online, and shape the online environment to obtain a seamless online innovation journey.

We've chosen the following ten rules out of dozens we've tested based on their effect on the online innovation process.

They result from our online experience and many mistakes, but mistakes are part of life, aren't they? And this is how we learn.

You'll find the ten rules in a logical order of before, during, and after your innovation workshops or journey.

Start applying the ones you feel are the most suitable for your situation and challenge.

CHART RULES BEFORE, DURING, AND AFTER YOUR INNOVATION WORKSHOPS OR JOURNEY

BEFORE	DURING	AFTER
1 DO A TECH ONBOARDING	**4** CO-FACILITATE	**10** MOVE TO ACTION WITH THE FOLLOW UP
2 KEEP THE DIGITAL BOARDS SIMPLE	**5** LET PEOPLE INTERACT FREELY	
3 SEND STUFF FOR ENGAGEMENT, INSPIRATION, AND FUN	**6** USE A 'STAR-MODEL' FACILITATION	
	7 ENGAGE PARTICIPANTS EMOTIONALLY	
	8 MANAGE THE ONLINE TIME	
	9 SET CLEAR INSTRUCTIONS (TO DIRECT THE RIDER)	

The online preparation phase aims to create all the enabling conditions in your technical set up, effective planning, and knowledge. Online workshops require more careful preparation than in-person ones because there are so many more issues that can jeopardize your workshop's success.

1. Do a tech onboarding

Depending on whether you are using a methodology that is applied in a three-hour workshop or during a 12-weeks series, the onboarding workshop can be longer or shorter, from ten minutes before the workshop starts, up to one hour, or two or three days before the beginning of your online innovation project.

Why? To ensure that the participants know the tools so they may be fully involved in the workshop and that participants' unexpected tech issues won't slow down your workshop.

> *Online workshops are significantly more reliant on technology than in-person. Technology-issues can have a ripple effect on your innovation journey.*

Even if you are only using a video conferencing tool, there are several audio, video, and connection issues you may encounter when facilitating. The question is not if they will happen, but which ones and to what extent. So, when facilitating online, you need to be prepared for these types of issues and have a plan in mind in case they happen.

Send the participants all the information they need, both in terms of hardware, log-ins, sign-up pages, links, and tips, and then check synchronously. In our experience, the four main things to check are:

Connection, of course. A high-speed connection allows participants to have the video on and use collaboration tools. Otherwise, you will have 'variable-geometry' workshops with people coming in and out. There are ways to increase bandwidth to suggest to your participants before the workshop: check the router's location because it can encounter interferences like other wireless devices or obstructions like doors and walls, reboot it before starting and shut down background apps that are consuming bandwidth. A quick solution to suggest is to set the mobile phone to a data network for the videoconference tool and the computer uses wifi to access the collaboration board, to free up the bandwidth. If you have the possibility, use a cable connection because wired connections have better internet speed than wireless ones.

Audio and video. Do a quick check to make sure everyone can be seen and heard clearly. Interacting with impassive or live-but-soundless pictures hinders engagement.
Again, use mobile phones for videoconferencing and computers with wifi for collaboration boards, or you can use computers for video and phone for audio to increase your audio quality.

Browser. Some browsers match better with specific tools, for example Chrome for Miro, Mozilla for Jitsy. Also, check that everybody has updated the browser to the latest version. Check it before the workshop rather than in the middle of the process when someone says, 'Help! My board is frozen. I can't move anything anymore.' In some cases, participants will have to download it on the spot, so consider the time needed.

Participant's experience. The tools-ability level of your participants may vary. Check the people's practice with it on some basic features you will use:

1. Raise a virtual hand, chat writing, screen sharing on video-conferencing.
2. Effectively navigate and use the essential features on a digital collaboration board.
3. Let them experiment how to switch from videoconferencing to the board, as you will probably do so often during your workshop. These checks will allow you to redesign some of the interaction forms or, if you do this just before the workshop, to quickly switch to more straightforward ways.

Plan at least a twenty-minute buffer in each workshop for tech-reasons. Prepare an alternative plan, tech-wise, and be sure you have agreed beforehand with your stakeholders what to do if you can't solve the technical problem.

TIP
Do a trial run with colleagues or friends to get an idea of the whole experience.

2. Keep the digital boards simple

Environment shapes behaviours. So, create an environment that helps participants have a pleasant online journey. Remove frictions and set up tasks in the simplest way possible. Digital collaboration boards are one of the main tools in online innovation for solving problems and generating ideas. Everyone needs to be able to work on them quickly and be productive.

However, working on online collaboration boards is potentially more difficult for many reasons. If you don't have two screens, you have to continually change your view, from the Zoom or whatever videoconference tool you are using to the board to read the instructions and do the assignments. To follow the process and work on a board, you have to zoom in and zoom out all the time, which is fatiguing for your eyes. Finally, the risk of miscommunication is higher in online processes because there are fewer opportunities to ask questions.

> *Keeping a digital board simple means essentially to care about three aspects: design, activities, and instructions.*

Design. For beginners, the route of the process should be straightforward and intuitive. Design your board in a compact working space, limit it to what is necessary, and make sure that people move around as little as possible. Define a logical flow, for example from left to right and from top to bottom, so that participants can predict where the next step will be without feeling 'lost in space' on the board. Display the different workshop steps on the board, separated into boxes, since they are on the agenda you sent in advance. If people have to brainstorm, set up a dedicated working space for each person so that while they are writing post-its, they don't overlap with each other. When you divide people into break out rooms, prepare in advance the board work areas: write the group's number or nickname and insert the participants' names and photos.

Activities. Start with simple tasks that require minimal actions from the participants, for example drag and drop items that you have already placed on the boards. When they become more confident, you can ask them for more complex actions. If participants need to upload files, consider having them sent to you via chat or even by email, if that is easier for them, so that you can upload them. Set up all the elements needed for the task: post-its, grids, kanban, and mind maps, so that people do not have to copy or duplicate them.

Instructions. Write instructions in a simple way next to the space to be used by the participants; if you have many groups working simultaneously, copy the instructions next to each workspace. In the instructions, especially if asynchronous work is required, you should always write and show information visually.

WHAT – e.g. Find the space with your name and photo. Write down as many ideas as you can think of related to the problem statement.
HOW – e.g. Select the arrow on the toolbar to the left of the screen to write on a post-it.
WHEN – e.g. Ten minutes. You can use the boards' timer to make time apparent to everyone.

The board's design defines the *modus operandi* with your users and can determine whether or not a workshop is useful. Spend some time on this phase; three or four hours to set up a board for a workshop that lasts two hours is not too long, especially if you are a beginner. You can design templates and then improve and adapt them from time to time.

After a while, you will be impressed by your design power and take on more challenges. The leading collaboration tools have ready-made templates that you can import or take inspiration from; a smart tool is Boardle, with which you can find templates divided by workshop type.

> **TIP**
> Set the 'board's start view for newly invited members' whenever possible so that your participants won't get lost on the board at the beginning. Block all elements on the board – boxes, graphics, instructions – to keep the layout as you imagined it.

3. Send stuff for engagement, inspiration, and fun

What is the thing we most suffer from having been catapulted into an online life? The lack of in-person relationships, of course. And the second one? Second is the lack of tactile experience: the objects we used during our workshops, markers, papers to hang on the walls, billions of post-it notes, and artefacts of various kinds. Nostalgia aside, objects serve to inspire, develop creativity, give a sense of solidity, and feel a 'real' connection to what we are doing.

Touch, taste, and smell are the senses that are missing in the online world.

Especially if you are about to embark on a long innovation journey, you can send participants at the beginning of the trip a physical toolbox. It will be a pleasant surprise, an act of care, and a call to concreteness.

To inspire you, below are some ideas for composing your five senses toolbox (more on this in Chapter 5) to send before kickoff. It will make participants feel like they are present in the room by sharing a concrete 'live' experience. Ensure the objects activate all five senses, take care of the packaging and enclose an intriguing note. Use the common unwrapping moment together in the kickoff to present each step of the route!

A wellness kit (scented candles, bath salts, room aromas, oils, soaps).

A book connected to the methodology you use, or this one ;-).

A novel related to the places, the environment, the trip or simply that has inspired you and you want to share. We like Raymond Queneau's novel, *Exercises in Style* – the same story retold in 99 different ways to look at things from different perspectives.

Posters with canvas templates to use in asynchronous work:
the FORTH innovation map, the Lean Canvas, the Business Model Canvas.

One whiteboard for creative activity or a prototype.

Card decks to use during icebreaking or creative tasks, for example, Dixit[2], Method cards[3], or Superpower cards[4].

Objects to use during tasks for inspiration: an innovative object, the storyteller cubes.

Gadgets: an hourglass to measure time as the ancients used to do, a magnifying glass to observe reality better.

A notebook, a bullet journal with pencils, stickers and washi tape for artistic notes.

Delicatessen for the palate's joy, a sweet and savoury mix representing your land or something related to the company or the route.

TIP
Send your box in time to the various destinations to ensure that everyone has received it before the kickoff and can participate in the magical unwrapping moment.

DURING

These rules serve to immerse participants in an online environment where they can feel at ease, share, generate ideas, co-create, and enjoy a seamless experience to the fullest.

4. Co-facilitate

No matter how much of a tech lover, expert, or nerd you are, running a remote workshop is a hard job. Therefore, we recommend always having a second person facilitating the workshop to help you with the technical issues. In this way, one of the facilitators can focus on the process, looking at the participants' more or less weak signals, and decide if there is something that needs to change.

We have experimented a lot with both. It's not impossible to run an online workshop on your own, even for groups of 20 people; it's just that a large part of your attention will be on making sure the flow is smooth from a technological point of view. You'll have to answer all the questions on how to use the tools. Plus, any technical problems with one of the participants will stop the flow of the workshop.

A tech facilitator is a person who also knows the process and can identify alternative solutions on the spot to guarantee results at any stage of the process. Here is a checklist of the primary tech facilitator's activities. The important thing is that you have rehearsed the flow first and have agreed on an effective way of dealing with each other during the workshop and how to deal with the most common contingencies. Watch out. Even tech facilitators may also suddenly disappear from the workshop; make sure they have a wired connection and be prepared.

TIP
If you can't have technical support, you might get light help from one or two persons in the group that helps keep things running smoothly and improve team cohesiveness and engagement. The activities you can assign to them are to chat check, set times, and support the less experienced participants in using the tools.

CHART: TECH FACILITATOR ACTIVITIES CHECKLIST

BEFORE	
1.	Supports the facilitator in preparing the boards and other necessary tools like polls and surveys.
2.	Facilitates the tech check.
3.	Sends an email to the participants explaining the facilitator's role.

DURING	
1.	At the beginning of the workshop, explains how video conferencing works and how to use chat, reactions, and polls.
2.	Checks that people are on mute and, if necessary, puts them on mute.
3.	Asks people to unmute, if necessary.
4.	Reads the chat continuously to see if there are any requests or difficulties.

5. Makes links and other resources available to the participants via the chat.

6. Shares the screen to show slides, boards, or other tools.

7. Sets music if scheduled when people are working in together-alone mode, after checking that nobody gets disturbed by the music.

8. Sets the timer for activities.

9. Manages icebreakers and some of the energizers.

10. Imports documents to be entered by participants if they fail to do so themselves.

11. If needed, prepares and launches voting workshops and supports people voting and shows the results.

12. Can write post-it notes for participants to make the flow smoother.

13. When using break out rooms, prepares and activates the BORs, checks that everyone is in, supports people, sends broadcast messages, warns five minutes before closing them, and checks everyone has logged in. And during BORs, the tech facilitator monitors that people are able to work with the tools.

14. Sets up the boards after the exercises.

AFTER

1. Updates the boards with new tasks.

2. Supports people in asynchronous work.

3. Sends materials after the workshop.

5. Let people interact freely

Innovation is a co-creation process for which people have to interact, confront each other, generate ideas, test solutions, and define actions together. Compared to in-person workshops, it is more critical to change settings in online innovation processes because, in the plenary, the interaction is regulated in a very structured way to not slide into delirium. People are sitting in front of a screen and, depending on the tool you use, they may or may not see each other, there is little movement, no informal communication, it's challenging to wink at your neighbour without being seen by everyone, and the idea of always being on stage, even if you are participating in a meeting are all very relevant. That's why Rule 5 is to recreate differentiated online settings to allow people to interact freely in small groups. You can do this with break out rooms, virtual rooms where you can split your group into subgroups.

What can people do in BORs?
- ▶ Look each other in the face.
- ▶ Interact informally.
- ▶ Explain their doubts.
- ▶ Come up with crazy ideas.
- ▶ Collaborate synchronously on a tool.
- ▶ Laugh.
- ▶ Comment on one's personal environment.

In particular, this is a chance for introverts to have their say and for people from more and less disciplined cultures to interact together.

You can find this feature in Zoom, which was the first to implement it successfully and, in our experience, the easiest and most flexible way. From early 2021 it has also been possible in Microsoft Teams and Butter. You can find an overview of these tools in Chapter 12. We recommend choosing tools that offer the BOR option in an online innovation process. If your group is bigger than eight people, in a two-hour workshop, you have to foresee at least one moment of free interaction in a BOR. When people don't know each other, always provide break out rooms of two in a moment during the workshop because it allows everybody to interact in the workshop.

In the online tools, you can set a casual mode that randomly puts people in the BOR or can define how to divide people into subgroups. And with most of the tools, you can prepare the rooms in advance. You can use the random option for a big group in which people do not know each other and you want to allow a more personal exchange, in pairs or triplets. Homogeneous groups allow people to have more confidence and interact. However, to have different perspectives, new ideas and contamination, you have to mix all these elements and make heterogeneous groups by hierarchical level, functions, technical skills, and nationality.

How long in the BORs?
It may seem like magic to you to make five, ten, or twenty groups with a simple click and with the same ease to make them return to the plenary sitting, avoiding scanning names, repeating them, going around the groups, and calling everyone back. These actions are more or less time consuming depending on the level of tech savoir and discipline of the group. However, the process is less fluid than in-person: people find themselves thrown into a virtual space without the reference group and facilitator. So, start with simple tasks and little time, three to four minutes. To continue, make sure people have time to interact, even in a less structured way. In the following table, we have indicated the time intervals needed to interact effectively in the BOR, based on our experience. The actual time planned depends on the topic and task you assign and how clear, simple, and structured it is.

Number of people Per BOR	Times (In minutes)
2 to 3	From 3 to 10
4 to 5	From 5 to 15
6 to 8	From 10 to 20
9 to 10	From 15 to 25

With groups of more than four people, define a moderator per group to keep time and structure and report on the group's results when needed.

> **TIP**
> **Have the BORs scheme ready during the workshop and prepare the first set in advance.**
> **Use broadcast messages to give necessary timing or instructions, go around the rooms to facilitate the work.**

6. Use a 'star-model' facilitation
Even if you have extended experience as a facilitator of in-person innovation processes, you should rethink your facilitation style to be effective online.

Why?
Silence with people looking at the screen can become awkward and immediately divert attention to the reality in which people find themselves. There can also be audio delays causing overlapping speech. Suppose people talk freely with all microphones on. In that case, it creates much confusion

and a disturbing environment, with the unwanted side-effect that introverts may never find their space to contribute if nobody gives them the floor.

What is star model facilitation about?

It means a centralized model in which interactions among people in the group are mainly the moderator's responsibility. As a facilitator, you have to 'direct' communications to create a smooth and equally clear and neat flow.

What are the best practices for doing this online?

Turn-taking – the facilitator calls the participants one at a time, avoiding overlapping. This is not saying that you should ban online horizontal conversations. Instead, it would be best if you facilitated discussions between participants to make them smoother. For example, you can ask one person in the group to answer a question or stimulate a comment by taking over the process.

Use (also) non-verbal methods of communication – In this way, there can be many questions and comments among the group and the facilitator will decide what to bring to everyone's attention.

Ask for frequent feedback – This is one method that works best online and allows you to get ideas, reactions, and moods quickly. Use quick polls and surveys to promptly and efficiently collect group feedback.

TIP
During the workshop, especially if you are using a together-alone technique, which we discuss in chapter 4, keep the board chat open to facilitate non-verbal interaction without going to the video conference chat. Have a list of people's names available, since you may not have all of them visible on the screen.

7. Engage participants emotionally

An innovative mindset grows according to the team members' focus and energy. Without feeling emotions, there's no energy for change and innovation. Engaging online is more difficult because people don't breathe the same atmosphere, never entirely in the same setting, as would be the case with in-person workshops.

Zoom fatigue is also a real phenomenon – as we discussed in Chapter 1 – linked to the difficulty of accessing non-verbal language, which causes stress in our brains. People are engaging in multitasking activities, checking emails or chat, and being distracted by their environment, as you read in the previous chapter. It's easy to get overwhelmed by online tasks and tools, switching from videoconferencing to other tools, and back again.

How can you facilitate emotions supporting your change and motivate 'the elephant' to focus its energy on the target?

Allow participants to share their feelings

There are several ways to facilitate the emotional experience. When you use a methodology, which lasts only a few hours, a short moment of sharing 'how do you feel' can be enough. You could ask to share an emoji on the video chat or share it on a simple mood board on your digital collaboration board. If you are using a longer methodology, we recommend spending more time to enable conversations about emotions and give them their rightful place in an innovation journey. Use different tools to collect feedback in real-time, for example, a quick Mentimeter survey to display answers in fun, visual ways.

Surprise and create a WOW effect – You can do that by creating an immersive and personalized experience, which enhances a sense of belonging. Create an environment that combines functionality and beauty. *Activate the child side, the repository of emotions, through play.* Collaboration boards are a very suitable tool for this purpose, where you can include cartoons, images, and videos, or create virtual rooms with Wonder.me, Spatialchat, or Butter to make people feel connected, as explained in Chapter 4.

Plan moments of informal exchange during the journey – Plan informal moments during which people can talk over coffee or a glass of wine. Get people to drop the cognitive part a bit and engage the body – our emotion detector! Creativity also needs a change of perspective, looking from the outside rather than from the centre, visualizing. In an in-person workshop, the setting changes are also physical, when you move from plenary to small groups, in a horseshoe arrangement or around tables in small groups. This is not the case online where people are sitting or standing but always looking at the screen and not moving. Getting up and moving away from the computer makes everyone feel much more connected and positively affects wellbeing. So, you can ask people to connect by their phones and go for a walk together or ask them to get up from their chairs to pick up objects in the shortest possible time and show them to the group. Use music as a togetherness enabler for energizers and informal moments. When you know each other better, you can even dance altogether.

> *Video off is not an option when trying to engage people!*

8. Manage the online time

Forget in-person time and enter another dimension.

Why?
In terms of fatigue, one hour in-person feels like two hours online, so our remote workshops need to be shorter. When taking our FORTH innovation methodology online, we learned that eight-hour online workshops were a disaster. Time online waiting to do something is boring and has the immediate effect of getting people into multitasking, reading emails, and typing WhatsApp, or WeChat messages. The initial ten minutes of talking as introduction in an in-person workshop, with everyone together in a room, can be only three minutes maximum online. As people organize back-to-back meetings online, you have to start and finish sharply on-time, and we strongly suggest you schedule the length of your online innovation workshops to a maximum of three hours.

It means that you might have to rethink your innovation process and redesign your workflow to include synchronous and asynchronous activities depending on the tools' objectives, the participants, and their knowledge.

During synchronous online workshops the pace has to be faster because people interact less and multitask much more quickly than in-person. Plan short and frequent activities; four to six exercises can be done in a three-hour workshop, divided into more straightforward five ten-minute steps.

Time is king, and the agenda is the queen, so be accurate to the minute.

In the online agenda, you must also plan slack time for technical issues, difficulties in using tools, and transitions between tools and devices.

As you are dealing with humans, you have to include the unexpected in your agenda. Let's see how. In Rule 1, we said that a buffer of 20 minutes should be left for additional tech issues, let's say ten minutes per hour. In concrete terms, this means putting a few extra minutes for each task on the agenda. If one person fails to complete a task, the workshop slows down for everyone, so include detailed explanations of how to use the tools in your agenda. Switching from one tool to the next, entering and exiting virtual rooms, swiping from a conversation in Zoom to Miro and vice versa, sharing the screen, and even unmuting are all time-consuming activities. Consider these transitions in your schedule as well. In our experience, you need to add three to five minutes to each transition, depending on the participants' experience with the tools and the number of people present. With eight people, three minutes is sufficient, but allow five minutes if you have more than fifteen people in the online workshop.

Have frequent breaks! Take breaks more often than when you do in-person workshops: at least one break every 40 to 60 minutes because the rhythm is tight and people are engaged in short and frequent activities.

Timebox – How often have you heard this word? It gives you an idea of what you have to do to facilitate online. Define timeboxes and get people to move from one to another. Using shared timers that everyone can see is a great resource to keep activities to their planned duration. You can find them on Miro or Mural. When it looks like a hyper-structured

process, reconsider the whole flow in the diary is smoother. An innovation workshop couldn't be only a succession of timeboxed tasks. Check the engagement activities from Rule 5 of this chapter, and see how the magic comes true!

TIP
Put activities on the agenda that you know you can skip without affecting results, because they will also constitute a time buffer.

9. Set clear instructions (to direct the rider)
Do you remember the introduction story? Direct the rider!

To ensure a seamless experience, you need to be clear every step of the way.

Be redundant – Say it, make an example, show it, and repeat and explain how the final output will look. Don't be afraid of over-communication. Write the instructions on the digital collaboration board as well, as explained in Rule 5.
Share your screen to show the necessary steps online and to avoid questions and interruptions.

Let's take an example of one of the most useful techniques, online voting. It always takes more time than scheduled. After all, it is only a few clicks. As soon as you start voting, people ask you where the 'thumb up' is because they don't see it in the bar at the bottom of the screen. Participants in the online workshop who were not active need to refresh. Someone will vote and close the screen without having clicked the 'done' button. The result is that often at the end of the given time, some have voted, others not. So, share the screen and show all the necessary clicks calmly. You will save a lot of time and frustration on the part of your participants.

Show the outputs – Share the canvasses, the matrixes, and the mind maps you need to use and explain how to do it practically.

▸ How do I write on a post-it?
▸ How do I copy a link in the chat?
▸ How do I add branches to mind maps?

Share the rules – Depending on your workshop, you can either communicate the three essential rules – Video on, mute on, use the chat to communicate – or send a complete document with proper online etiquette. Choose all the options between. We have collected and selected practices from which you can choose. Depending on the countries' culture and organisation you are working with, you can decide how many items to include in your netiquette checklist. We suggest you start with a maximum of six items to avoid the paralyzing effect of receiving a list of 20 rules. Then, if you see that you need more, you can always update your list. Here are some of the items you can have in your online meeting etiquette.

CHART: NETIQUETTE CHECKLIST

1. Read the agenda and the instructions beforehand and come to the meeting prepared.

2. Familiarise yourself with the tools you're going to be using. Have a quick tour of the video chat or online whiteboard tool so you can be productive in the workshop.

3. Call in from a quiet, well-lit location.

4. Arrive on time, if not a little early, so you can iron out any audio/visual equipment issues before starting.

5. Test your audio so you can be heard just after logging in.

6. Use a headset or earphones when possible to minimize echo and background noise.

7. Turn off notification sounds (also for the facilitator).

8. Set microphones to mute when not speaking.

9. Shut down other devices taking up bandwidth, if possible, to help ensure a stable connection.

10. Turn webcams on whenever possible – it's nice to see your face! Though bear in mind that in low-bandwidth environments turning off the camera can help with call quality!

11. Keep the video chat open to interact with people.

12. If you participate in the office with your colleagues, be sure that each of you is connected with its PC .

13. Use nonverbal means to indicate when you would like to speak, for example raising your hand in your video conferencing software or using built-in hand-up features.

14. Respect break time to the minute.

15. Be engaged. Listen to whoever is speaking, communicate in the chat channels, and use the online collaboration tools.

16. Close extra tabs unless necessary and remove distractions, like email notifications.

17. When speaking, do so slowly and clearly. Practice brevity whenever possible.

18. During presentations or longer discussions, try to add questions or thoughts to the chat channel and avoid interrupting.

19. Please wait for the facilitator to give you the floor; online, it only takes two people overlapping to create confusion.

20. Read what's in the chat, so as to not repeat questions.

21. Giving feedback, nod and real thumbs up are signs that you are listening!

Source: Adapted from Workshoplab https://www.workshoplab.com/blog/online-energizers/#set-good-online-meeting-etiquette

AFTER

Now that you have done an outstanding workshop, keep up the energy and engagement of your participants and keep the pace up in the next stages!

10 . Move to action with the follow up
An online experience is both short and intensive. What happens after the workshop is just as important as the activities you have done during the workshop. The innovation process cannot end at this stage; you must review the work done, gain more insight, engage people for the asynchronous work between the workshops, and get feedback to improve subsequent experience workshops. Online follow-up is more manageable than in-person because all outputs are available in digital format, which makes further use very easy.

Define virtual spaces to share resources
Whether you are using a short or long process, you need to follow up to continue the discussion after the meeting is over to bring the action to life. Find channels where you can continue the asynchronous work. These can be a MS Teams channel or the digital boards you have collaborated on or with tools like Padlet and Trello. Share the results and topics for discussion with the participants and share the video recording with those who could not make it to your workshop or other interested relevant stakeholders.

Download or screenshot all significant board outputs and put them in a shared space. Update them on the progress of the asynchronous work, showing screenshots.

Set up the board so that participants can retrace the workshop's flow whenever they return to it.

Be open to having an additional workshop to support people in using the tools. It can be a 45-minute plenary meeting with the whole group or an optional workshop involving only those who feel they need more practice to participate. It will speed up and smoothen your follow-up process.

Keep a virtual water cooler open. A virtual watercooler is a channel where people can stay connected after the end of the project, learn, and have fun. It could be done via a MS Teams channel, or with apps that you can add to your Slack, like Donut, Watercooler, or even a WhatsApp group, as we often do, to make it extremely easy. You just need to provide the space without facilitating it; the more spontaneous, the better.

Use the following chart to keep to the rules that are most important to your innovation process.

RULE	WHY	WHEN	TECHNIQUE	TOOLS
1. Tech Onboarding workshop.	Because technology can make either your dreams or worst nightmares come true.	Always!	Use the chat function.	All tools used during your workshops
2. Keep the board simple.	To encourage everyone to interact and make the innovation journey seamless.	When people use collaboration boards for the first time.	Design a virtual room. Visualize.	Boardle Klaxoon Miro Mural Trello
3. Send people real-life stuff.	To surprise and create a WOW effect.	At the beginning of the journey.	Wrap it in a charming way!	Post offices and express couriers
4. Don't facilitate it alone.	Because you need to be focused on the process.	Always!	Co-facilitation.	SessionLab Calendly
5. Let people interact freely in small groups online.	To give the opportunity to interact for more introverted participants, and to have more informal conversations.	When the group is bigger than six people.	Break out rooms.	Zoom MS Teams Butter Wonder.me Spatialchat
6. Use a star-model facilitation in plenary settings.	To be more inclusive and to speed the process.	When people don't know each other.	Questionnaires/surveys. Anonymous voting. Bulk mode (in Miro) to generate ideas without distraction.	Klaxoon Miro Mural Tscheck.In

RULE	WHY	WHEN	TECHNIQUES	TOOLS
7. Engage participants emotionally.	Because emotions enable change and innovation.	When your innovation journey is longer than a three-hour workshop.	Using questionnaires/ surveys. Design a Virtual Room. Use Music.	Howspace Wonder.Me Butter Miro Mural Spatial.Chat Spotify
8. Manage time more strictly online.	Because workshops are shorter and you're less flexible.	Always!	Agenda. Working synchronous and asynchronous. Anonymous voting. Use Bulk mode (in Miro) to generate ideas without distraction.	Sessionlab Miro Mural
9. Set clear instructions.	To prevent people from interrupting the workshop with continu-ous requests.	Especially when people use tools for the first time.	Record videos to explain tasks or to instruct participants.	Loom Toonly SessionLab Speechelo
10. Follow up.	To keep energy and engagement high and move to action.	When you have asynchronous work.	Using questionnaires/ surveys. Working synchronous and asynchronous.	Dropbox Google Form Howspace Mentimeter Miro Mural Padlet Slack Trello

KEY MESSAGES FROM THIS CHAPTER

▸ **Online innovation is a new process with many potential pitfalls linked to technical issues you often can't control.** *Having rules to follow makes the journey more straightforward for you and your participants.*

▸ *In setting your online environment, you need to consider both the rational and the emotional sides to be effective.* **Because of the lack of social interaction among people, emotional engagement is challenging online, so you need to use the right rules.**

▸ *You cannot control technology, so have a plan b, c, and d.*

▸ **You can put each of the rules into practise with different tools and techniques. You can find them in Chapters 3 and 4;** *choose the ones you feel most comfortable with.*

▸ **To understand which steps are the most critical for you,** *you have to experiment.*

▸ **There are many ways to co-create online with participants, even if they have few technological skills.** *Choose rules that allow you to do it quickly.*

▸ *The simpler, the better* **(based on your participants' technological skills and habits). Calibrate the use of technology. The possibilities are endless even in simplicity.**

[1] C. Heat and D. Heat, Switch, how to change things when change is hard, Random House Business Books, GB, 2010
[2] https://print-and-play.asmodee.fun/dixit/
[3] https://www.ideo.com/post/method-cards
[4] https://madeby.sypartners.com/products/superpowers-card-deck?variant=1098868541
[5] https://www.ideo.com/blog/how-to-get-free-and-feel-inspired-when-workshops-are-remote

CONTENTS

CHAPTER 7

ONLINE INNOVATION METHODS

INNOVATION METHODS CREATE COMMON LEARNINGS

More elephants: the blind men and an elephant

The parable of the blind men and an elephant originated in the ancient Indian subcontinent, from where it has been widely diffused. It is a story of a group of blind men who have never come across an elephant before and who learn and conceptualise what the elephant is like by touching it. Each blind man feels a different part of the elephant's body, but only one part, such as the side or the tusk. They then describe the elephant based on their limited experience, and their descriptions of the elephant are different from each other. In some versions, they come to suspect that the other person is dishonest, and they come to blows. The parable's moral is that humans tend to claim absolute truth based on their limited, subjective experience as they ignore other people's limited, subjective experiences, which may be equally valid.

From a Wikipedia search for 'Blind men and an elephant.'

Innovation requires a method: to expand your perception of reality, to develop many ideas, to hold on when you feel lost on your journey, to get feedback from customers, and to co-create in a structured way. Innovation is a shared learning process from which its participants get an open mind and a greater awareness of the business, the market, the customers, and even themselves. Exchanging, challenging, and working together is the basis of the 'We-innovation' process, as we like to call it, instead of 'Innovation'. Quoting Gijs van Wulfen: 'you can invent alone, but you can only innovate together.'

Since there are no in-person connections among the team when innovating online, using structured methods helps to guide you, keep the pace, and monitor your progress on the innovation journey.

Remote working limits the exchange and cross-pollination between individuals, making serendipity difficult, and creates obstacles against effective innovation processes. And, since we work remotely, the innovation methods we use are also online. Working remotely powerfully affects established organisations' innovation processes. The lack of in-person connection gives more freedom, flexibility, and quality of life. However, you run the risk of anarchy. Rigorous and structured methodologies will prevent that.

You cannot use innovation methods tout court without tailoring and adapting them to the online setting.

Innovating online means maintaining the creative power of each method in a remote setting. It is more important to modify activities, times, and tools to keep the strength of a method intact than to remain faithful to it in an online setting. You cannot copy a method from in-person to online, but you need to understand the essence of transforming and adapting it for online use.

Using online methodologies allows you to control simultaneity and complexity, and to stay more connected.

With online methods, you can work efficiently in different settings with tools that amplify and enhance people's skills by giving them the possibility to be creative in an easy and inspiring way. With fewer costs and effort comes the opportunity to have more diversified teams in terms of experience, culture, and skills, with the ability to deliver much more creative power. Chapters 3 and 4 described tools and techniques to work synchronously and asynchronously, to stay connected, and to govern complex innovation processes.

Online innovation enhances iterative and fast-paced methodologies.

The methods described below are iterative, have rapid and repeated cycles, and give continuous feedback. From this point of view, online methods empower these processes because they provide teams – whether in a company or a startup – with tools to collaborate simultaneously and rapidly, share work immediately, combine parts of the process asynchronously, and moments of decision-making and alignment synchronously. Many startups already know this because their teams are dispersed worldwide, but it repre-sents a quantum leap for organisations to work in-person.

We have experienced directly, and through the experience of other practitioners around the world, that online innovation works and is consistent with a lean way of working. We've chosen ten online innovation methods that can bring you innovation in a structured, rigorous way:

- ▶ Three innovation methods for short online workshops: Problem Framing, the Customer Experience Deck (CXD), and the Lightning Decision Jam (LDJ).
- ▶ Two methods for online innovation sprints of a week or less: Pretotyping and the Design Sprint.
- ▶ Five methods for online innovation projects in which we feature the FORTH innovation method: Lean Startup, the Business Model Canvas, the Purpose Launchpad, and the Circular design process.

You will find seven methodologies in this chapter. The Lightning Decision Jam, Design Sprint, and the FORTH innovation method have dedicated chapters, respectively Chapters 8, 9, and 10, because we consider them very critical for online innovation.

CHART: OVERVIEW TEN ONLINE INNOVATION METHODS

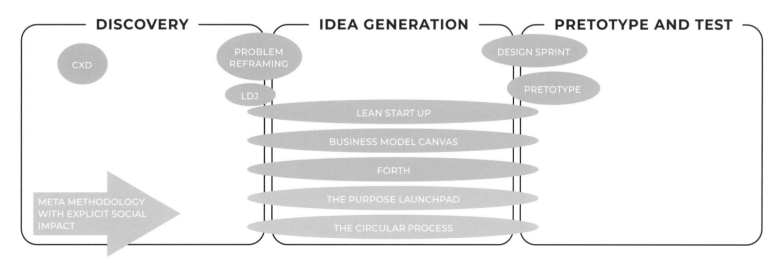

All these methods have incorporated the principles of design thinking. Design thinking is a multidisciplinary human-centred approach with (at least) three phases:
1. Discovery by listening and observing.
2. Idea Generation, leading to out-of-the-box ideas.
3. Prototype and Testing of new solutions with users.

CXD, Problem Framing, and LDJ are more focused on the discovery phase, Pretotype more on the pretotype and test phase, while all the other methods embrace all the three phases. Some of them are for startups or specific phases of a company , such as Purpose Launchpad and Lean Sprint. But they can very well be used by organisations that want to innovate products or services. Others, such as the CXD, give insights into the way people within teams perceive their customers. Some, like the FORTH innovation methodology, effectively boost an effective start of innovation. The Purpose Launchpad and the Circular Process are meta-methodologies, combining various other methods to thrive social impact.

How is this chapter structured?

In this chapter, you will find a brief overview of each method and why to use it. As our focus is online innovation, we explain the online process describing tools and techniques you need to apply to run any one of them successfully. For each of the methods, you will find a chart in which we list the method's steps, the online techniques used, the timeframe, and the outcomes. The listed steps are specific for each method. We do not describe all the activities, for example check-ins, energisers, and breaks that are necessary for every online innovation process. For this, you can check Chapter 6, which gives you an overview of the ten rules you need to apply in all online innovation processes. The Lightning Decision Jam, the Design Sprint, and FORTH are explained in Chapters 8, 9,

and 10. Our focus is on how to apply the methods and facilitate them online, maintaining their effectiveness.

METHOD 1. PROBLEM FRAMING

Don't use it if you quickly fall in love with solutions.

'If I had an hour to solve a problem, I'd spend 55 minutes thinking about the problem and five minutes thinking about solutions.' This quote of Albert Einstein explains the 55/5 rule, which is the superpower of problem framing.

What is Problem Framing, and why use it?
Problem framing helps to define the right problem at the beginning of an innovation process. Many of you experienced the situation in your own company or as a consultant that the problem you're trying to solve seems to not be the right one, which you discovered only after spending time and money. In business, we have many examples of products or services not addressing the right problem. This usually happens because we are doers; instead of living the discomfort of addressing the problem, we'd start working toward a solution. Additionally, solutions are usually copies of our past successful experiences. However, it is not wise to assume that what worked in a certain situation in the past will work again in the future. Thinking about our switch from in-person to online collaboration, for example, the right question wasn't how to replicate methodologies using video conferencing but how to brainstorm at a distance while engaging people online.

D. Spradlin first explained the idea of problem framing in Harvard Business Review[1]. The Design Sprint Academy then developed it as a preliminary step in running Design Sprints to ensure effective outcomes.

'Problem Framing is a framework, based on design thinking principles and methods, used to understand, define, and prioritise complex business problems and help stakeholders make better decisions, fast.'[2]

Use it before any innovation process to determine whether a problem is relevant or not for the company and the market, build alignment among the team over the problem, and have a clear, shared definition of the real issue you're going to work on.

The Problem Framing Power

You can apply problem framing to attain alignment and a shared vision before an innovation process so that you may better explore a defined problem or explore the company's future vision.

The Challenge

The challenge is to frame a real problem. Don't stop at the first statement. Try to reach the essence of the problem by asking yourself more 'Why' questions. Investigate your assumptions during the process and verify that your team is convinced about the outcome.

The three main phases are:

1. Establish a business need. The goal is to deliver a shared definition of the requirements in a factual statement.
2. Contextualise the business and user perspective by gaining insights into how this problem affects your organisation and your customers.
3. Reframe the Problem.

> *The output is a clear and shared problem statement to start the ideation phase.*

The Slow Elevator Problem[3]

Imagine this: You are the owner of an office building and your tenants complain about the elevator. It's old and slow and they often have to wait. Several tenants are threatening to cancel their leases if you don't fix the problem.

When asked, most people quickly identify some solutions: replace the lift, install a stronger motor, or perhaps upgrade the algorithm that runs the lift. These suggestions fall into what I call a solution space: a cluster of solutions that share assumptions about what the problem is – in this case, the elevator is slow. This framing is illustrated below.

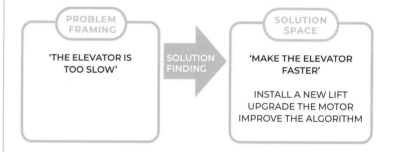

However, when the problem is presented to building managers, they suggest a much more elegant solution: Put up mirrors next to the elevator. This simple measure has proved wonderfully effective in reducing complaints because people tend to lose track of time when given something utterly fascinating to look at – namely, themselves.

The mirror solution is particularly interesting because it is not a solution to the stated problem: It doesn't make the elevator faster. Instead, it proposes a different understanding of the problem. Note that the initial framing of the problem is not necessarily wrong. Installing a new lift would probably work. The point of reframing is not to find the 'real' problem but, rather, to see if there is a better one to solve. The very idea that a single root problem exists may be misleading; problems are typically multicausal and can be addressed in many ways. The elevator issue, for example, could be reframed as a peak demand problem – too many people need the lift at the same time – leading to a solution that focuses on spreading out the demand, such as by staggering people's lunch breaks. Identifying a different aspect of the problem can sometimes deliver radical improvement and even spark solutions to problems that have seemed intractable for decades.

Source: Thomas Wedell-Wedellsborg, Are You Solving the Right Problems? Reframing them can reveal unexpected solutions, HBR January-February, 2017

Who should be involved in a problem framing workshop?

You should aim to include a diverse mix of relevant stakeholders in the company: those who can make decisions afterward, people who are bringing different perspectives and competencies, those who are struggling or have been working for an extended period with the problem, and people with a fresh view. It's essential to have enough diversity of opinion as problem framing works best with different perspectives and when people don't drive straight to the solutions. Both vision and expertise are needed.

Online Problem Framing

This methodology works exceptionally well online. The advantages are that you can quickly connect relevant stakeholders with no travel costs and scheduling complications. You can send in advance research or data should you need it for the internal or external analysis. You have all the steps in a digital format. And you can apply many of the online techniques, as we'll explain later.

Which tools do you need?

Online Whiteboard tools for realtime collaboration

You can use Miro or Mural to collaborate online in realtime with all participants. These tools have handy features like digital post-it notes, voting, and a timer. And a great feature in Miro is the 'Bulk mode', which allows participants to contribute individually without being distracted from what others are writing. When preparing your board in advance, follow the general rules on setting your board as mentioned in Chapter 6. You can also find a predefined template for Problem Framing in Miro and one for problem statement in Mural. You can upload them and adapt them to your needs. There's also a predefined template on Trello, an easy collaboration board upon which the team can share ideas.

Videoconferencing for communicating

During your workshops, you can use a video conferencing tool. We suggest Zoom or Butter. These tools have break out rooms to split participants into smaller groups.

Collaboration in execution

To follow-up with the team, you can use a tool like Slack, which offers various communication options such as channels, private groups, and direct messaging. You can share documents and files across teams and in a one-on-one format. Also, Google drive fits the purpose of sharing files.

Another tool is Padlet, where you can compile documents, links, and images with team members.

Tools for preparation and instruction.

In one possible set up among many, you can use SessionLab to set your agenda and share it beforehand with your team, Calendly to book the workshop with the team, and Loom, a video messaging tool, to get your message across through instantly shareable videos about how to use the tools or to illustrate the steps.

Tools for making the workshop interactive

You can use Tscheck.in, a simple tool to start a conversation on a personal level by asking questions, or Mentimeter to do instant pools and Q&As, to make your online workshop interactive. You can find a complete description of these tools in Chapter 3.

The online duration of problem framing can vary enormously, from a short 90-minute workshop to a six-hour workshop divided into two sessions. Here we explain the 90-minute to three-hour process. For the longer sessions, you would spend the additional time going deeper into the contextualisation phase to better understand its issues and customers.

Problem framing can be divided into three phases to fit the online setting:
1. Establish the business need.
2. Contextualise it into the business, and into the user perspective.
3. Problem reframing.

1. ESTABLISH THE BUSINESS NEED

In this phase, you have to understand what the needs of any given business are that you are prepared to address. The goal is to deliver a shared definition of the requirements in a factual statement. It is important that everybody is on board and that participants have both time to express their ideas and to discuss and challenge them.

You can divide this phase into four steps:

1. Individual brainwriting on the business needs. Participants think individually and get inspired by what others write.
2. First problem framing. The facilitator asks Why and How questions to get to the root of the problems, transforming vague statements into more concrete ones.
3. Affinity mapping. The facilitator asks the group to cluster all the items into similar groups to see if the team can add more elements to the problem.
4. Choosing criteria; using, for example, the business impact/effort matrix, and then voting on it. At the end of this phase, you will have drafted a concrete problem statement.

2. CONTEXTUALISE THE PROBLEM ON YOUR BUSINESS/CUSTOMERS

The two steps of this phase are:

1. Understand the impact on your organisation. Here you can use a great variety of tools like SWOT analysis or Business Model Canvas to answer the effects of the problem on your business and set a future vision. You can do this by individual brainwriting to fill in the matrix or canvas.

2. Customer insights. The main questions to ask are, Which customers are affected by the problem? And, How are they achieving their goals today? You can use Proto-Personas or an Empathy Map to describe your customer.

Again, you will do online brainwriting on each of the templates. Place participants in pairs in break out rooms to do the affinity mapping and then have them issue a report. To answer the How question, you may use the Customer Journey Map Template.

PROTO-PERSONA

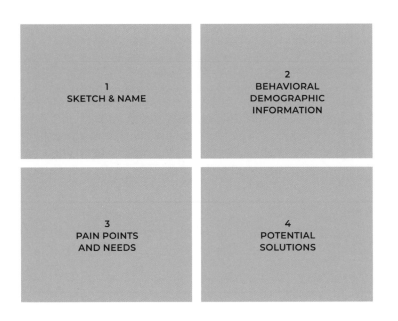

EMPATHY MAP

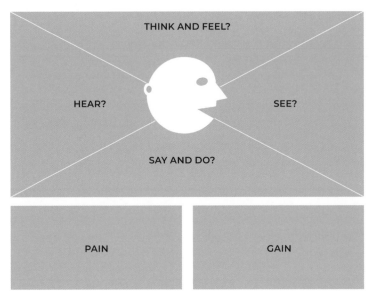

CUSTOMER JOURNEY MAPPING

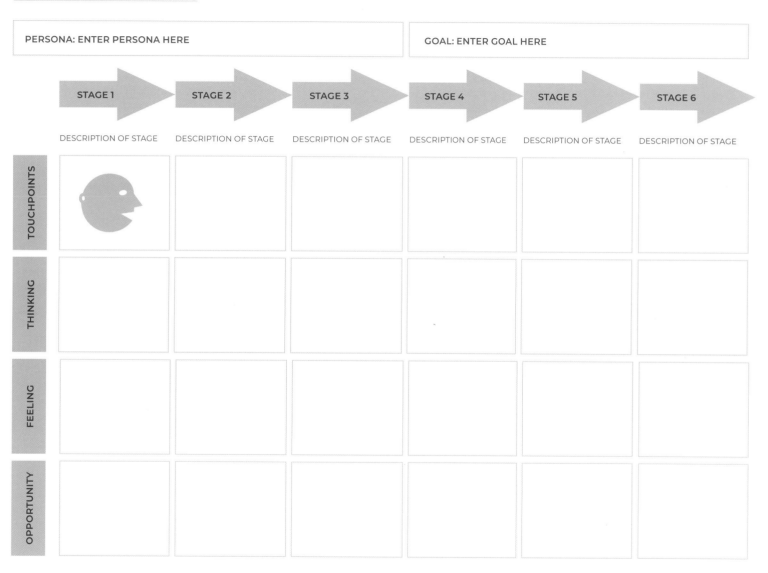

PERSONA: ENTER PERSONA HERE

GOAL: ENTER GOAL HERE

STAGE 1 | STAGE 2 | STAGE 3 | STAGE 4 | STAGE 5 | STAGE 6

DESCRIPTION OF STAGE | DESCRIPTION OF STAGE | DESCRIPTION OF STAGE | DESCRIPTION OF STAGE | DESCRIPTION OF STAGE | DESCRIPTION OF STAGE

TOUCHPOINTS

THINKING

FEELING

OPPORTUNITY

You can use brainwriting for the different steps of the Customer Journey Map. Now you need to match the 'business' and 'customers' to see the overlap. Use the insights gained to transform the problems into challenges with the 'How Might We' questions. The 'How Might We' (HMW) question template is popular in Design Thinking. The HMW-questions should be specific and linked to what you learned during this phase. Define them broad enough not to address the solution too small and positively draft the question; after collecting all the HMW-questions, the team votes for the more relevant one.

CHART: ONLINE PROBLEM FRAMING TECHNIQUES AND OUTCOMES

3. WRITE A PROBLEM STATEMENT

Now it's time to reframe your problem using the top-voted HMW-question to write a problem statement. There are two steps to take:

1. Write problem statements. Each person in the team writes a problem statement individually and then shares it with the team.

A good, complete problem statement should contain four elements: Who is having the problem? What is the problem? When is it happening/what is the context? Why is it important to solve/why will we or our users care? Please apply the 40-20-10-5 rule. State your problem in 40 words. Cut it down to 20, then to 10 and end up with a 5-word problem statement.

PHASE	STEPS/TEMPLATES	ONLINE TECHNIQUES	TIME 90 min/3 hours	OUTCOMES
1. ESTABLISH THE NEED	▸ Brainwriting. ▸ First framing. ▸ Affinity Mapping. ▸ Vote.	▸ Together-alone and Bulk mode for brain-writing. ▸ Anonymous voting.	15 to 30 minutes	A shared definition of the needs in a concrete statement.
2. CONTEXTUALISE THE PROBLEM EXPERIENCED BY YOUR BUSINESS/ CUSTOMERS	▸ Understand the organisation impact/SWOT Business Model Canvas. ▸ Customer Insights/Proto-persona, Empathy map, Customer Journey Map.	▸ Lightning Demo. ▸ Break out rooms to work on the different part of the templates. ▸ Bulk mode. ▸ Chat function.	60 to 120 minutes	▸ Impact on the organ-isation. ▸ Persona description. ▸ Overlaps between the two.
3. WRITE A PROBLEM STATEMENT	▸ Individual writing. ▸ Voting.	▸ Together-alone to write the problem statement. ▸ Anonymous voting.	15 to 30 minutes	A clear problem statement with a common language to share.

2. Participants vote for the most relevant problem statement.

In the chart on previous page , you can find the phases of problem framing with the techniques you can use online. For a complete description of all techniques, check Chapter 4.

METHOD 2. THE CUSTOMER EXPERIENCE DECK

Don't use this if you think that feelings are merely hairdressers' chat.

What is the Customer Experience Deck, and why use it?

The Customer Experience Deck (CXD) was created in 2019 by Jeremy Dean to 'help teams build a shared understanding of their customers.'[4] It's a simple nine-step process to build your customers' shared vision and start innovating the customer experience. You can apply it to create a shared understanding of the client's needs and get insights on the critical elements of the desired customer experience and how you can work together to shape it. You can then integrate it in other more structured methodologies: in the FORTH innovation method in the Observe and Learn phase, before the customer friction interviews, or in the Business Model Canvas in the Customer relationship section. Another way of using the CXD is to innovate internal practices and working starting from the customer experience. So, it's the first step in the discovery phase. Afterwards, use other online innovation methods to continue.

The CXD is a nine micro-step process that leads a group to identify a customer segment they want to work with and understand the customers' desired and undesired feelings. In the first seven steps, participants individually address the question:

How do we want our customers to feel and how do we want them not to feel?

This question triggers a process of description, discovery, and sharing of the team's customer experience, aiming to align the vision. Through the detailed description of the emotions you want to elicit with your product or service, you create a common language and gain valuable insights. The Customer Experience Deck workshop must be attended both by people involved in the customer experience and others whose work is not related to it. It is also essential that decision-makers join in to follow up on the actions defined.

The first phase involves identifying a customer segment or proto-persona on which to focus the trigger questions. Individuals work in subgroups to choose the relevant emotions, explain their vision, share the facts and evidence upon which they base it, and verify assumptions. It ensures that there is alignment on the desired experience at the end of the workshop and how to detect it. When the groups come back to the plenary workshop, vote to identify the five top emotions they want to focus on in two areas: the one they would like their customer to feel and the one they don't want their customers to feel.

In the next phase, the team works on a canvas to identify the signals, which detect emotions among customers and the actions and good practices to introduce. You can complete the workshop by reconstructing the customer journey map to identify the three most important moments in your customer's journey or interaction with your business.

The CXD Power
The CXD can be a great starting point for developing innovation based on the client's needs. It helps organisations to adopt a customer-centric approach in all areas.

The Challenge
CXD is a method of gaining insights into one's customers, but on its own, it is unlikely to trigger a process of innovation. Keep the focus on the evidence the team has. Don't let too many assumptions invalidate the process. Invite people to ask customers directly.

Applying the Customer Experience Deck online
You can apply CXD via a two to three-hour online workshop, depending on the group size. That could be between 10 to 20 people if you're able to divide them into break out rooms. If you are working with a large team and want to add the Customer Journey Map, you need to run another 60-minute workshop the following day.

Which tools do you need?

Online Whiteboard tools for realtime collaboration
We use Miro to run the CXD, but Mural works just as well to collaborate online in realtime. On the board, you need to upload the card and the canvas template, then set up each phase at a different area of the board to allow sufficient space for participants to work on. You can read general rules on how to set your whiteboard in Chapter 6.

Videoconferencing for communicating
As for the Problem Framing method, you can use video conferencing tools with break out rooms as you need to divide participants into smaller groups. Zoom or Butter work well.

Tools for preparation and instruction

You can use SessionLab to set your agenda. It is not necessary to explain the process in advance because it is very simple and made to be entirely synchronous.

Tools for making the workshop interactive

As with every innovation method, making the workshop interactive requires an onboarding phase. It should be concise and could encompass the storytelling of experiences with clients in different situations. You can use Mentimeter for a quick poll.
In the following chart, you can find the main steps and techniques for the Customer Experience Deck for each phase.

CHART: ONLINE CUSTOMER EXPERIENCE TECHNIQUES AND OUTCOMES ➜

PHASE	STEPS	ONLINE TECHNIQUES	TIME 2 h/4 h (3h + 1h)	OUTCOMES
OUR CUSTOMERS	▸ IDENTIFY YOUR CUSTOMERS ▸ PERSONIFY	▸ Together-alone to brainwriting in silence. ▸ Anonymous voting to choose the customer segment.	10 to 15 minutes	The customer segment or the Proto-persona is selected.
HOW DO WE WANT OUR CUSTOMERS TO FEEL?	▸ PRIMARY FEELINGS ▸ FRINGE FEELINGS	▸ Participants split into break out rooms to sort out the related feeling cards. ▸ Synchronous sharing with the large group. ▸ Anonymous vote. ▸ Chat function to communicate during the workshop.	30 to 60 minutes	Agreement on the top five primary feelings and top five fringe feelings the team or organisation wants customers to feel.
HOW DO WE WANT OUR CUSTOMERS NOT TO FEEL?	▸ PRIMARY FEELINGS ▸ FRINGE FEELINGS	▸ Participants split into break out rooms to sort out the related feeling cards. ▸ Synchronous sharing with the large group. ▸ Anonymous vote. ▸ Chat function to communicate during the workshop.	30 to 60 minutes	Agreement on the top five primary feelings and top five fringe feelings the team or organisation doesn't want your customers to feel.
CANVAS	▸ EMPATHY How do we know our customers are feeling this? ▸ ACTIONS To help our customers feel (insert feeling), we need…	▸ Participants split into break out rooms complete the Customer Experience Canvas. ▸ Share synchronously with the large group. ▸ Anonymous vote. ▸ Chat function to communicate during the workshop.	20 to 45 minutes	
CUSTOMER JOURNEY MAP	▸ The most important moment of the customer journey. ▸ Ways to amplify positive feelings and remove the negative ones.	▸ Participants work together-alone, writing the three most important moments in their customer journey of interaction with their business. ▸ Choose cards on different journey steps. Anonymous vote. ▸ Synchronous work to ideate ways to amplify positive feelings and eliminate negative ones. ▸ Chat function to communicate during the workshop.	30 to 60 minutes	Three most important moments of the Customer Journey and ideas to amplify the positive feelings.

METHOD 3. LEAN STARTUP

*Don't use it if you want to slow down
and take your time.*

What is Lean Startup, and why use it?

Lean Startup is a methodology for developing businesses and products. The Lean Startup method was originated in 2008 by Eric Ries[5] using his personal experiences adapting lean management and customer development principles to high-tech startups. The method combines experimentation, iterative product releases, and validated learning. The Lean Startup method seeks to increase value-producing practices during the earliest phases of a company to have a better chance of success. It emphasises customer feedback over intuition and flexibility over planning.

The five principles of Lean Startups are

1. Entrepreneurs are everywhere.
2. Entrepreneurship is management.
3. Validated learning.
4. Innovation accounting.
5. Build-measure-learn.

Lean Startup aims to shorten product development cycles and avoid developing a product nobody wants. 'The Lean Startup method is not about cost; it's about speed.' But how long it takes to go from an idea to a successful business will vary greatly among sectors. Unlike typical yearlong product development cycles, Lean Startup eliminates wasted time and resources by developing the product iteratively and incrementally. The iterative feedback loop is a three-step process

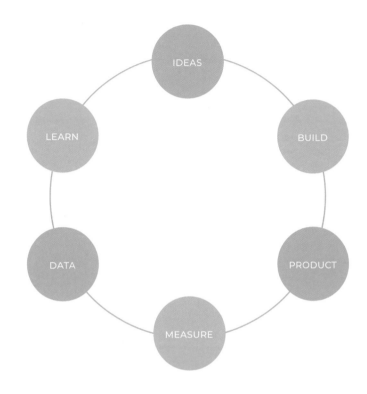

Developing a minimum viable product (MVP), the 'version of a new product which allows a team to collect the maximum amount of validated learning about customers with the least effort', plays a crucial role in Lean Startup. The goodness of the MVP is not measured by its efficiency but by its ability to generate learning. The measure of a startup's progress is, in fact, learning. The speed of execution serves to transform leap-of-faith assumptions into metrics to be validated rapidly. The validation of the assumptions takes place through innovation accounting. This method requires acquiring accurate data through feedback from cohorts (homogeneous clusters) on the MVP, identifying the relationship between improvements made to the product and the drivers of the growth model. Based on the data, it is decided whether to persevere with continuous improvements or to make a major change to test a new hypothesis.

The Lean Startup Power
In this method you learn by doing, and what you learn comes from the most important source: your market and customers.

The Challenge
You always need to have a clear broad view; you'll be pushed to explore as many directions as possible, which might create chaos that is very hard to deal with for you, for the development team, for management, and eventually even for your customers. The Lean Startup process has four phases and is supported by the Lean Canvas, a template designed and tested by Ash Mayura to guide and monitor the process. In four phases, the solution is developed in line with the customer problem and validated.

PROBLEM-SOLUTION FIT
1. Understand the problem or, better, 'love the problem'.
2. Define the solution.

PRODUCT-MARKET FIT
3. Validate qualitatively.
4. Verify quantitatively.

Based on the results of the validation and the lessons learned, the process is reiterated. The Lean Canvas[6] is a model adapted from the Business Model Canvas by Ash Mayura, containing the following nine boxes:

a. The problem: a list of the three main problems and existing alternatives in other market segments.

b. Target customers and the early adopters.
c. The unique value proposition. It will be revised several times. In the initial phase, you must define the broad and specific scope not calibrated in the middle of the market to catch everyone.
d. The solution to solve the problem for one or more target customers. At this stage, the solution does not have all the details of implementation.
e. The channels of distribution.
f. The revenue streams. They already include price because it is an important element of the MVP validation, defining the target customers.
g. The cost structure with the current operational costs.
h. Key metrics.
i. The unfair advantage. It's something that cannot be easily copied or bought by your competitors.

As you can imagine, the canvas's design is also an iterative process, so not every box has to be filled at the first shot when developing your idea. In defining the solution, the next step is to rank your business model to three types of risks:

Product Risks	Technical feasibility
Customer Risks	Customer Pain Level
	Ease of reach
	Market Size
Market Risks	Price/Gross Margins
	Assemble the Problem Team/Solution Team

Before moving on to Product/Market Fit, you formulate a falsifiable hypothesis, 'a statement that can be proven wrong'. It means that it should be measurable and contains numbers. Validate qualitatively and verify quantitatively. In this method, as in prototyping, there is no need to have a lot of quantitative data but to proceed by approximations. Strong negative signals tell us to change something, and positive signs urge us to continue to verify through quantitative data. In the validation phase, the most important element is to correlate the feedback to characteristics and features because the final product does not yet exist. It is necessary to know in which direction to go. Furthermore, validation data must be accessible to all involved. The validation process continues parallel to the development of the solution in an ongoing process.

Online Lean Sprint

Although it was born for startups, this methodology can be usefully applied to companies that need to innovate their offer. The team must be diversified and include people with complementary experience, skills, and thinking attitudes. The enthusiasts and the critics and, above all, the decision-makers should all be involved.

Which tools do you need?

Online Whiteboard tools for realtime collaboration. Use an online whiteboard tool like Miro or Mural to collaborate online with all the participants. You need to prepare all your boards in advance and upload the templates you need, for example, the Lean Canvas.

Videoconferencing for communicating. We already mentioned Zoom and Butter because they are easy to use and provide breakout rooms.

Collaboration in execution. As mentioned at page 118 some useful tools to follow up with the team involved are Slack, Google drive, Dropbox, and Padlet.

Tools for Prototyping and Testing. Here you can use a great variety of tools, like social media: YouTube to make a video explaining your new product or service and Linkedin to publish a landing page and a video or an article explaining your offer. There are also tools developed to help you design your pretotype and prototype. Some examples, described in Chapter 3, include Marvel, which allows you to turn any sketch or image into an interactive prototype for an app or website and Toonly, which is an animated explainer video creator that you can use to create simple videos to provide information on your solution and how it works. When you need to test your ideas online and collect feedback from customers, Google Forms allow you to do this in a simple and versatile way.

The various online phases, models, and techniques are described below from a remote Lean Startup team's perspective.

PHASE/QUESTIONS	STEPS	MODEL/TEMPLATES	ONLINE TECNIQUES / TOOLS	TIME	OUTCOMES
PROBLEM-SOLUTION FIT ▸ Do I have a problem worth solving? ▸ Will they pay for it? ▸ Can It be solved?	▸ Understand the problem. ▸ Define the solution.	▸ Problem framing or Job To Be Done.[7] ▸ Lean Canvas.	▸ The ones used in Problem Framing. ▸ Synchronous team brainwriting on each section of the canvas. ▸ Together-alone on the Unique Value Proposition. ▸ Lightning Demo to collect data. ▸ Leave the Canvas available so team members can add resources afterwards. ▸ Visualise.	Two-hour online workshop, having the problem framing workshop/Job To Be Done interviews.	▸ Top three problems. ▸ Existing alternatives.
PROBLEM-SOLUTION FIT Identify the riskiest parts.	Rank your business model to product risks, customer risks and market risks.	Lean Canvas.	Synchronous work with break out rooms to identify the product, customer, and market risks.	Two-hour online workshop.	Top three solutions.
PRODUCT-MARKET FIT Have I built something people want?	▸ Validate qualitatively. ▸ Verify quantitatively.	▸ Pretotype. ▸ Problem Interview. ▸ Solution Interview. ▸ Dashboard.	▸ Pretotyping. ▸ Make a Video. ▸ Virtual Room.	Every three to five days, an online meeting to share results and iterate the model.	A continuous feedback loop with the customer.

METHOD 4. BUSINESS MODEL CANVAS

Don't use it if you want to think outside the nine 'boxes'.

What is the Business Model Canvas, and why use it?
The business model generation process is a well-known methodology developed in the 2000s by Alexander Oster-walder[8]. His best-known tool is the Business Model Canvas (BMC), used to map business models and understand where the competitive advantages, risks, and opportunities lie. It's applied to make better-shared decisions on an everyday basis, monitor the evolution of different areas of the model, and make incremental changes in your offerings.
The well-known nine blocks of a BMC are:

1. **Customer Segments**. You can have one or several. *For whom are we creating value?*
2. **The Value Proposition**. The way an organisation solves customer problems and satisfies customer needs. *What value do we deliver to our customers?*
3. **Channels**. The way an organisation delivers its value proposition through communications, distribution, and sales channels. *Through which channels can we reach our customer segments?*
4. **Customer relationship**. The way the organisation communicates with the customers. *What type of relationship does each of our customer segments expect us to establish and maintain with them?*
5. **Revenue streams**. The revenue streams generated by the value proposition. *For what value are our customers willing to pay?*
6. **Key resources**. The resources are necessary to create and deliver the value proposition. *What key resources do our value propositions require?*
7. **Key Activities**. *What key activities do our value propositions require?*

8. **Key partnerships**. *Who are our key partners? Who are our key suppliers?*
9. **The Cost Structure**. The fixed and variable costs. *What are the most important costs inherent to our business?*

The BMC is also a methodology to innovate a company's offer or business model because it allows us to identify specific areas from which to innovate. There are four areas of the canvas from which innovation can spark:

1. **Resource-driven**, when an organisation expands its business model using existing infrastructure or partnerships. For example, during the first phase of the pandemic, *Innova*[9], an Italian startup from Brescia, had the idea of installing 3D-printed respiratory valves on Decathlon diving masks, thus making up for the lack of respiratory machines. Decathlon supported the company by providing the CAD model and supporting engineers to integrate the project in the best possible way.
2. **Offer-driven**, when innovation starts from your offer. For example, schools in many countries have changed their teaching processes through online teaching because of Covid-19.
3. **Customer-driven**, based on customer needs, such as the apps created to manage queues at supermarkets where there were restricted entrances due to the pandemic's safety measure.
4. **Finance-driven**, innovations driven by new revenue streams pricing mechanisms or reduced cost structure. On a newspaper website, the customer does not have to have a subscription anymore but can pay for each article he wants to read at a minimal fee, invoiced immediately.

The Business Model Process Power

The BMC can be applied in a lot of ways: for ideation, for visual thinking or for scenario analysis. Moreover, the canvas itself can be integrated with other innovation methodologies. In Problem Framing, you can apply it in the initial phase of defining the problem to be solved. In the Blue Ocean strategy, you can use the canvas to identify which strategy to create value and not compete on costs.

The Challenge

As the business model process is structured and integrates many models and tools, you could get stuck in the analysis phase. We suggest implementing it in an iterative way to build better versions of itself every time.
You define a new business model in five steps:
1. Mobilise, when you prepare, create awareness, and momentum, defining the team.
2. Understand, when you 'research and analyse' elements needed for your business model design.
3. Design, when you transform your ideas into a pretotype to validate them.
4. Implement, when you put into practice what you've designed in your model.
5. Manage, when you adapt and modify your business model in response to market feedback.

There's no fixed duration. It could take you a few hours, a few days, or a few weeks when you iterate the process. The Business Model Process's output is a clear, complete, and shared canvas with nine essential elements of the new business model, plus pretotypes or prototypes to be tested, and clear and defined actions with the team on how to proceed.

Online Business Model Canvas Process

The Business Model Canvas process is already used online in the case of remote teams. From this point of view, all the ten techniques described in Chapter 4 can be applied because, in the process, there are moments of alignment and engagement of the team, ideation, visualisation and storytelling, decision, and design of the solution.

Tools

You can use many of the tools already mentioned when explaining the previous methods on this chapter:

Online Whiteboard tools for realtime collaboration, we suggest Miro or Mural. On Boardle you can find a ready-to-use Mural Canvas template; other templates are available in Miroverse by Miro.

Videoconferencing for communicating
During your BMC workshops, you can use a video conferencing tool providing break out rooms. We suggest Zoom or Butter.

Collaboration in execution
Slack, Google drive, Dropbox or Padlet work well.

Tools for preparation and instruction
Use SessionLab to set your agenda and co-create with co-facilitators, Calendly if you need to share your calendar with the team, and Loom to make nice videos about how to use the tools or to illustrate the steps.

Tools for making the workshop interactive
You can use Tscheck.in, a simple tool to start a conversation at a personal level by asking questions.

Tools for Prototyping and Testing
Here you can use a great variety of tools, already mentioned on page 128 of this chapter: social media to communicate your new offering; tools developed to help you design your prototype and pretotype, like Marvel and Toonly; Canva to create graphical pretotype in an easy way; Google Forms for when you need to test your ideas online and collect feedback from customers.

CHART: ONLINE BUSINESS MODEL CANVAS STEPS, TECHNIQUES AND OUTCOMES

Source: our elaboration from A. Osterwalder, Y. Pigneur – Business Model Generation, John Wiley & Sons, Inc., Hoboken, New Jersey, 2010. Page 255-265

PHASE	ACTIVITIES	MODELS	ONLINE TECHNIQUES	TIME	OUTCOMES
MOBILISE	▸ Frame project objectives. ▸ Test preliminary business ideas. ▸ Plan. ▸ Assemble team.	▸ Business Model Canvas. ▸ Storytelling. ▸ Problem framing.	▸ Team and engagement building through synchronous work and engagement tools. ▸ Visualisation for the storytelling phase. ▸ Make videos to explain the process and the tools.	One to two-hour workshop.	▸ An energised innovation team. ▸ Shared objectives, methodology, and tools. ▸ Common language. ▸ An engaging story.
UNDERSTAND	▸ Scan environment. ▸ Study potential customers. ▸ Interview experts. ▸ Research what has already been tried. ▸ Collect ideas and opinions.	▸ Business Model Canvas. ▸ Business Model Patterns. ▸ Customer Insights. ▸ Visual Thinking. ▸ Scenarios Business Model Environment Evaluating Business Models.	▸ Asynchronous work: people collect and sharing data. ▸ Synchronous collect learnings. ▸ Break out rooms. ▸ Lightning Demo.	It depends.	▸ Shared learning on the market, customers, and technology. ▸ New business model patterns.

PHASE	ACTIVITIES	MODELS	ONLINE TECHNIQUES	TIME	OUTCOMES
DESIGN	▸ Brainstorm. ▸ Prototype. ▸ Test. ▸ Select.	▸ Business Model Canvas. ▸ Business Model Patterns. ▸ Ideation. ▸ Visual Thinking. ▸ Prototyping. ▸ Pretotyping. ▸ Scenarios. ▸ Evaluating Business Models. ▸ Strategy Managing Multiple Business Models.	▸ Synchronous and Asynchronous brainstorming. ▸ Anonymous voting. ▸ Visualisation. ▸ Break out rooms. ▸ Together-alone	Two to three-hour workshop.	▸ New ideas. ▸ Pretoptype. ▸ Prototype.
IMPLEMENT	▸ Communicate and involve. ▸ Execute.	▸ Business Model Canvas ▸ Visual Thinking ▸ Storytelling ▸ Managing Multiple Business Models	All the techniques explained in Chapter 4 are suitable for this phase.	It depends.	Business Model implementation.
MANAGE	▸ Scan the environment. ▸ Continuously assess your business model. ▸ Rejuvenate or rethink your model. ▸ Align business models throughout the enterprise. ▸ Manage synergies or conflicts between models.	▸ Business Model Canvas. ▸ Visual Thinking. ▸ Scenarios. ▸ Business Model Environment. ▸ Evaluating Business Models.	All the techniques explained in Chapter 4 are suitable for this phase.	Ongoing.	An ongoing process of validation and adaption.

METHOD 5. PRETOTYPING

Don't use it if you want to rely on your dreams for a long time; the reality check could be hard.

What is Pretotyping, and why use it

Pretotyping is a method to quickly and economically validate whether your idea is worth pursuing in your innovation process. The word Pretotype is a neologism created by Alberto Savoia[10]. It is a fake product or service you want to realise that simulates and precedes the real one. The main reason to use it is 'to make sure you are building the right It before you build It right.' It aims to see if the market is interested in a product or service before investing too much time and resources in developing an innovative idea.

Pretotyping is also a way to test if you are suitable for the product: that you possess the energy, commitment, and motivation in the case it happens to be a success. The starting point of a pretotype process is that you have an idea and write it as a simple concept with a target customer and an ideal price. Before investing much money in a real prototype and a launching campaign, you collect feedback from your potential market by doing market experiments.

Pretotyping was initially developed at Google in 2010. Since then, it has evolved by the continuous practice of many organisations and practitioners worldwide. There's an online professional community[11] that is spreading and experimenting with the method, developing tools to apply it, and extending its scope to everyday life. Instead of getting lost in thoughts and procrastinating, you can also try to pretotype your habits before deciding whether they are the right ones, as Saibelle Khaibeh says in the first episode of the official Pretotype podcast on Spotify.

Let's start from the beginning. In his lecture at Stanford[12], Alberto Savoia describes seven main elements:

1. Obey the law of market failure, as data show that most of the new ideas will fail in the market even if competently executed.
2. Make sure you are building the right It before you built It right. The right It is a product that, if competently executed, will have success.
3. Don't get lost in 'thoughtland', the land of opinion, because opinions are biased and have no value without data.
4. Trust only on Your DAta (YODA). Data collected yourself satisfy the criteria of 'freshness, relevance, trustworthiness, and significance'.
5. Pretotype it. Build a simple artefact or technique to collect YODA very quickly and inexpensively.
6. Say it with numbers. Concretely express your hypothesis; for example, X% of Y (market) will do this.
7. Think global, test local. Start as soon as possible to test and to get your first data.

The Pretotype Power

The power of pretotipying is to reverse the classical approach from, 'If we build it, will you buy it?' to 'If you buy it, we will build it' You can do that by putting together intuition and math rules to get relevant data quickly and cheaply.

The Challenge

One pretotype experiment is not enough to validate an idea, depending on how much you have to invest; you need to do at least three to five. You also need to choose the right market in which to test the pretotype, and to not make the pretotype-phase last too long.

Pretotyping is a five-step process.

1. **Isolate the key assumption: define what the premises of the new idea are**.
   The first step would be to write your idea in a simple statement, for example, The Magic Mirror, displaying music, news, and the day's agenda. Then it would help if you wrote a market engagement hypothesis, for example,

   In the morning, instead of watching your phone or tablet while preparing yourself for the day, you can have music, news, and your agenda written on your mirror so when you brush your teeth, shave or apply makeup, you can comfortably read it.

   We suppose this is the output of using the problem framing methodology, a design sprint, or divergent idea generation phase and a convergent phase where people chose the ideas, refined the concept, and put it down transparently.

2. **Make your market engagement hypothesis concrete and verifiable by clear and quantifiable assumptions.**
   You need to transform this market engagement hypothesis into numbers, and a specific testable market hypothesis: the XYZ hypothesis. This is a tricky step because it's not easy to preview your market share. So, what you need to do is to identify the minimum percentage of the market you need to make your product worth developing. Accordingly, write your XYZ hypothesis this way:

   At least X% of Y (market) will do Z. For example, 'At least 10% of people with a two-bathroom house will buy a mirror with a display for 100 euros'.

   How can this be tested it in the world? Check out the next phase.

3. **Hypozoom: think about how you might test locally, quickly, and inexpensively while staying true.**
   Hypozoom means to zoom in on your potential market until you find a representative XYZ on a smaller scale that you can test quickly and more comfortably, with participants not being your friends and family. For example, 'At least 10% of the people living in San Siro, Milan will buy a 100 euros magic mirror'. In this way, you can collect data that satisfy the criteria of freshness, relevance, trustworthiness, and significance. At this point, you have the market hypothesis, and you should find an easy, quick, and effective way of testing with a pretotype.

4. **Choose a type of pretotype. Plan it. Test it.**
   In this phase, you choose the best technique to validate the data and build the pretotype, costs, and time. There are different types of pretotyping techniques, depending on the product, service, or target audience; you can find them in the book, The Right It, and choose the most suitable one for you. The crucial point here is that when you think of a technique, you have to evaluate so-called skin-in-the-game: an engagement action made by your potential client that shows interest in the product and validates your hypothesis. That's the critical point, together with the XYZ hypothesis of this method because almost everyone is so in love with their ideas and doesn't like having them disconfirmed by others. That's why when pretotyping the facilitator will explicitly ask the group to think about 'skin-in-the-game' – concrete actions of you and your future customers.

   What are examples of skin-in-the-game? Give a personal email address or phone number, give time and attention, pre-order something, provide money to buy something right now, introduce the pretotype in your offer and share with clients. The most valuable skin-in-the-game actions would be giving money to have the product, as Tesla customers did to ensure they will have a model. Still, it could also be considered valuable to provide a real email address, a telephone number, or giving time to talk about the product or even show them to your client. Thumbs up or down, likes, and smiling faces on social media are not relevant as these reactions' conversion rates are unproven.

Amazon's Build It: how to get skin-in-the-game from future customers

'Build It' is a brilliant example of pretotyping from the world's e-commerce leader. Amazon announced that periodically they would present some concepts asking customers which they want to see built. It not only requests an opinion to enter the program, but also that you should also put skin in the game by pre-ordering it.

If a concept reaches its pre-order goal in 30 days, Amazon will build it and those who pre-ordered it will be among the first to get their hands on it at a special price. Customers will be charged if and when the product ships. If the pre-order goal is not met, the product will not be built, and people won't be charged. It's low risk, high reward, and a whole lot of fun. Below, you will find two examples from their first-day edition.

Smart Sticky Note Printer

Using voice-to-print technology, this hands-free smart sticky note printer that works with Alexa makes it easy to print your shopping lists, to-do lists, reminders, calendar events, or fun items like puzzles. All you have to do is ask. The printer uses thermal technology, so it never needs ink or toner, and paper rolls are easy to refill.

Smart Nutrition Scale

Smart Scale works with Alexa to offer hands-free, instant access to nutritional information for thousands of ingredients and food based on weight. Paired with an Echo Show, you can also view nutritional information at a glance. Alexa remembers your frequently used foods and defaults to those items. Simply say, 'Alexa, ask Smart Scale how much sugar is in these blueberries,' or 'Alexa, ask Smart Scale to weigh 200 calories of blueberries.'

Source: www.aboutamazon.com

5. **Analyse the data, make tweaks, repeat the process.**
   The last phase of the method is data analysis. You can do it by rating the feedback you had from your sample in terms of skin-in-the-game intensity from the zero-value opinion or comments on social media to a small-value validated email (1 point), a cash deposit (50 points), or a real paid order (250 points). Time is also considered a way of putting skin in the game because people's time is precious. The basic idea here is that quality data connected to your hypothesis and linked to engaged potential customers are infinitely more valuable than a tremendous amount of data with no skin in the game.

   At the end of the process, you put your data on a TRI-meter (The-Right-It-meter) to interpret the data you collect as objectively as possible. This is a five-scale metric for the likelihood of success varying from very unlikely (10%) to very likely (90%). At this point, you have to look at the results of the pretotyping experiment and place them on the ladder according to whether they are far below your hypothesis, in line, or far above. Since it is not a question of applying a mathematical formula, it is crucial to remain objective in interpreting the results. The best way is to compare them with the group that designed the product and the pretotype and with someone else in the company.

Pretotyping is used to obtain the rapid validation of your hypotheses. It is an iterative method, so be ready to repeat it, change features, attributes, turn it inside out, and use all the creative techniques that can be useful to adjust it after the first results. The exciting thing is that you do this after you have your relevant data from the market.

Pretotyping amazon gift cards

'Here we go…. I joined Amazon as a data engineer on the gift-card team. It bothered me that gift cards and the emotions attached had such a short lifespan. After claiming the balance, the gift card had no use. I had an idea. I chugged a coffee and grabbed a stack of builder tools: napkins, straws, and scrap paper. After a couple of hours, I had the prototype you see. A napkin as a 'book' and a folded napkin as a 'bookmark gift card' saying, 'Keep reading! -Love Mom', and I was embarrassed. But I stopped random people in random buildings for feedback over the next hour to get my go/no-go data. People loved it. I had the right It.

Within months we launched our new Gift marks in five countries and were awarded two patents. They are still available. I truly believe innovation can be paralysed due to fear of embarrassment. How many ideas never become something, anything tangible? Are they all terrible ideas, or are we too scared to take that first step?

As Alberto Savoia quotes, Reid Hoffman, the founder of LinkedIn, said, 'If you are not embarrassed by the first version of your product, you've launched too late.'

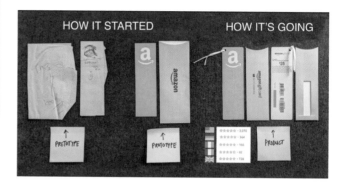

Source: LinkedIn post by Farzad Darouian, Principal Product Manager: Data Engineering Core | Inventor and Patent Holder | ex-Amazon[13].

Online Pretotyping

Let's take the pretotyping process online. The team consist of those who came up with the idea and all those who can present elements to falsify it. Therefore, mix experts in technology, market segment, product, service, people with a higher vision of the business, and people from other departments and business areas. For a startup, this is more difficult because the whole team is firmly committed to the cause. Still, you can decide to invite some outsiders in some of the phases, for example, the one when you perform hypozoom or when you analyse the results of the first experiments and put them in a TRI-meter. In applying this method, you can use all the online innovation techniques described in Chapter 4 to work and co-create together.

Which tools do you need?

Online Whiteboard tools for realtime collaboration, mentioned on page 118 of this chapter, for example, in Boardle you can find a predefined template for pretotyping made on Mural (see the box the pretotype Canvas).

Videoconferencing for communicating with break out rooms, like Zoom or Butter.

Collaboration in execution, like Slack, Google drive, Dropbox, Padlet.

Tools for making the workshop interactive, like Tscheck.in or Mentimeter

Tools for Prototyping and Testing, mentioned on page...of this chapter, like YouTube, Linkedin, Marvel, Toonly, Canva, and Google forms.

The online steps could be done both in synchronous and asynchronous ways, as shown in the picture.

PRETOTYPING PROCESS

IDEA MEH

Output of
Ideation
process
or other
innovation
methods

XYZ WORKSHOP

PRETOTYPING EXPERIMENTS

TRI METER WORKSHOP

GO FOR IT

DROP IT

SYNCHRONOUS

ASYNCHRONOUS

SYNCHRONOUS

TWEAK IT

Here you find a way to go through the different steps. If you're pretotyping inside a company, share the approach, method, techniques, and tools upfront. Collect concerns to understand which phases you need to focus on most.

PHASE/QUESTIONS	STEPS	MODEL/TEMPLATES	ONLINE TECHNIQUES	TIME	OUTCOMES
TURN AN IDEA INTO AN OBJECTIVE What is your X% of Y (market) that will do Z (something at a certain price)?	XYZ WORKSHOP ▸ Formulate the XYZ hypothesis. ▸ Hypozoom to formulate an XYZ.	PRETOTYPE CANVAS (see box in this chapter)	▸ Working synchronously. ▸ Asynchronous vote the XYZ hypothesis. ▸ Working in small groups in break out rooms. ▸ Lightning Demo to collect data to formulate the hypothesis.	One to two hours	Make a market engagement hypothesis that is concrete and verifiable by clear and quantifiable assumptions.
PRETOTYPE Which pretotype best suits my experiment?	▸ Define the pretotype technique. ▸ Set up the pretotype. ▸ Define the skin-in-the-game.	Basic Pretotype techniques.	▸ Asynchronous work. ▸ Making Videos to show how the pretotype works.	30 to 60 minutes	A pretotype to collect YODA with skin-in-the-game.
PRETOTYPE EXPERIMENT Are customers buying it?	▸ Experiment. ▸ Experiment. ▸ Experiment.		Asynchronous workgroups in competition to gain quicker and more relevant YODA.	It depends on how long it takes to build a pretotype and get data that makes sense.	YODA.
TRI-meter How likely is it that this pretotype experiment would generate this data?	▸ TRI – Meter WORKSHOP. ▸ Share YODA. ▸ Put it into the TRI-meter. ▸ Decide.	TRI-Meter	Break out rooms where subgroups share the YODA they have and decide where to put it in the meter.	Two hours	▸ Go for it. ▸ Drop it. ▸ Tweak it.

Pretotype Planning Canvas v1

Adapted from The Right It: Why So Many Ideas Fail and How to Make Sure Yours Succeed, by Alberto Savoia

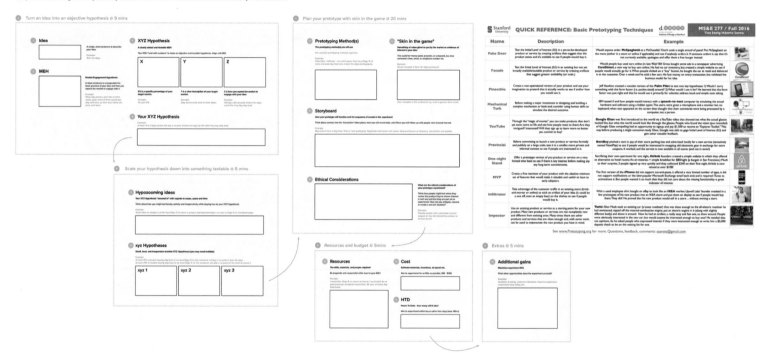

We Interviewed Chris Callaghan, UX Director at McCann Manchester, who designed a Canvas to go through the different phases of the pretotype method. You can use it, since it is on Boardle[14]. He taught it to a remote team of 20 students at Hyper Island Manchester in a two-hour workshop where students designed a set of pretotypes to be tested in the following hours. Immediately following the workshop, one group of students launched a pretotype with the fake-door pretotyping method. They used Facebook ads to drive people to a landing page with sign-up as a measure of interest.

In the Canvas below, you can see the phases and how he divided them into chunks and timebox . As you can see, 'boxes' are pretty short. Although it was an educational setting, when developing 'real preto-types' (it seems like an oxymoron), time should be short because the hypothesis is a first guess, something that makes sense to your business but not necessarily the result of an extended analysis and research process. Chris divided the team into subgroups of four, each of which developed a different idea going through the phases. When they were in subgroups, they briefly discussed the assign-ment then the plenary shared the results to be put on the canvas. So, at the end of the workshop, each group had a ready-to-test pretotype. One of the students' challenges in the room was to think about the pretotype to develop. This may require additional time and asynchronous thinking in a dedicated pretotype ideation phase.

Don't use it if you think *the purpose is a buzzword*

What is Purpose Launchpad, and why use it?
Purpose Launchpad is an open methodology and a mindset to generate and evolve early-stage initiatives into purpose-driven organisations to make a significant difference. It was developed by Francisco Palao, with the input of more than 150 contributors around the world[15]. It was designed to help people build purpose-driven organisations and evolve their mindsets to become explorers who will discover the right path to create a new organisation, business, product, or service that will make a positive impact in the world. It works for startups or teams with an early-stage idea. It is also appli-cable to established organisations that want to transform themselves into purpose-driven organisations. It is a meta-methodology, meaning that it includes many innovation frameworks and methods like design thinking, design sprints, agile, and scrum. It's like having a toolkit with all the tools inside, and you only take certain tools when applicable, depending on the situation within the organisation.

The Purpose Launchpad is a holistic approach meaning that you work on eight interconnected key areas: Purpose, People, Customer, Abundance, Viability, Processes, Product, and Metrics. There is no clear linear order of development. It is, however, true that one should not move on to the next stage without having evolved all of the key eight areas. They don't necessarily evolve in the order of appearance in the spiral diagram. The assessment might show that, for example, Viability is further developed than People and Customer. In such a case, focussing on the People and Customer axes in the next sprints is advisable to help evolve all axes evenly outward on the radar. The reason to do this is to ensure that it is not a 'false sense of viability'. An organisation might be successfully selling products, giving them the belief that they've obtained a successful value proposition and business model. Still, until this is validated against the pains, gains, and needs of both the internal organisation, the wider community, and the (potential) customers, it remains a hypothesis. To ensure successful long-term viability and growth, and prevent a possible crash-and-burn scenario when going mainstream, evolution takes place along all the axes. In each evolutionary phase (Explore, Evaluation, and Impact), different tools and strategies are applied along each of the eight key areas.

The Purpose Launchpad Power
The Purpose Launchpad aims at transforming team culture and making a positive impact on the world. So, it not only innovates products, services, or business models but also evolves a team culture. It combines the power of scrum and sprints with other proven methods and frameworks, such as design thinking, Lean Startup, and customer development processes, embracing complexity while keeping things together at the same time.

The Challenge
It is new for many organisations to operate with a larger purpose in mind. Most organisations have designed all of their processes around profit and loss, not positively impacting the world. Even our economic models measure progress based on revenues and cost.

There are four key components in the process of Purpose Launchpad. It is an iterative model, which means that you might (have to) pivot your product and/or business model numerous times on your journey to growth. The insights you gain by the use of the components will help you ensure validated growth.

1. The first phase is to understand the so-called 'Massive Transformation Purpose' of the initiative. Such a Purpose covers what your team and organisation want to bring to the world and how you and your organisation would like to affect the world in a positive way, like TED's 'Ideas Worth Spreading'.

2. Then, the team goes through the online assessment made up of 24 questions covering all the eight interconnected key areas. The assessment outcome is outlined on a radar graph with a score for each of those eight key areas. The overall outcome of the graph will also indicate the evolutionary stage you are currently in. There are three evolutionary stages.

   ▸ *Exploration* – focused on finding the key elements of the initiative.
   ▸ *Evaluation* – focused on evaluating the key hypotheses of the initiative.
   ▸ *Impact* – focused on growing the organisation to maximise its impact in the world.

   The Purpose Launchpad mentor determines the required focus points (backlog items) and what framework might be useful in the upcoming sprint, trying to create a perfect circle and making the circle bigger and bigger all the time.

3. The central component is a Sprint. Each sprint begins with an assessment. The sprint focus is a result of the assessment. If your score is very good on product but low in the customer area, you will run a design thinking process talking to customers, assessing the pains and the gains. Based on the assessment, you determine the methodology. If you score low on people, your sprint will focus on this using the Team Canvas to create insights into the organisation's gaps.

4. After the first sprint, you can complete the first Purpose Launchpad Scorecard when you measure the eight areas of actions to be done to evolve. It is a scorecard and dashboard managed by the certified Purpose Launchpad mentor, where you measure each sprint's progress. It is a central component during each online mentoring meeting between the team and the mentor. The progress is not measured based on completion of the backlog tasks but based on how much you have learned during each of the backlog steps and which new insights you have gained. Every week you monitor the scorecard progress visualised in graphs. The Purpose Launchpad Board provides the mentor and the organisation with valuable insight into how to help rapidly evolve the team and organisation as a whole, as the people are a critical element in the initiative's successful growth. After closing every sprint before opening a new one, you check the mood among the team.

Then you start a new iterative process on the eight areas of the model. The goal is to evolve each of the eight areas of the launchpad and grow the initiative and organisation from Exploration to Evaluation to the exponential impact phase.

The Purpose Launchpad Process Online
This Purpose Launchpad process has been designed for online innovation. It does not have a fixed timeframe, nor are there fixed scheduled workshops. It is dependent on the stage that your initiative is in, the skillset and mindset of your people, and the need of the project based on the regular Purpose Launchpad Assessments by the mentor. Depending on all these factors, it can take weeks, months, or longer to evolve your initiative and organisation towards (exponential) growth. The Purpose Launchpad can be applied as a set of principles, tools, or a structured, iterative process. This makes the method highly flexible and perfect for online innovation.

The team meets with the mentor regularly, often weekly. Depending on the progress and need, the team can move bi-weekly during the Evaluation and Impact phase of the Purpose Launchpad process. The process starts with a kick-off workshop. The mentor facilitates the team through a series of tools and activities designed to help the team define the initiative's Massive Transformative Purpose and find alignment around the individual and organisational values.

At the start of the process, the mentor and team agree on a fixed meeting time during which they will close the running sprint and open a new one. This is usually on a weekly basis and at the beginning of the week. During this meeting, varying from one to one-and-a-half hours, the team updates the mentor on their progress of the backlog items assigned to them by the mentor. The insights are measured and recorded on the Purpose Launchpad Board; the mentor closes the current sprint and opens it based on a new

Purpose Launchpad Assessment performed by the mentor. During the sprints, the team members work asynchronously with the mentor. On a need-basis, additional training master-classes or coaching workshops on the provided tools and frameworks are scheduled during which one or more of the backlog items are covered under the mentor's guidance.

We interviewed Michael Smits, a Dutch Certified Purpose Launchpad Mentor, about this methodology's online experience.

Who is this online Purpose Launchpad method for?
'It's for those that believe in empowering their employees and colleagues, who believe in strengthening collaboration, seek alignment in values, and believe they are in business to contribute to society and advance humanity and life as a whole. It's for those organisations that believe in autonomous teams and wish to transform into a purpose-driven exponential organisation.'

How does the Purpose Launchpad process work?
'After facilitating the definition of the Purpose and Values, I generally work with the team on the alignment of their strengths and facilitate the appointment of a team coordina-tor, who is responsible for organising teamwork during the sprints and mobilising the team to prepare efficient updates for the mentor during their recurring mentoring meetings. Some teams are more autonomous than others; some need more guidance. If needed, I provide them with additional help, either by providing additional tools, setting up templates for them, or providing them with self-learn resources. This is not always enough, and a team might require additional training and coaching. In such cases, I assign the coordinator the task to coordinate and schedule the required additional workshops with the team. I try to help them as much as I can, as it is also part of my purpose to help

them grow. But it is also the purpose of the method itself, as it is equally important that the process helps to evolve the initiative to exponential growth as it is to realise exponential growth among the team and its team members.'

Which tools do you need?
'Depending on the skillset and current way of working of the team, I decide to use templates I have prepared in Google Docs/Slides and Sheets or, when the team has worked with tools like Miro before, I set up collaboration boards for them in which they can work on the different templates.'

For communication with the teams, Michael always has an easy and quick communication channel open with them, like a WhatsApp or Slack channel.

A smaller team not as familiar with the different tools and principles, like design thinking, customer development et cetera will move slower in the beginning, but from experi-ence, will create traction quite quickly, as they tend to develop the right entrepreneurial mindset quicker than teams who are accustomed to work in set ways already.

What about time? Is it different in an online setting?
'In the Purpose Launchpad, there's not a predefined time-lapse, and because you don't have fixed workshops or activi-ties, you can easily adapt to the online shift. Ideally, an organisation adopts the Purpose Launchpad as their agile workflow process forever, as it is, as far as I know, the most comprehensive methodology thus far. And you do not have to apply it continuously as a rigid iterative process. However, I recommend using the Sprint framework embedded in it, even if you run two or three-week sprints. But if you do not want to, you can also apply the purpose launchpad as a set of principles or a framework with the different tools the mentor provides you. However, if you want to experience the

method's power as a structured, iterative process towards growth and impact, I recommend committing a year to it, because it is not just about the transformation of product and services. After one year, you'll start to see the real priceless value: the evolution and transformation of the team and its team members. Often, this is already visible after a month or two, but after one year, the mindset shift will have created ripples throughout the organisation.'

How does the process work for established organisations?
'In an established organisation, it is often different compared to startups. You often have to deal with a set way of working, scheduling meetings, and already established internal processes. The same rule applies there. If the organisation wants to experience the method's true power, they should commit to it for at least one year. However, you can already achieve great results by applying the method as a set of principles of a framework under the mentor's guidance. You don't have to do it the startup way. Besides, in my experience, in an established organisation, people generally are much more stuck in their day-to-day. They often need to be accompanied a little more if you want to achieve the maximum feasible growth. They tend to, especially in the beginning, treat the backlog items like tasks when the key element is not about completion but about maximising learning and gaining insights. You take the next steps and develop your innovation further based on those learnings and insights. It takes you from an inside-out approach to an outside-in approach. Customer value, customer experiences, and even employee value and experiences are designed and developed based on continuous and real conversations and learnings from the customer and other stakeholders. It is not so evident in most organisations. Also, often the project tends to be one of the many other tasks the team members have. That too is not beneficial, but a reality. So, in such cases, I tend to schedule workshops with the team to facilitate amplified

learning and growth along all of the eight key areas. Usually, they start to experience that it works after four to five weeks. That's when the mind shift starts to happen, and you can gradually work towards the setup with weekly mentoring meetings.'

In the box below, there's an example of the evolution path of a startup in education.

Purpose Launchpad evolution of a startup in education

The evolution of a startup in education is visualised by means of the outcome of each assessment. The organisation had an idea of what they wanted to do but had no idea where to start. I helped them clarify their purpose, values, and even their Moonshot, Mission, and Vision, even though this is not critical, since they were clearly still in the Exploration phase. They had done a lot of groundwork, but much of it was (are) hypotheses until validated with real customers and stakeholders.

The pictures show an overview of their evolution in a couple of weeks from the Exploration to the Evaluation phase. They are not further evolving with real paying customers (early adopters), so the methodology does help to move quickly towards experimenting with paying customers, and all of the development is done with hardly any investment. That's the power of this methodology because you are almost co-creating with customers and the community.

This startup in education was mentored by Michael Smits, a certified Purpose Launchpad Mentor.

PL Explore Phase

PL Evaluation Phase

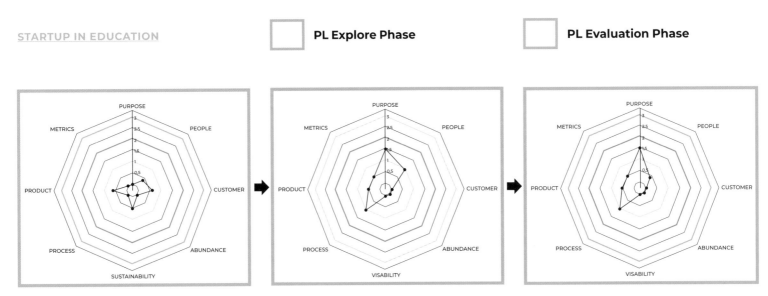

Before Purpose Workshop

Start of Sprint #1

Start of Sprint #2

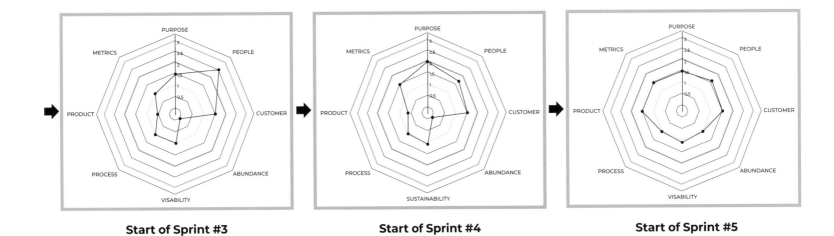

Start of Sprint #3

Start of Sprint #4

Start of Sprint #5

METHOD 7. THE CIRCULAR DESIGN PROCESS[16]

Don't use it if you think that we have endless resources on our planet.

What is the Circular Design process, and why use it?

The Circular Design Process is a meta-methodology. The aim is to innovate products that reflect the principles of the circular economy. It is a design thinking process specialising in creating circular design products, services, and business models, originated by IDEO and the Ellen Macarthur Foundation. Premises of the methodology are that pressure to sell has led to a disregard for products' environmental impact, resulting in the need to extract more and more resources from the planet, increasing waste, worsening pollution, and consumerist behaviour. The European Commission estimated that 80% of a product's environmental impact is determined during its design stage[17]. According to journalist Richard Girling, we throw away 80% of what we purchase within six months of buying it[18].

'McKinsey and Company have estimated the economic benefit of moving towards a closed-loop economy by examining the following durable goods industries in the European Union: The automotive sector and other transport; machinery and equipment; furniture; radio, TV and communication; medical precision and optical equipment; and finally, office machinery and computers. By studying these industries, they found that: "(...) the circular economy represents a net materials cost savings opportunity of US$ 340 to 380 billion per year."' (World Economic Forum 2014, p. 20)[19]

The Circular Design Process Power

This aims to solve local problems but with a large-scale impact. The process uses expertise and experience from all over the world, and therefore, the possibility to work remotely is of great value.

Challenges

Make sure that people are aligned on the circular economy principles and definitions. Make sure you, as a facilitator, understand the *why* and *for what* of the single methods to pick the right one. Go quickly into the first loop using learning loops, rapid prototyping, and circular buy-in to validate your circular innovation early.

The circular design process has a butterfly shape, showing that instead of ending the product lifecycle in the landfill, four loops can be used in the following order: reuse, refurbish, remanufacture, and recycle.

The circular design process comprises four stages and incorporates approaches such as design thinking and human-centred design.

- ▶ **Understand** – Get to know the user and the system.
- ▶ **Define** – Put into words the design challenge and your intention as a designer.
- ▶ **Make** – Ideate, design, and prototype as many iterations and versions as you can.
- ▶ **Release** – Launch your design into the wild and build your narrative; create loyalty in customers and deepen investment from stakeholders by telling a compelling story.

For each of the four phases, there are six methods with templates available on the Circular Design Guide, adapted to the Circular economy principles. In addition to these twenty-four, there are four advanced ones concerning the use of materials. The process may last from a couple of days to a month. It depends on the output you want to design. It's an iterative process, so many loops will be taken to develop learning and the right output.

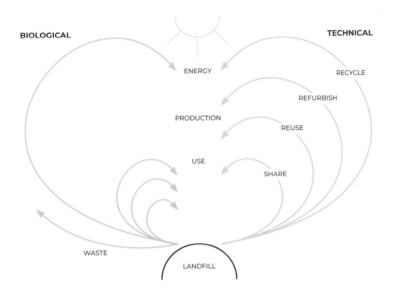

BIOLOGICAL

TECHNICAL

ENERGY

RECYCLE

REFURBISH

PRODUCTION

REUSE

USE

SHARE

WASTE

LANDFILL

Source: Ellen Mcarthur foundation/

The Online Circular Design Process

In the Circular Design toolkit[20], you will find many templates for the innovation journey's four phases. Each phase can be implemented online. It is an iterative process, so it is important to be quick with the first release, use online techniques to engage.

Which tools do you need?

The online techniques can all be used depending on the methods you use, and the same can be said of the tools. Digital whiteboards (Miro, Mural, Klaxoon) work fine, and to get connected, Zoom or Butter make sense. Loom and SessionLab help to prepare the workshops. And with Canva and Google Forms, you can prepare prototypes for simple tests. In addition to these, you can also use tools for prototyping and design, including YouTube videos.

The Milan Food Policy

The need: Every second, the equivalent of six garbage trucks of edible food is wasted globally. Less than 2% of the valuable nutrients in food by-products and human waste are recovered for productive use in cities. The modern food system is degrading and unhealthy, but cities could hold the key to changing this.

The solution: The Municipality of Milan and Fondazione Cariplo has taken a bold new strategic approach to support a new food system by developing the Milan Food Policy, a tool to support the city's food industry players to manage food-related challenges.

What makes the Milan Food Policy circular: Through local procurement, developing logistics for distributing surplus food, and valorising discarded organic material, Milan is making the most of its food resources while supporting the regeneration of natural systems.

The benefits: By working with local public and private organisations and supporting innovation, Milan has seen important reductions in food waste and the associated costs. Through awareness-raising and capacity building, local organisations involved with food are also able to evolve and benefit from this positive shift.

Source: www.ellenmacarthurfoundation.org/case-studies/the-milan-food-policy / CHART Case study – The Milan Food Policy – BOX

In this chapter, we have presented you with seven methodologies to innovate online. Because of their massive impact, we are great fans of the Lightning Decision Jam, the Design Sprint, and the FORTH innovation method and we dedicate separate chapters to them. We start by introducing the Lightning Decision Jam to you in Chapter 8.

KEY MESSAGES FROM THIS CHAPTER

▸ **Innovation methods create common learnings.**

▸ **Using online methodologies allows you to control simultaneity and contemporaneity and to stay more connected.**

▸ **Because there's no in-person connection among the online team, use structured and rigorous methods to keep pace and monitor your results.**

▸ **You cannot use in-person innovation methods *tout court* without tailoring and adapting to the online setting.**

▸ **Online innovation enhances iterative and fast-paced methodologies.**

▸ **Don't use a method just because of the method itself. Match the purpose of your initiative and your organisation's characteristics with the superpower and benefits of the online methods presented.**

[1] Dwayne Spradlin, Are You Solving the Right Problem?, HBR September, 2012
[2] https://designsprint.academy/about-problem-framing/
[3] Thomas Wedell-Wedellsborg, Are You Solving the Right Problems? Reframing them can reveal unexpected solutions, HBR January-February 2017
[4] https://www.ridersandelephants.com/thecustomerexperiencedeck
[5] Eric Ries, The Lean Startup, Penguin Random House, UK; 2011
[6] Ash Mayura, Running Lean, O' Really Media Inc. California, 2012
[7] JTBD It's a method to understand customer behaviours by focusing on the job a specific product should do for a customer instead of on the product. Clayton Christensen first used the name in an HBR article describing a fast-food chain wanting to improve milkshake sales.
[8] A. Osterwalder, Y. Pigneur – Business Model Generation, John Wiley & Sons, Inc., Hoboken, New Jersey, 2010
[9] Innova is a heterogeneous team of engineers, designers, and communication experts who collect ideas from all sectors and turn them into concrete objects. https://www.industriaitaliana.it/isinnova-stampa-3d-di-valvole-per-respiratori-polmonari-componenti-meccanici-e/
[10] Alberto Savoia: 'The right It, why so many ideas Fail and How to Make Sure Yours Succeed', Harpers Collins Publishers, New York, 2019
[11] You can find interesting discussions, videos, and experiments on pretotyping on the following social media outlets: the YouTube Channel, 'The Right it – Video Lessons by Alberto Savoia'; Linkedin group, 'Pretotyping Professionals', ignited by Robert Skrobe; the Spotify channel, 'The official Pretotyping Podcast', by Jonathan Sun and Robert Strobe
[12] You can watch the full lecture on YouTube at https://www.youtube.com/watch?v=3sUozPcH4fY
[13] https://www.linkedin.com/posts/farzaddarouian_pretoyping-beembarassed-activity-6765359977457696768-1n41/
[14] The template has been designed on MURAL, and you can find it on Boardle
https://www.boardle.io/boards/222
[15] https://www.purposelaunchpad.com
[16] https://www.ellenmacarthurfoundation.org
[17] http://www.buildup.eu/sites/default/files/content/Brochure-Ecodesign-Your-Future-15022012.pdf
[18] Rubbish!: Dirt On Our Hands and Crisis Ahead 0th Edition by Richard Girling
[19] Ministry of food and agriculture of Denmark – Best Practice Examples of Circular Business Models
[20] https://www.circulardesignguide.com

CONTENTS

CHAPTER 8

THE LIGHTNING DECISION JAM

Overview of the 9 steps of the Lightning Decision Jam
Minutes in black: 60 minutes session
Minutes in blue: 90 minutes session

STEP 9
MAKE SOLUTIONS ACTIONABLE
10 MINUTES / 12 MINUTES

STEP 8
DECIDE WHICH SOLUTION TO EXECUTE
10 MINUTES / 12 MINUTES

STEP 7
PRIORITISE SOLUTIONS
6 MINUTES / 11 MINUTES

STEP 6
IDEATE SOLUTIONS
7 MINUTES / 15 MINUTES

STEP 5
REFRAME THE PROBLEM
4 MINUTES / 8 MINUTES

STEP 4
PRIORITISE PROBLEMS
6 MINUTES / 11 MINUTES

STEP 3
CAPTURE PROBLEMS AND CHALENGES
6 MINUTES / 8 MINUTES

STEP 2
START POSITIVE
6 MINUTES / 8 MINUTES

STEP 1
DEFINE THE GOAL
5 MINUTES / 5 MINUTES

One of the main obstacles for innovation in organisations is that there's a lot of unstructured discussion on it with unclear outcomes. Instead, follow a structured method that leads to more ideas, decisions and clear action steps with internal support. A process that helps you to start DOING things. The Lightning Decision Jam (LDJ)[1] is an excellent method to get your team in action mode. It is a fast exercise; it eliminates discussion; it allows all team members to contribute, leading to tangible action steps to get started NOW.

ONLINE INNOVATION

WHAT IS THE LIGHTNING DECISION JAM?

The Lightning Decision Jam (LDJ) is a 60 to 90-minute exercise generating solutions to a problem you face with a product or service, for trying to come up with new product features, to solve a problem within a team or process – any problem you can imagine. It helps to identify problems and challenges participants in the workshop have in mind. It gives the organisation insights into what employees see happening. And it triggers them to come up with ideas to solve those problems, and above that, generate action steps to start testing solutions directly. No writing memos, no reports and no plans, but clear, measurable activities that will give insights into what works and what doesn't. So, it is about taking action fast. That is why the process is called Lightning Decision Jam: it is fast (like lightning), and it is aimed at gathering input from all participants to make decisions.

The process can also help familiarise those new to innovation to the characteristic way of working and thinking needed to be successful: having no discussions and everyone can contribute. So, it is not about those with the loudest voice getting the most attention, but group work where all person-alities can give their input and share their ideas. Since the Lightning Decision Jam is a process of only 60 to 90 minutes, it is very easy to try without risk. As soon as participants experience working in a very structured way with short timeboxed activities, most of them – if not all – will see the power of it. This opens the door to more extensive online innovation methods like the Design Sprint and the FORTH innovation method described in Chapters 9 and 10.

WHY RUN A LIGHTNING DECISION JAM?

In a fast-changing world, you must adapt to quickly changing circumstances. You simply can't spend days on extensive conversations and discussions if you want to make progress. The Lightning Decision Jam significantly speeds up decision-making processes, especially those concerning innovation. The key to successful innovation is to start DOING things instead of just talking. As Gijs van Wulfen describes it, 'Innova-tion is doing new things or things in a new way', which means no one knows beforehand what will work. The only way to find out is to come up with solutions and turn them into (small) experiments so you can start testing in practice.

The highly structured process of the LDJ is aimed at coming up with a lot of solutions fast, especially very creative ones or those that may have been overlooked for years. By using the impact/effort selection matrix, deciding on which idea(s) to put forward becomes a straightforward exercise. After identi-fying the best solution(s), the workshop ends with a shortlist of clear action steps, with names of those responsible to take those steps and a timeline for executing them. So, no meetings with open ends and just a wall full of post-it notes with ideas that have not been curated. No unclarity on the next steps. The LDJ sets you and your team in action mode!

WHO IS THE PROCESS FOR?

The Lightning Decision Jam can be used in any type of organ-isation. Whether you work in (or with) a five-person company or a multinational corporation, this exercise is useful in any workshop where you want to put an end to useless, unstruc-tured discussions and want to kick-start innovation.

The ideal team size for the process is three to eight people. If you have more participants, break them into smaller groups and work through the same process simultaneously. For this, you can use the break out rooms feature of a videoconferencing tool like Zoom or Butter. Ensure that the facilitator jumps in and out of each break out room regularly to make sure participants are making progress and do not get caught up in extensive conversations or discussions. It is advisable to have one or more co-facilitators who can moderate a group next to a tech facilitator.

The process can also be used to familiarise people with the way online collaboration – and especially innovating remotely – can be done. It will help develop a positive mindset in your way of working and the fact that innovation can easily be done online. This may open the doors for more intensive online innovation methods and processes mentioned in Appendix 2, where we give you an overview of online innovation methods.

Running a Lightning Decision Jam is a relatively simple way for a facilitator to build experience for running innovation workshops online. It helps you get familiar with the tools used, the types of processes, and how they are run best, taking into account that it is all about having a clear and structured process with timeboxed workshops, each aimed at specific outcomes and decisions to be made. Last but not least, an LDJ is very helpful for aligning a team. Especially now that more people work remotely, chances are higher for miscommunication, and it is harder to keep track of what everybody is doing.

FOR WHAT TOPICS CAN THE LDJ BE USED?

Whether you need new, innovative ideas for improving your office environment or to decide on improvements in an existing product or service, the Lightning Decision Jam can be used for a wide range of topics. For your inspiration, here is a list of topics you could think of:

▸ Improving the office environment.
▸ Making working from home more personal (or 'human').
▸ Improving a product, service, experience, or business model.
▸ Finding new revenue streams.
▸ Increasing the number of visitors to the website.
▸ Improving internal collaboration.
▸ Eliminating redundant processes across teams.

This is just a shortlist to trigger your ideas about topics to use. Whether you want to work on an internal problem, a simple or a more complex problem, if you want to make decisions fast, the LDJ is your method.

We appreciate the fact that more complex problems require more time than 60 to 90 minutes to be solved. There is no magic to this method that makes issues with a high degree of complexity simpler. But it does help to make your journey towards solutions simple. You can break down a complex problem into smaller chunks first and run an LDJ on each chunk. After running the method, once you have experimented with the action steps, you can run a next LDJ to make an inventory of barriers and problems faced in the experiment to come up with solutions to the most important issues.

'Everything should be made as simple as possible. But not simpler.' – Albert Einstein

RUNNING A LIGHTNING DECISION JAM WILL BRING YOU THE FOLLOWING OUTPUTS:

1. An inventory of problems, prioritised by the participants.
2. Solutions to solve the top-voted problem.
3. Decisions made about which solution to test first.
4. Action steps to start an experiment with the top-voted solution.
5. An overview of next best solutions to try if the prioritised solution doesn't work in the experiment.

TRY IT YOURSELF!

Since the Lightning Decision Jam is a relatively simple process, it is a great process to try yourself! You can easily schedule it in an already planned meeting, so it doesn't eat up extra time for your team. On the other hand, since you can run the process in 60 to 90 minutes, it should not be hard to find a gap in your team's agenda to schedule an LDJ.

To help you on your way, below, you find a full description of the nine steps of the process. It is your guideline to follow for your workshop. So, there is no reason NOT to start today. Just plan a workshop with your colleagues or team and try out the method!

CHART SIX TIPS FOR RUNNING A SUCCESSFUL LIGHTNING DECISION JAM

1. Be strict on timing
Participants may feel limited now and then, but the timeboxed steps force them to decide, even though those decisions may sometimes be based on gut feel. But that is better than making no decisions at all, isn't it?

2. No discussions
Make sure to manage expectations before you start. The strict timing and silent way of working help to avoid discussions and endless conversations.

3. Run the workshop with teams of three to eight people
Do you have a bigger team? Then work in break out rooms and have a co-facilitator to help manage the teams in their break out rooms.

4. Work together-alone
To allow every participant to contribute and to avoid discussions, it is essential to let everyone work individually in a timeboxed workshop when generating input. This means working in silence. When time is up, participants can read the input of others. By anonymous voting, everyone can express their preferences.

5. Claim your role as facilitator
Your team or colleagues may be new to you facilitating a workshop like this. Make clear that you take on this role for the outcome. Alternatively, you can consider asking someone else (who is not in your team or not in your organisation) to facilitate or hire a professional innovation facilitator.

6. Start DOING it!
Since getting started is the most important, just try out the Lightning Decision Jam yourself! For the first time, you can start with a low-risk, easy topic just to experience the method.

THE NINE STEPS OF THE LIGHTNING DECISION JAM

The Lightning Decision Jam contains nine steps. We will describe each step to be your guide to run a workshop yourself. If you want to familiarise yourself with the method, it is recommended to schedule a workshop with your team on a low-risk topic as a try-out.

BEFORE YOU START

Facilitator
Make one of the team members the facilitator or reach out to an external facilitator to moderate the workshop. The advantage of having an external facilitator is that this person has no interest in the workshop outcomes at all, which helps to eliminate politics and company culture in the process.

Online whiteboard tools for realtime collaboration
Online whiteboard tools like Miro or Mural, as you read in Chapter 3, are great to collaborate online in realtime with all the participants. These tools have very useful features like digital post-it notes, voting, and a timer. If you don't want to introduce new tools (yet), be creative and use a collaboration tool you are familiar with (for example Google Slides). A great feature in Miro is the so-called Bulk Mode which allows participants to contribute individually without being distracted from what others are writing, which improves the principle of working together-alone.

Videoconferencing for communication
For communication during your workshop, you can use a videoconferencing tool like Zoom or Butter. With these tools it is very easy to make break out rooms, which is recommended if you have a bigger group (more than eight participants) since you can make smaller teams easily. If you use Miro as your online whiteboard, you can also use its built-in video conferencing feature. You can use Microsoft Teams too. Your choice may depend on company policy or restrictions.

Collaboration in execution
For a follow-up with the team involved in the solution's execution phase, you may use a tool like Slack. This is a communication medium that is positioned as an alternative to email. Slack offers various options of communication such

as channels, private groups and direct messaging. As with email, you can share documents and files across teams and in a one-on-one format.

Prepare your online whiteboard
Prepare a whiteboard in Miro or Mural with areas for participants to work in. You need the following areas:

CHART: OVERVIEW OF THE NINE STEPS AND WHAT YOU NEED PER STEP

STEP 1	STEP 2	STEP 3	STEP 4	STEP 5	STEP 6	STEP 7	STEP 8	STEP 9
DEFINE THE GOAL	**START POSITIVE**	**CAPTURE PROBLEMS AND CHALENGES**	**PRIORITISE PROBLEMS**	**REFRAME THE PROBLEM**	**IDEATE SOLUTIONS**	**PRIORITISE SOLUTIONS**	**DECIDE WHICH SOLUTION TO EXECUTE**	**MAKE SOLUTIONS ACTIONABLE**
An area on a digital whiteboard like Mural or Miro to state the goal of the workshop.	A picture of a sailboat. An ideation area per participant to write input individually on digital post-its.	An ideation area per participant to write input individually on digital post-its (this can be next to the area used in Step 2).	An area on the whiteboard to copy the prioritised post-its from Step 3, too.	A big post-it with the reframed problem (for the brainstorm).	An ideation area per participant to write solutions individually on digital post-its.	An area on the whiteboard to copy the prioritised post-its from Step 6, too.	The impact-effort matrix for stating the prioritised solutions.	An area to write action steps (and when the steps will be executed and who is responsible).

Please note that we have added our suggested number of minutes to take for the specific action with each step. The first number of minutes mentioned (in green) is for a 60-minute LDJ; the second number (in blue) is for a 90-minute LDJ. Where there is a number of minutes mentioned in the description of a particular step, it's based on a 60-minute workshop. You can adjust the timing if your workshop runs 90 minutes.

STEP 1: DEFINE THE GOAL
5 MINUTES / 5 MINUTES

At the start of the workshop, introduce the topic or goal to the participants. Why are we here today? Goals can be anything: increasing the number of visitors to the website, reducing the number of errors made in a specific process, increasing revenue, et cetera.

In Steps 2 and 3, start using the sailboat picture. The upper part (above the wavy line that represents the waterline) represents Step 2, 'having the wind in the sail', where you identify what is going well ('What is moving us forward [towards our goal]?'). Use the bottom part with the anchor ('What is holding us back?') in step 3 for defining challenges and problems.

STEP 2: START POSITIVE
6 MINUTES / 8 MINUTES

Instead of starting to identify challenges or problems, start with an inventory of what is going well around the chosen topic. This helps to get participants in a positive mood and to share successes. It is also a nice warm-up for the workshop.

Each participant writes down – individually, in silence, and without discussion – all the successes he or she can think of. Make sure to write each topic on a new post-it note. Encourage everyone to write down as many topics as they can. There is no right or wrong; it is all about getting everyone's thoughts out there. When working with an online collaboration tool like Miro or Mural, all participants can work simultaneously on the same whiteboard.

> **TIP**
> ask everyone to use the same colour post-it notes (no worries if people still use another colour since with one click, you can change the colour of the sticky notes afterwards). The standard soft yellow colour is advisable since it doesn't stand out. The reason for using the same colour is that you want all input to be neutral and anonymous.

To focus and not get distracted by what others are writing on the online whiteboard, you can either prepare a workspace for each participant (when they zoom in on their workspace, they don't see what others are writing), or – when using Miro – participants can use the so-called Bulk Mode. Using this, you cannot see what others are writing since the board will be covered with a blank screen. When you click 'done', all your input will appear on the board in separate post-it notes.

After two minutes, let all participants put their post-its on the sailboat picture in the 'above the water' area. Then every participant will present their positive aspects to the group. Also, here applies the rule: no discussion, just listen. It's okay to ask a clarifying question if something is not clear, but make sure you don't end up in a discussion.

After this step, the positive sticky notes will not be used anymore. They have done their job: you created a positive vibe for moving forward, and everyone is warmed up for the rest of the workshop.

STEP 3: CAPTURE PROBLEMS AND CHALLENGES
6 MINUTES / 8 MINUTES

In this step, everyone writes frustrations, barriers, concerns, mistakes, and problems regarding the topic. Again, it is all about writing in silence and one topic per post-it note. Encourage all participants to write as many things as they can think of; there is no right or wrong.

Since there may be people reluctant to write negative things, to encourage everyone to contribute, this time, make sure there is a 'safe' way for all participants to do so. Give everyone their spot on the online whiteboard or, when using Miro, use Bulk Mode again. Let everyone wait to bring over their written post-its to the 'under water' area of the sailboat picture or click 'done' when using the sailboat. Encourage everyone to use the same light yellow post-its again to make the input anonymous.

This time, don't ask participants to read out their post-its since some may feel they are attacking someone. Let the post-its speak for themselves. As the facilitator, read through the post-its and take out any doubles. If in doubt, ask in the group who has written the post-its and agree on which to take out.

STEP 4: PRIORITISE PROBLEMS –
6 MINUTES / 11 MINUTES

Now ask everybody to vote for the problems they think are the most relevant to solve (only vote for the negatives, NOT for the positives). To do this, all participants get three votes. This can be either green 'dots' (small circle shapes – all in the same colour – on the online whiteboard) or using the powerful voting feature in Miro or Mural. Using this feature makes the voting the most anonymous. This can be very helpful since participants are not being influenced by what others are voting for (they can't see who is voting for what problem). Besides that, it avoids participants being reluctant to vote for a specific problem if everyone else can see them. Everybody can vote for three different sticky notes, but they can also put all three votes on the one they think is the most relevant. They can again vote for the sticky notes they wrote themselves.

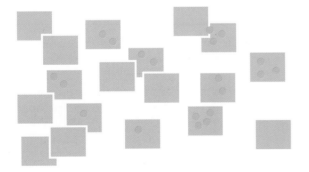

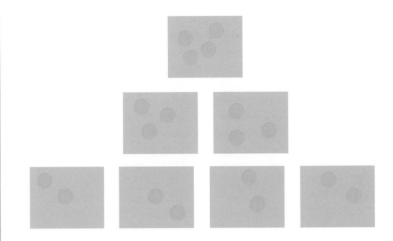

Now prioritise the post-its that were voted for in a triangle shape with the post-it(s) with the most votes at the top.

STEP 5: REFRAME THE PROBLEM
4 MINUTES / 8 MINUTES

In this step, reframe the problem with the most votes into a challenging question that triggers ideas. The moderator can do this, but if you have a bit more time for your Lightning Decision Jam, you can ask participants to reframe individually and vote for the best question the same way as the voting for prioritising problems is done.

Phrase the challenge as a so-called 'How Might We ' (HMW) question. The reason is that these three words have an important meaning in a process like this:

How

triggers your brain to find solutions.

Might

means there may be more possible solutions, and it says we are going to try to solve the problem, but we don't know yet if we will succeed. We are looking for new ways to solve it, which implies we will be running experiments to find out if a solution works.

We

says that we are collaborating to be inspired by the other participants and build upon each other's ideas.

Here is an example. Let's say the top voted problem was 'It is hard to keep in touch with our team when working remotely'. If we reframe this into an HMW-question, it could be 'How might we improve the team spirit when working remotely?'. Now the problem has been reframed into a question that participants can find solutions for.

If you have the time in your workshop, you can address more than one problem from the priority list. It is advisable to limit this to the ones on the top of the triangle with the most votes and ignore the ones that only had one vote since otherwise you will lose voting and prioritising effectiveness. We advise you to work on no more than three to five topics to keep the workshop's energy up. Problems that are not chosen in the workshop can stay on the online whiteboard to look at in the next workshop.

STEP 6: IDEATE SOLUTIONS
7 MINUTES / 15 MINUTES

In this step, you are going to brainstorm solutions to the HMW-question. Before you start, make sure the HMW-question is visible for all participants, for example, by placing it at the top of the area on your online whiteboard where you will put the sticky-notes with solutions. This is important since you want to make sure everyone is thinking of solutions for the same HWM-question.

As in the previous steps, ask participants to write their solutions in silence. Participants can again work on a separate part of the whiteboard or use Bulk Mode.

The focus is on quantity over quality; make this clear to all participants. When brainstorming, our brain tends to judge an idea instantly. We don't want that at this stage of the process. Every good idea starts with many ideas, so postponement of judgement is essential! You can curate later.

Make sure solutions are written in simple, clear language and keep it short and concise. Participants will not present their solutions since the ones presented best can get the most attraction when voting.

After five minutes, ask everyone to place their sticky notes in the brainstorm area on the whiteboard without any discussion. There is no need to sort them; just make sure all solutions are visible. As a facilitator, check if there are any doubles. If so, ask the group who has written those post-its to agree on which one(s) to take out.

STEP 7: PRIORITISE SOLUTIONS
6 MINUTES / 11 MINUTES

Now do a voting session again. Give all participants five votes. As during the voting workshop for problems, you can use small circle-shaped coloured dots in Miro or Mural or use the voting feature. When the time is up, organise the post-its in the same way as done with the problems while ignoring all post-its with only one vote.

You will end up with something like:

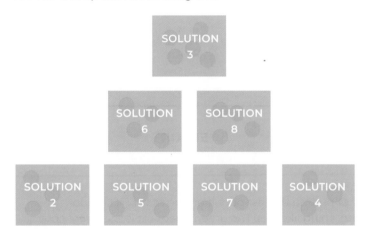

STEP 8: DECIDE WHICH SOLUTION TO EXECUTE
10 MINUTES / 12 MINUTES

This step is crucial for success. Many brainstorming workshops end with a lot of ideas, but no decisions on what solution(s) will be executed, who will do it, or when it will be done!

To make a decision, you don't want to end up in a conversation or discussion where someone is trying to convince others to go for a specific solution. What you want is to compare the solutions to see which one has the biggest chance for success. To do this, you want to use variables against which you can 'measure' each idea.

In the Lightning Decision Jam, we use the so-called 'Impact-Effort Matrix'. In this matrix, we use the horizontal Effort axis and the vertical Impact axis. 'Impact' means to what extent we think the solution will solve the problem (from 'not at all' to 'completely'). 'Effort' describes how much time and work we think it will take to execute the solution (from 'very little' to 'a lot').

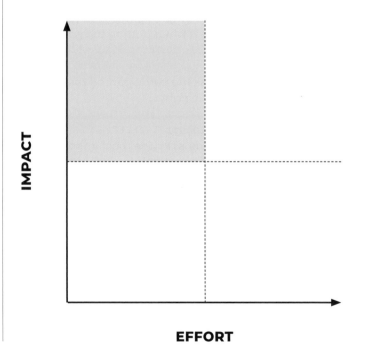

The Impact-Effort Matrix helps make sure you use execution time efficiently. It will help you gain insight into what solution to implement right away, which might evolve into a more significant project, and what idea(s) should be kept on the shelf for later use.

Now it is time to start using the matrix. Take the top-voted solutions (the five to eight solutions with the most votes) and pick the one with the most votes (if there is more than one on the top, work from left to right, so start with the one at the top-left). Now put it in the middle of the matrix. Start with 'Impact' and ask the participants if the post-it should be higher or lower on the axis. Make sure not to end up in long conversations or discussions. Remember you are looking for new solutions that you need to try out. Based on practice, you will know if it works or not. So, trust your gut and common sense at this point in the process when putting the post-its on the matrix.

Now do the same for 'Effort': ask the participants if the post-it should go more to the left or the right.

Please note the following two things:
▸ The exact position on the axis is not the most important; it is about what quadrant the post-it is in.
▸ This exercise will become easier as soon as there is one post-it on the matrix, since from that point onwards, you have something to compare the next post-its to.

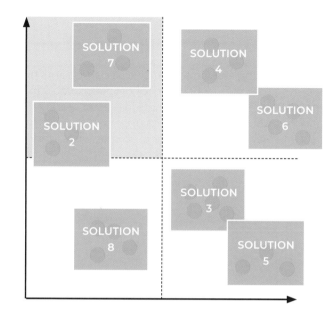

After putting the last post-it on the matrix, it will look something like this. The green quadrant is the sweet spot: here are the solutions that have the most impact and are expected to take the least amount of effort to implement. These can be tested and executed quickly. In the top-right quadrant are the solutions that will have high impact and take more effort to execute. At the bottom-right are the solutions to leave for now;

IMPACT

SOLUTION 7 — **DO NOW**

SOLUTION 4 — **MAKE A PROJECT** — SOLUTION 6

SOLUTION 2

SOLUTION 3 — **FORGET**

MAKE A TASK

SOLUTION 8

SOLUTION 5

EFFORT

STEP 9: MAKE SOLUTIONS ACTIONABLE
10 MINUTES / 12 MINUTES

The Lightning Decision Jam's last step is defining what actions should be taken for the solutions in the 'sweet spot'. Take the solutions in this quadrant and ask the participants to come up with three action steps for testing each solution. You can ask the person who wrote the post-it to suggest these action steps, or all participants can write individually so the team can then vote for the key steps. Keep this simple, and don't overthink; you don't have to execute the whole solution from day one. A prototype is enough for testing. Keeping it small will be easier to start executing, and if something doesn't work, it is easy to pivot. Make sure the first step is something that can be done easily right after the Lightning Decision Jam. This keeps the fire burning! The action steps should be actionable within one or two weeks after the workshop.

Let's look at an example. The HMW-question we formulated was 'How might we improve the team spirit when working remotely?'. A solution in the sweet spot may have been to ask team members who live (relatively) close to each other to meet in-person and drink coffee or go for a walk. This is easy to execute. Another solution may be organising a weekly online café on a set day and time in the week. Everyone brings their drinks and snacks and can chat about anything but work. With many people joining, you can create break out rooms with specific themes participants can join free of choice. This is something you can organise quickly by sending invitation emails and setting up an online workshop in a tool that allows using break out rooms like Zoom or Butter. A bit more effort but relatively easy to prototype is making a weekly radio show for the whole organisation with interviews with employees or experts in the industry, a word from the CEO, and personal stories from colleagues. The show can be

these take a lot of effort to execute and have a low impact. On the bottom-left quadrant are solutions that take low effort to execute and have a low impact. These could be valuable to look into but are probably easy to turn into tasks for someone to do. Please note that the solution(s) with the most impact and the lowest effort (the green area) are NOT necessarily the ones with the most votes! This shows that this matrix helps make 'neutral' decisions where the influence of individual preferences is reduced to a minimum; solutions are compared to objective variables.

shared through internal platforms like an Intranet, a file-sharing platform, or a private YouTube channel.

Once you have decided on the action steps, assign one participant to each step responsible for the execution (either alone or in collaboration with other team members). The most important thing is to take small steps to find what works (and what not) as soon as possible. The sooner you can start sharing successes in your organisation, the better. If something works, you can roll it out on a larger scale.

AFTER THE LIGHTNING DECISION JAM

To make the team's efforts worthwhile, it is important to keep track of the execution. Schedule short check-ins when everyone working on an experiment shares what they have done, what the results are, and if they encountered any barriers with which they need help. These check-ins can be short online meetings (about 10 to 15 minutes). Alternatively, you can make a workspace in an online collaboration tool like Slack.

After the one or two-week experiment, you can get the team back together in a new Lightning Decision Jam and run it exactly like the first one. Only this time, the topic is about the results of the last LDJ. What went well ('What is moving us forward?') and what barriers or problems did you encounter ('What is holding us back?'). This way, you keep the process alive, and you can create new experiments which in the end will bring you to an implemented end-solution or you decide to pivot or leave a solution behind, based on results.

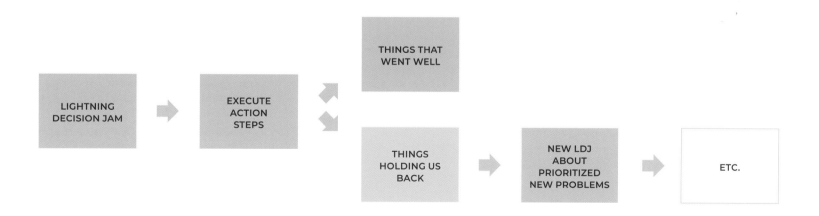

LIGHTNING DECISION JAM → EXECUTE ACTION STEPS →

THINGS THAT WENT WELL

THINGS HOLDING US BACK → NEW LDJ ABOUT PRIORITIZED NEW PROBLEMS → ETC.

If a solution proves to not work, then it isn't that hard to abandon it since you didn't spend too much time (and perhaps money) on it yet. Just pick the next best solution from the Impact-Effort Matrix and start testing it. And don't forget: it is better to get started and fail fast than to do nothing at all! Experimenting like this means some things will work and others won't. You will only find out by DOING!

In the next chapter, we share with you another effective, fast method to help you innovate. It's the Design Sprint that will take you five days from a challenge to a tested prototype.

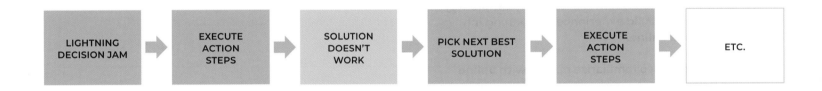

KEY MESSAGES FROM THIS CHAPTER

▶ **Use the Lightning Decision Jam to identify the participants' problems on their minds and define the most important problem to solve in 60 to 90 minutes.**

▶ **The most important output of an LDJ is actionable steps that can be executed right away.**

▶ **Be strict in facilitation; the timeboxed exercises are aimed at avoiding discussions.**

▶ **The Lightning Decision Jam is a relatively simple way for a facilitator to build experience for running innovation workshops online.**

▶ **The process can also familiarise people with online collaboration for innovation, which can help get buy-in for a bigger online innovation project.**

[1] The Lightning Decision Jam is a process developed by AJ&Smart, a Global Innovation and Product Design Agency based in Berlin – https://ajsmart.com/ldj

In this chapter we have made some minor changes to the original process.

CONTENTS

CHAPTER 9

THE DESIGN SPRINT

A Design Sprint is an innovation process for validating ideas and solving significant challenges. It involves various techniques included in the process that, depending on the format, can span between three to five days. This chapter will explore the five-day version of the sprint, covering each day to allow you to gain a solid understanding of how you can apply this within your organisation or with your clients.

WHAT IS THE DESIGN SPRINT?

In his book, 'How to Solve Big Problems and Test New Ideas in Just Five Days', the creator of the Design Sprint, Jake Knapp, described the Design Sprint Process as 'The greatest hits of business strategy, innovation, behavioural science, and more. All packaged into a step-by-step process that any team can follow'[1].

A Design Sprint is a time-boxed, five-stage process that has design thinking as its foundation. It aims to reduce the risk of bringing a new product, service, or feature to the market. The process helps teams to define clear goals, validate assumptions, and agree on a road map that the product will take before starting development. The process aims to address strategic issues using interdisciplinary, rapid prototyping, and useability testing.

The high-level five-day process is defined below

- ▶ Understand: Discover the business opportunity, the audience, the competition, and the value proposition, and define success metrics.
- ▶ Diverge: Explore, develop and iterate creative ways of solving the problem, regardless of feasibility.
- ▶ Converge: Identify ideas that fit the next product cycle and explore them in further detail through storyboarding.
- ▶ Prototype: Design and prepare prototypes that are tested with people.
- ▶ Test: Conduct 1:1 usability testing with five to six people from the product's primary target audience. Ask good questions.

Former Google Ventures design partner Jake Knapp devised the planning sprint process for Google in 2010. He drew inspiration from such areas as Google's development culture and IDEO's design thinking workshops[1]. In design sprints, teams work on problems and goals differently than when siloed within the product development departments in the traditional waterfall process. A carefully selected team from across the organisation focuses on themselves. They manage their time to systematically collaborate and define a user problem to test a possible solution within five days. Sprints are also integral to agile development. Self-organised, cross-functional teams work to supply short-term deliverables and improve quality while keeping a careful watch on current user needs and any changing circumstances[1].

The primary value of sprints is the speed at which design teams can concentrate on key objectives and come up with validated ideas quickly. Under time-boxed conditions, team members work first to know these, then progressively ideate, critique, and fine-tune their way towards a testable prototype. Eliminating distractions is vital to the current process, and therefore the intense specialisation in specific user needs and goals involves dedicated time away from regular everyday business. Since the planning sprint process is streamlined and enables teams to supply deliverables and ensure or discard users' assumptions quickly, it helps to keep costs down.

WHY SHOULD WE RUN A DESIGN SPRINT?

We have all been in a brainstorming session where we developed thousands of ideas, selected our preferred option, and then started thinking about how we could develop it. This usually takes considerable time to ideate, prioritise, discuss, and then develop, but the question is, 'How do you know if this is something that your customers would want?'. This is why the design sprint was developed, to cut down the time it takes to validate a business idea with customers compared to the traditional innovation process outlined at the start of this paragraph.

Good ideas that are a real-world success are hard to find as they face an uncertain road in their development journey. This is the case whether the organisation has just started or is mature in its approach. We need to answer questions such as, 'where and how should we focus our efforts?'. With whom should we test the product, and who should be part of the development team? The design sprint looks to shortcut the endless-debate cycles in organisations and compresses months of work into a single week. Think of the design sprint as a time machine for your product development process. It allows organisations to engage warp speed to enable your customers to see your product in a tangible form, display what your product will do, and gauge reactions without wasting both time and money along the way[1].

The online form of the design sprint was developed ahead of its time and was a pioneer in online innovation development. Agencies such as AJ&Smart[2] in Germany, in partnership with Jake Knapp, pushed the boundaries further and adapted the process to suit the online form using tools such as Miro, Mural, and Zoom, to name a few. While online communities have developed around the methodology, it truly has a global presence, all aided by online forms. This global presence has developed different design sprint forms, from a short three-day sprint to the traditional five-day process, and variations have further developed the methodology. There are now strategy sprints, brand sprints, service sprints, but underneath they are all designed around the initial method that Jake Knapp developed in 2010. To be very clear in our approach, we will focus on the five-day design sprint focusing on the method's online delivery, covering everything including pre-sprint, set up, and focus points throughout the week of the sprint.

We set up each day differently depending on your time commitments and the guidelines you use, and, of course, this may vary how you approach it yourself. But the high-level goals of each day are that we map out the problem on Monday and pick an important place to start. On Tuesday, we sketch our solutions on paper. On Wednesday, we review and make decisions based on the pre-defined sprint questions and then turn our ideas into testable hypotheses. On Thursday, we hand over the prototype's development to the designers who build a realistic example of our concept. Finally, on Friday, we test with our selected users to gain their feedback[3]. Before we get into each day of the process, we need to look at why you would run an online design sprint when compared to an in-person event.

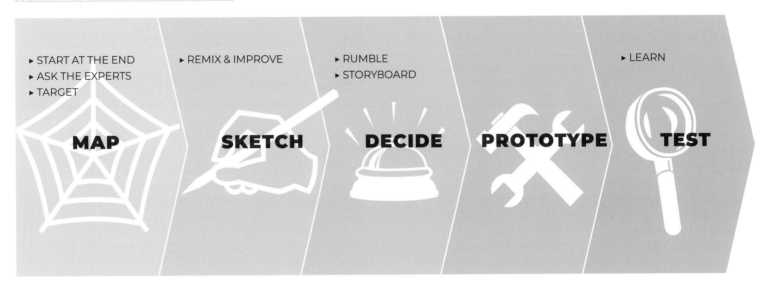

- ▸ START AT THE END
- ▸ ASK THE EXPERTS
- ▸ TARGET

MAP

- ▸ REMIX & IMPROVE

SKETCH

- ▸ RUMBLE
- ▸ STORYBOARD

DECIDE

PROTOTYPE

- ▸ LEARN

TEST

ADVANTAGES OF AN ONLINE DESIGN SPRINT

Both online and in-person design sprints have their advantages and challenges. Still, as this is a book about online innovation, we will focus on the benefits and challenges of the online form and how you can mitigate them.

The below are taken from The Ultimate Guide to Remote Design Sprints[2].

It doesn't matter where you are.
Your development team is spread globally, and you usually would book expensive flights and pay hotel bills and expenses. This is where online design sprints add in both flexibilities, saving time and money. Using online tools, you can work in synchronous and asynchronous forms and access individuals with a global perspective. This also aids in recruiting user testers; using platforms such as UserTesting.com, you can access a massive pool of testers that you wouldn't have access to if you were to recruit in person.

Contributing ideas is easier, faster, and more anonymous. Online design sprints allow the participants to focus on coming up with ideas without the pressure of being seen to put them on the board. In tools such as Miro, you can write your thoughts on your digital post-it notes in anonymous form using the bulk upload function. This allows the participants to feel less pressure to take ownership of the idea at this stage.

The sessions tend to be more focused and quicker.
In-person sessions are great and can lead to great conversations, essential for team building. Although this can come as a distraction in the session, people might be late returning to the room; breaks slip, et cetera . The online sessions are more focused on the session's output, and because it is facilitated, it can make managing the group harder compared to in-person sessions.

Last, you don't need any particular area for innovation.
We have all arrived at an innovation session to be presented with a cold, dark room that leaves both the facilitator and the participants feeling less than inspired. Using digital tools allows us to remove this constraint by using a bright, fast digital board and other communication tools. Another factor is the Covid-19 pandemic; more and more companies are looking to reduce their office space leading to a lack of suitable meeting rooms. Again, online design sprints lessen this problem.

So, these are some of the advantages of running an online design sprint, but what are the challenges that we need to face and ensure that we mitigate?

CHALLENGES OF AN ONLINE DESIGN SPRINT

Although online design sprints were a pioneer of online innovation, there is still a learning curve that needs to be reduced. As we have discussed in this book, running an online session can be challenging and hard work.

Working across different time zones
Although, as outlined, an online design sprint makes it easier to include your team from anywhere in the world, this does become a challenge. Managing multiple time zones is very demanding and identifying suitable times is also a challenge. Tools such as World Time Buddy (www.worldtimebuddy.com) help mitigate this, but you need to be aware of setting up a session[2].

Lower engagement and lack of interpersonal dynamics
A bond develops when people are in the same room and we can read body language. As discussed in previous chapters, the lack of such a bond online can be mitigated, but it's essential to keep the team focused as the internet does have thousands of distractions that can ruin the session's flow.

Technical issues
This can make or break your session and can lead to the process becoming frustrating and counterproductive. Always ensure that you have had a run-through with the participants before the sessions to ensure that all systems such as online whiteboards and video conferencing tools work with the organisation. It's also essential that you take time to ensure that everyone has a level of understanding of how to use the tools, and again this should be a focal point before the session.

Working remotely can feel strange at first.
It can feel strange when you start an online design sprint; people are so used to working in the same location, using post-it notes and other physical materials that it can feel like a big step to move to the digital form. But using the right collaboration tools is outlined in this book, and the onboarding process will help the individuals quickly become used to the new environment[2].

SO, HOW DO YOU RUN A SUCCESSFUL ONLINE DESIGN SPRINT?

Running an online design sprint comes down to understanding four primary areas of focus. These are preparation, onboarding, using the right tools, and running the session. We will cover each in turn to allow you to gain a good, actionable understanding.

First, we need to ensure that we have prepared correctly for the session and onboarded the participants to help with the session's future success. The preparation stage is vital for everything to run smoothly, and it allows you to focus your time on actually running a session.

Set up your workspace.

As discussed in previous chapters, numerous tools can run an online design sprint, one of the most critical elements that you need to ensure you have covered. The digital space can be confusing, and this applies to running your session. If you are running the session, we would strongly suggest that you invest in two screens as this helps to ensure that you can see the digital boards and all the participants. We use one screen for the board and the other for the participants. This allows you to read the room better, check if someone looks confused or distracted or is having technical problems. We would also suggest getting a timer, as you will need this to keep the time of the exercises in the workshop to ensure you manage to fit everything in.

As this book has suggested, you can use specific tools for different types of actions that you are looking to apply. When running a design sprint, we would suggest that you use the below.

Miro

Miro is a cloud-based collaboration tool. It features a digital whiteboard on which you can go from ideation to execution on an infinite canvas. It's scalable, includes more than a hundred pre-built templates, and works cross-device. Together with Mural, it's one of today's most popular and trusted tools to create together online. There is a free version for you to try and ready-made design sprint boards for you to start with. Refer to Chapter 3 to understand more about this.

Zoom

Zoom, also described in Chapter 3, is a cloud-based videoconferencing tool that allows you to set up virtual video and audio conferencing. It has a chat option as well as screen-sharing, break out rooms, and other collaborative capabilities. For more interaction, there is the option to do an online poll. Zoom has the Gallery View mode that allows you to see every person on the call at once.

Calendly

Calendly is an app offering you a versatile set of features that allow you to schedule one-on-one appointments, group events, and team meetings. There is a free version available. This is great to book the sessions for each day and to provide recurring meetings. As the design sprint team has a number of participants, using a tool such as Calendly allows you to arrange a suitable time for all meetings, customer testing, and other aspects. You can find more on Calendly in Appendix 1.

Loom

Loom is a video messaging tool that helps you get your message across through instantly shareable videos. With Loom, you can record your camera, microphone, and desktop simultaneously. This allows you to record simple messages to the participants to help them with an understanding of tools and the techniques used in the design sprint. Refer to Chapter 3 again to understand more about Loom.

Google Forms

Google Forms is a tool for conducting online surveys and is completely free of charge. All the information gathered with the survey is automatically recorded in an Excel spreadsheet in real-time. When you need to test your ideas online and collect feedback from customers, Google Forms allows you to do so in a simple and versatile way.

For a full breakdown of these tools, plus many more, please check the toolkit in Appendix 1.

Set up your Miro board.

The whiteboard will become the session's focal point, so we need to ensure we take the time to prepare this for the sprint. You can create ad-hoc, beautiful templates, but if you are new to running a design sprint, you should use one of the design sprints templates available in Miro. You will find the official design sprint template[5] that Jake Knapp has approved for use across the different platforms. The board contains all the activities you will be running over the next five days, with detailed instructions to focus on running the session.

If you create your board, we recommend that you create a separate frame for each exercise and for each part of the workshop to aid the participants' visual appearance and understanding[2]. Not only does this allow you to structure your workshop clearly, but it also allows the participants to feel a sense of accomplishment as they move through the frames.

Digital whiteboards, like Miro, include several important features that you will be using in your workshops. Examples would be brainstorming ideas, voting for your preferred options, and grouping your post-it notes to see patterns. They are the workshop's heart and soul, so you want to be sure to have spent time ensuring your board is right for your workshop.

Video conferencing

Zoom is our preferred choice as a video conferencing medium; this is mainly due to the ease of use and the ability to run break out rooms, which is a key function of your session. Ensure that you have checked your zoom account before the workshop, as the basic account only allows for a 40-minute session and recording. Therefore, you will need to upgrade to the premium package option to record the whole session. When you do run the session, encourage participants to switch on their webcams and share their video.

This will help you to see if engagement is low or if any of the participants seem confused. It will also encourage the participants to work from a quiet place instead of just dialling in and muting while driving. This is a common misconception of online workshops; people still think they are in a meeting where they can join from anywhere. Having the camera on will allow you and the other stakeholders to monitor this.

A bonus is that you will have more fun when you see each other. For example, Zoom offers virtual backgrounds, which can lighten the mood at the start of an online workshop.

Onboarding

You have set up your workspace, and are nearly ready to run your workshop, but you mustn't forget the onboarding stage. The onboarding of participants is essential if you want your session to run as smoothly as possible. We cannot emphasise the importance of this step enough; it can make a huge difference to your session success.

There are two main functions of onboarding: first, to ensure the participants understand what will happen, when, and where, et cetera; and to ensure that all participants are set up correctly for the sprint. During the onboarding, your role is a combination of a pilot and a flight attendant on a passenger plane. Similarly to a pilot, you run technical checks and ensure that everything is going according to plan. On top of that, you welcome the participants on board, make sure they feel comfortable and know what they can expect, just like a flight attendant would.

Brief the participants on your Miro board.

The worst thing that can happen on the day of the design sprint is that no one knows how to use the Miro board. Therefore, we always suggest that you book in some time with each person in the sprint to run through the Miro board and outline the key features. This will allow you to answer any questions, fix any technical issues, and get them accustomed to the board[2]. A tip is to include in your board an area where the participants can enter their name, details, and any emoji of a topic of their choice. This is important because it addresses two functions. First, you get their details on the board, allowing others to read these before the session. Second, it enables the participants to use the other functions of the board in preparation for the workshop.

Brief the participants on Zoom.

Ensure that the participants can check that Zoom is working correctly and their microphones are compatible with their system. We always state that during the session the participants should find a comfortable, quiet place either in their home or in the office where they can focus on the workshop, and the microphone picks up no background noise. You want to have a minimal number of distractions in the session; therefore, strongly enforce this.

Give them an overview of the design sprint[2].

Yes, we know that you know what the design sprint is, but there is a good chance that the participants will not have heard of it and will need to be briefed. Provide a high-level overview of the process, what's included on each day and what to expect. This will reduce the participants' anxiety and allow them to be more focused on the actual workshop instead of second-guessing what it is. This can be part of a wider group conference call to brief everyone to save time before the session.

Last, send the meeting invitation and links to the board and zoom.

You are nearly ready to start the design sprint, you understand the problem you want to solve, and you have completed the preparation and onboarding. It's now time to discuss the dates of the design sprint with the main stakeholder and then send out the meeting invitations using Calendly, Outlook, Gmail, et cetera to ensure everyone is aware of the plan accordingly.

Workshop timing

In general, we recommend keeping remote workshops shorter than their in-person counterparts. Sitting in front of a screen is surprisingly exhausting, and after a while, it gets tough to stay focused. We always limit them to a maximum duration of four hours per session – this includes breaks and an overtime buffer, so realistically you should be able to finish earlier. A couple of natural breaking points in the workshop structure make sense to end the session and continue the next morning[2].

So, it's now time for the sprint itself...

THE ACTUAL SPRINT

Following your discussions with the internal decision-maker, all invitations have been sent out to run the sprint from Monday to Friday.

MONDAY

Monday is to hold a series of structured conversations to build a foundation – and a focus – for the sprint week. The structure allows the team to 'boot up' as much information as possible[1] while preventing the usual meandering conversations. On Monday, you will be covering your long-term goal; then, you go on to map the challenge. In the afternoon, you will ask the experts within your company or your client's company to share what they know about the challenge. Lastly, you pick a target on the map of a problem you can solve in one week.

It's always good to start any session with a warmup exercise. It is a great way to make people feel at ease and to break the ice. It also performs a second function, allowing the participants to get used to the Miro board. We always ask them to find a GIF image of how they feel at the start of the meeting, as this gets them used to the board and allows the facilitator to gauge the mood in the room.

You can use lots of different warmup exercises, depending on your personal preference. I have a few which I like to use.

My first job
We ask participants to write on post-it notes their name, their first job, and what they learned that they still use today. This normally creates a good, welcoming environment and reduces the session anxiety for the participants, and it can create a laugh which is always good.

Superpowers
Again, similar to the above, ask the participants to write their name, who their superhero is, and their own superpower. This could be something like they are very good at team building, listening, coming up with new ideas, or the like. We tend to find this exercise allows the participants to open up.

30 circles
Create 30 circles on the Miro board and ask the participants to fill the circles with as many images as possible. These could be any image, or you can give them a theme such as football teams or movie stars. When the time is up, ask them to explain their pictures and look for any patterns. Patterns could be that everyone drew a similar image, with the same look and feel, et cetera. This is an excellent way to get the conversation going in the meeting.

Catch the basketball
Everyone switches on their camera and unmutes; the facilitator starts by saying 'one' and saying the person's name who is going to catch the ball. They pretend to catch and shout 'two', and so on. If someone says a different number, we start the whole process again. It's amazing when we play this that we struggle to get into double figures but again, it provides a great ice breaker for the group and generates plenty of laughter as we try to get into double figures.

As we said, there are numerous types of warmup exercises and what you choose is up to you, although you should ensure it works well online and that you can potentially use the board because it will give the participants more time to play around with the board as they start to get used to it.

The Design Sprint
The first exercise we start with is called, Start at the End; this places the team in a time machine to think about the future[1].

We want the team to step outside their current thinking and focus on questions such as, 'What will have improved about your business due to this project?'. This is important as it makes it more concrete in the participant's mind and sets them up for the long-term goal's critical exercise.

The Long-Term Goal

The long-term goal answers at the very beginning the ultimate question the team is trying to answer in a more formal manner; we ask the team the below questions[1].

'Why are we doing this project? Where do we want to be six months, a year, or even five years from now?'

This can and will lead to discussion within the sprint team and ensure that you take your time to listen to the various viewpoints so that everyone has been heard and has had their points listened to. Examples of long-term goals for Zoom, our video conferencing tool, could be, 'Bring a great online video experience to new customers' or, 'Be seen as the go-to app for video conferencing'. When completing your long-term goal, ensure that you are ambitious, reflecting your team's ethos and future aspirations once the team has written them on a digital post-it note and placed it at the top of the board. This will allow it to be seen throughout the sprint to remind you why you are doing this.

The goal doesn't have to be 100% perfect or accurate. If you find that the discussion is taking too long, ensure that you stop and use the long-term goal that has been discussed. You don't want to impact the rest of the sprint agenda. Do inform the team that the rest of the day's activities will help form a more concrete goal that you can carry throughout the sprint.

Now that you have your long-term goal, which is super optimistic, ambitious, and motivating, it's time to think about what could go wrong. It's time to jump back into the time machine and look at a future where you haven't met your long-term goal. What went wrong? Why didn't the project or product work? Why didn't customers like it? This is where the sprint questions come in.

List your sprint questions.

As a team, you will need to think about the potential roadblocks or reasons for failure. It's important to get the team thinking to prompt them to think about this constructively. We normally do this by setting the scene and asking open-ended questions such as, 'If we were to hit our goal, what must be true?', 'If we could jump into the future and the project failed, what were the reasons for this', and 'How will we define success?'

A vital part of this is rephrasing the assumptions into a set of questions that will allow us to record the answers more concisely and use them for reference when we start other exercises in the sprint. This is an important mindset shift as it turns the assumptions from worry to a more engaging challenge for the participants. To do this, we use the reframing question, 'Can we?' when outlining our assumptions on the Miro board. This instigates the mindset shift. Here's an example. Assumption: 'We struggle to build trust, making the project fail'. Re-phrased: 'Can we build trust with new customers?'.

The process allows us to think about the biggest risks to the project, which forms the basis of our sprint, and during the review at the end of the sprint, we go back to these questions to determine if we have answered them throughout the process. Using the sprint questions at the start of the process, the team has to face its fears and worries, but this allows these to be defined early in the process. Once the team has written their sprint questions, we vote on these and select the top three to take forward in the process.

Ask the expert questions.

It's now time to interview experts from your organisation and your client's organisation as a team. The design sprint is a collection of project team members who may or may not have the domain expertise required. Therefore, it's important that we understand the company's vision, what projects they have run before, and how things work. It's about becoming curious, acting in the manner of a reporter diving into details that will help us in the sprint.

There are certain methods for interviewing experts, although we prefer to interview the expert with the team engaged, and each person can take turns asking specific questions. This leads to free-flowing conversations, which can unearth some real nuggets of information that we can take forward[1]. When interviewing outside experts, only ask questions closely related to their expertise as this will allow them time to be maximised and provide more reliable information to be gained. We need to remember that each sprint and challenge is unique, and the questions asked will vary depending on this. Try to keep the conversation flowing and please do improvise as you go along or double down on certain topics.

An excellent method for extracting information is using the five-Ws-and-an-H method. This stands for Who, What, When, Where, Why, and How. This is so powerful because it is a proven formula for obtaining the complete story of a subject, and due to its nature, it allows for easy structuring of questions.

Examples of this type of questing are:

▸ Who is it about?
▸ What happened?
▸ When did it take place?
▸ Where did it take place?

▸ Why did it happen?
▸ How did it happen?

To ensure that the answers are as factual as possible, and as you can see from the example, the questions are open-ended. Avoid closed questions that can be answered by a simple yes or no because this can lead to weak insights, which will hamper your project. Each expert interview should take between 15 to 30 minutes, and due to the tight time constraints, I recommend not going over. As the interview is being conducted, the team should be taking notes in the form of 'How Might We' questions.

Using How Might We Questions

The 'How Might We', or HMW, questions are fundamental to the design thinking method and the design sprint methodology. The method allows the sprint team to record their insights from the expert interviews, reframing the insights and pain points as a series of questions to create a framework for resolving challenges. As a facilitator, it's important to explain how the HMW method works and inform the team that they are looking for opportunities and not solutions. This method is so powerful that it creates a mindset shift in the team.

Like we discussed in the previous chapter on the Lightning Decision Jam, the Google guide [6] to HMW questions breaks it down as, 'How' guides team members to believe the answer is out there. 'Might' lets team members know their HMW statement might or might not work, and either possibility is okay. And 'We' reminds team members that the design sprint is about teamwork and building on each other's ideas.

Come up with as many HMW post-it notes as possible and encourage little self-editing of what is said. Now that you have captured loads of HMW notes, it's time to think about prioritising these. Select a maximum of ten HMW's from your Miro board and, as a team, organise them into similar groups. Once you have columns of similar notes, you can place a post-it at the column's head to categorise this list. Example headers could be Operations, Sales, or Marketing. Now the team votes on both the HMW question and the category, and the top voted are taken forward to the next step of the process.

The User Journey Map
The journey mapping exercise enables the team to understand the process from the customer's viewpoint, identify touchpoints, and visualise the user's journey from start to finish. It's important to remember that this is to map out the 'As-Is' process.

Please think of the journey map as a simplified process that the user takes, that it's not about detail, more about understanding the overall process, and this will allow the team to target an area of the map to focus the sprint on. How you start the map depends on where you are in your product cycle. If you are running a new product sprint, you may want to explore a certain user journey from start to finish. If you have an existing product and are further along in the cycle, you may start your journey map when the user is first introduced to your product, searching for your product, or when they are onboarding and/or setting up an account.

The secret to mapping is to keep it simple; you don't want to get bogged down in every element's detail because this will draw the process out and confuse the participants. Several steps can be used to complete this exercise. Jake Knapp suggests in his book, 'Sprint: How to Solve Big Problems and Test New Ideas in Just Five Days'[1], the below steps are the most important.

List the actors on the left of the map.
The actors are all the important users that interact with your product. These can be customers, internal stakeholders, or whoever is the best using the current process.

Write the ending on the right.
It's much easier to write down the start and finish of a process, so ensure everyone agrees on how it ends before you move on to the middle of the map.

Words and arrows in between.
Remember, this is a simple map, so you do not want masses of detail; it doesn't have to be a masterpiece. The mapping exercise was developed when used for in-person workshops to mitigate any lack drawing expertise. It's easier with the online environment as you can quickly draw lines, arrows, and type words into Miro.

Keep the steps simple.
The map should have between five and fifteen steps. If there are any more than this, the map will become too complicated, and you should work towards making this simpler.

It's a team exercise.
Don't let just one person come up with the map. Yes, someone needs to start the process, but once it's defined, there should be some discussion to ensure this reflects the user journey you are trying to capture.

The decider gets the final say.
And yes, it's a team exercise, but we need to ensure that we have a decider to confirm that they are happy to proceed with the map you have produced. Therefore, once the exercise is complete, get them to agree to move on to the next step.

You have had a busy day so far, you have defined your long-term goal, and you have outlined the questions you need to be answered, your sprint questions. You have met with experts from the domain and completed the mapping exercise. You still have one last exercise to consider for the day: picking a target on the map to explore.

START	MIDDLE	END
GUEST		

GUEST	BOOKS ROOM	CHECK IN	CHECK OUT
HOUSE-KEEPING	PREPARES ROOM	DAILY CLEANING	STRIPS ROOM FOR NEXT GUEST

Pick a target.
This method allows the team to focus on a specific map area where the topic is the most critical to be accurate. You need to ensure that you select this correctly. Otherwise, the direction of the sprint will be misplaced, leading to a poor result and process. You need to think of this as finding the point in the customer journey that is most critical to get right. Although we advise that the decider decides on the point of focus, Jake Knapp[3] does suggest that there are other techniques to use to come to a decision. Remember, this dictates the rest of the sprint, the focus of the sketches, and the prototype, so ensure you take some time to decide.

Techniques that can be used [4]
Ask the decider
This is usually the best course of action because there tends to be less discussion. As you have covered a lot of ground today, the decider will be updated with everything and should be able to identify the area fairly easily.

Use an anonymous vote.
Ask everyone to vote on an area that they feel is the most important and review the results. This will allow the decider to understand the rest of the team's viewpoints and make a more informed decision.

However, I would always use option one with speed and ask the decider to decide on this[1]. Once the decider has chosen a target, look back at the sprint questions and ensure that one or more is in line with the chosen target. You have completed the long-term goal, the sprint questions, conducted the expert interviews, drawn a map, and now selected the sprint target. Tomorrow we will be covering the lightning demos and the sketching exercises.

TUESDAY

So, you have rested from the previous day, and it's now time to get into solutions. This is a day that can lead to many anxieties for the participants, and you must mitigate them early in the day. The design sprint's beauty is that you do not need to be great designers, illustrators, or writers. It's about being inclusive and allowing everyone to contribute in their way to the process. Today, you will start with the Lightning demo exercise, which helps the participants review existing ideas, take inspiration, and look at ways of bringing them into their ideas for the process. Then everyone will complete a 4-part sketch, an offline exercise, and upload them to the Miro board.

The Lightning demo

The secret to getting inspired is to look outside your current business or environment for examples of things that encourage you. The light demo exercise[1] further asks each participant to think of a product or service they can bring into the workshop to inspire the complete team to remove their blinders. It's built around the premise of building inspiration so that we can design more innovative concepts.

The three steps that we would advise to follow are:

1. Consider and list robust solutions from a range of companies and industries. Encourage participants to also look at their own organisation.
2. Give everyone 25 minutes to carry out their research and to place their ideas on the Miro board.
3. Once the research has been finished, limit each lightning demo to three minutes. That goes fast.

It's an excellent idea to set a timer for both exercises. The creative process can lead to extra conversations and the participants taking longer to find more and more examples. You can also use Lightning demos from videos, advertising, et cetera, and any links should be inserted into the Miro board. Before starting the demos, assign someone to take notes on Miro about each idea's key points. Another technique is to make a quick drawing of the inspiring component, write a simple headline above it, and note the source underneath.

You don't have to decide which ideas should be discarded or are worth remixing or improving at this stage. You can figure that out later when you sketch. For now, don't make decisions and don't debate. Just capture anything that might be useful. Once the exercise is over, you will have a Miro board full of inspiration. In a normal design sprint, you would have between 10 and 20 ideas listed. This should be enough to gain some good insights and allow the creative juices to flow before going into the 4-part sketch exercise.

4-part sketch

In the sketch phase, the team slowly builds up the level and detail of their drawings. This is similar to athletes. They would warm up before running a marathon, and we approach this in the same manner. The participants generate and share a broad range of ideas from both outside perspectives and the lightning demo exercise in the sketch stage. Start with simply reviewing the lightning demos, the ideas discussed, and then review the sprint questions. Then begin to doodle simple drawings, which are rough solutions to the sprint questions you have come up with. It's now time to speed up your creative mind and use crazy 8s to generate rapid variations of your solution. Last, bring it together to design the solution sketch.

Notes. This is the first technique to use to start the sketching process, and it's straightforward. This is the process of reviewing what's been generated, collecting thoughts, and preparing to sketch ideas based on the knowledge and opportunities shared in the design sprint so far. This is important because you have covered a lot of ground, and you need to allow the team to be relaxed and able to translate their ideas into visual form. Set a time limit of 20 minutes to complete notes[6].

Ideas. Now that the participants have completed their review, it's time to start bringing this together. Each person will draw and write down their rough ideas, doodles, diagrams, and other thoughts they feel are relevant. This should be a messy creative process, so do not try to be perfect; get stuff down on paper. We usually set a time limit of 20 minutes for this exercise[6].

Crazy 8s. This is a fast-sketching technique that challenges the participants to sketch eight distinct ideas in just eight minutes. Its focus is to push people past their first idea, which is usually the least innovative, and generate variations. Realise that ideas do not have to be perfect; this exercise is about pushing your creative levers further to develop some great and not-so-great solutions. We ask each participant to come up with eight variations of their initial idea in eight minutes. This pushes the participants past their first idea to sketch their minds.

Solution sketch. Each participant focuses more time on the one idea they are most interested in. It's okay to sketch a new idea or a mix of ideas, and also, you can include any of the other participant's ideas. The main purpose of this is to develop a solution that we feel is the best solution to the sprint's challenge. The sketch should include three pieces of A4 paper, with a frame on each page outlining how a user would use the product or service[6].

When completing the solution sketch, make it self-explanatory and keep it anonymous because we don't want this to influence the next stage. Include words in the drawing and finally give it a catchy title. Once everyone has finished their designs, ask them to upload these to the Miro board so, on Wednesday, you can focus on deciding what you are going to include in the final design.

Today is all about deciding what will be in the final prototype; several techniques can be used to determine this, and we will explore them here. You will be critiquing each solution using the lens of the long-term goal set on the first day. Once you have completed this step, it's time to move to storyboarding the prototype and passing the design to the team that will develop it.

Decide

In his book, 'Sprint', Jake Knapp states that the decision stage is one of the most difficult and something that he has refined while developing the process[1]. The decide stage contains five steps that allow a decision to be made constructively. Each participant will share their Solution Sketch, and the team will find consensus on a single idea through decision-making exercises. The final direction will aim to address the long-term goal and prototype direction. Jake Knapp states the process is as follows[1].

1. Art Museum
   a. Put the solution sketches in Miro from each person.
2. Heat map
   a. Everyone reviews all the solutions in silence and uses dot stickers to mark interesting parts of each design.
3. Speed critique
   a. Everyone has three minutes to discuss the highlights of the designs, using post-it notes to capture ideas.
4. Straw poll
   a. Each person chooses one solution and votes on their favourite elements of each design using Miro.
5. Supervote
   a. The decider makes the final decision by placing a large red sticker on the solution that is decided.

After the above process, you may find that you want to include elements of different designs into one prototype or, if you have more than one winning solution, which I wouldn't recommend, test both with your customers. If this is the case, discuss it and bring together the important elements, again with the decider making the final vote.

On to the storyboard...

Storyboard
The storyboard connects each of the solution concepts to map each step of the experience you want to test. It's important as this will be handed to the team that will be building the prototype, and it makes most sense for all concerned. The focus should be on what needs to be built for testing with users on the final day.

Storyboarding can be a challenging element of the design sprint both for the facilitator and the participants. So far you have not worried too much about getting into the fine detail, only ensuring that you have covered everything needed. I would advise against jumping right into a storyboard as a blank screen can intimate the participants. Instead, start with an exercise called User Test Flow.

The purpose of this is to write out at a high level the basic steps that will be included in the storyboard. When you complete the mapping exercise, it's easier to think of a start and endpoint. As the diagram above explains, you break this down into four post-it notes and outline on each note what the user will see. This could be a welcome screen, a newsletter, or a social media post etc. Once everyone has completed this exercise, vote on the best flow.

Next, following this exercise, take the voted-for user test flow and convert this into a storyboard. The storyboard contains

around ten to fifteen frames of the user interactions within your product, service, and process. Always start the process by outlining how the user found out about your product and the result. This exercise can take over an hour depending on the level of detail, but it's important to remember the below points when completing it; from 'Sprint':

- ▸ Work with what you have.
- ▸ Include enough detail.
- ▸ The decider decides.
- ▸ Keep the story to fifteen minutes or less.

Once you have designed your board, the workshop element of the design sprint is over. You have covered a lot, and your designs are now ready for the final two days, which we will cover briefly.

THURSDAY

Prototype
The developer's job is to build a high-fidelity prototype using an application like Figma to develop an interactive, testable prototype. We say developers, but it may be the case that your prototype will take the form of a presentation that the team members will complete. Although, usually, the storyboard is passed to a developer to build the final design. Time is tight on Thursday as you only have one day before the user testing. This is why the storyboard is so important if the developer always asks questions; this will delay the design's implementation.

The tool of choice for digital prototyping is Figma[7]. Figma is a graphical, web-based tool that allows various people to work on a single file. You can share the prototype with your client and team to get real-time feedback. Figma lets you create an interactive prototype with a few simple clicks, and you can share the URL with your user testers. A great feature of Figma is its ability to import a library of pre-made templates such as IOS and Android screens to add to the prototype's real feel.

There are a few simple rules we should follow when building a prototype:

1. You can prototype anything.
2. Prototypes are disposable.
3. Build just enough to learn.
4. The prototype must appear real.

I mentioned prototyping a presentation, and you may be wondering how this appears real. It depends on what you are prototyping. If you are prototyping a sales document or an advertising campaign, for example, then a presentation using PowerPoint or Keynote will be sufficient.

FRIDAY

Last, we will be testing the prototype with real users to identify any useability problems and determine the user's feedback on the product prototype. This can be conducted remotely using Zoom, Google Meet, or if you want to invest in a dedicated platform, then Usertesting.com is my preferred choice. Online user testing is more convenient and increases the chances of accessing a larger pool of candidates that you can recruit.

Interviewing users is outside this book's scope, but you want to ensure that the users match your target customer and record the session using the Loom tool. This will allow the team to review the tests afterwards to gain the greatest level of learning[3].

Once you have completed your interviews, the team needs to review the feedback and look for good and bad patterns in the prototype and concept. Another important element is to refer back to the sprint questions and ask, 'Did we achieve what we set out to do?'. After accruing the insights, the team can disband and celebrate a sprint completed, and they can build on learning further in future tests.

The design sprint is a versatile and innovative process that allows teams to devise and test a concept with real users in five days. This chapter was only an introduction to the method, and I would refer to the sources outlined to explore further. The next chapter will describe how you can ideate new products, services, business models, processes, and customer experiences 100% online with the FORTH innovation method.

KEY MESSAGES FROM THIS CHAPTER

▶ **The Design Sprint is focused on the user. Its entire process is user-centred. It is built on a solid understanding of the user wants and needs and seeks to validate ideas directly from your target users.**

▶ **Making a Design Sprint is a team sport. This means there are less back and forth discussions and fewer silos, which can delay implementing this innovation process.**

▶ **The Design Sprint is fast and efficient. It forces you to focus and work towards building a validated prototype in five days.**

▶ **Learn fast; fail fast. The sprint allows you to focus on your clear goals to make decisions quickly. This means that instead of taking months, your team can determine the desirability of your product very quickly, which allows you too then iterate quicker.**

▶ **The contents of this chapter have been taken from the below sources to pull together different perspectives on this method. All credit goes to the leading authorities outlined below.**

[1] Knapp, J., Zeratsky, J. and Kowitz, B., 2016. Sprint: How to Solve Big Problems and Test New Ideas in Just Five Days. Simon and Schuster.

[2] AJ&Smart, 2020, The Ultimate Guide to Remote Design Sprints. Retriever from https://ajsmart.com/remotedesignsprints

[3] Knapp, 2020, The Remote Design Sprint Guide. Retriever from https://www.thesprintbook.com/remote

[4] Sprint stories, 2020, Seven Tips for the First-Ever Design Sprint of a Company. Retriever from https://sprintstories.com/7-tips-for-the-first-ever-design-sprint-of-a-company-16682b307c1c

[5] Cruchon, 2020, The Official Remote Design Sprint Template Retriever from https://www.mural.co/templates/the-official-remote-design-sprint-template

[6] Google, 2020, The Design Sprint Kit Retriever from https://designsprintkit.withgoogle.com/

[7] Figma, 2020, Design Retriever from https://www.figma.com/design/

CONTENTS

CHAPTER 10

THE FORTH INNOVATION METHOD

FORTH is the innovation methodology that unites us as writers of this book. We are all certified online FORTH innovation facilitators and part of the FORTH family of over 250 innovation managers, project leaders, and facilitators worldwide.

WHAT IS THE FORTH INNOVATION METHOD?

FORTH is a method that helps organisations to become innovative by generating mini new business cases and empowering team members with an innovative mindset in a 12-week online-process. The method was created in 2005 by the global keynote speaker and innovation authority, Gijs van Wulfen. In 2013, he published 'The Innovation Expedition' (also BIS Publishers), which became a worldwide innovation bestseller that has been translated into nine languages.

FORTH is an acronym. It stands for the five phases of this method. Full Steam Ahead is about preparing yourself for a real innovation expedition. That means understanding why the innovation journey should start now, what you should you be looking for, and how innovation success is defined. Furthermore, you achieve full buy-in from all stakeholders from the beginning, plan the journey, engage a team, and kick off the expedition. In Observe and Learn, you get 'the blinders off' of all participants and reach out to customers to understand their needs and customer frictions. In Raise Ideas, you generate a lot, upwards of a thousand, ideas online and convert the 15 best ones into concepts. With real customer feedback, you improve the concepts in Test Ideas. In the final phase, Homecoming, you transform the three to five best concepts into mini new business cases. You end the journey with a decision that will be transferred into the organisations' innovation funnel of the three to five mini new business cases.

F ➡ FULL STEAM AHEAD
O ➡ OBSERVE AND LEARN
R ➡ RAISE IDEAS
T ➡ TEST IDEAS
H ➡ HOMECOMING.

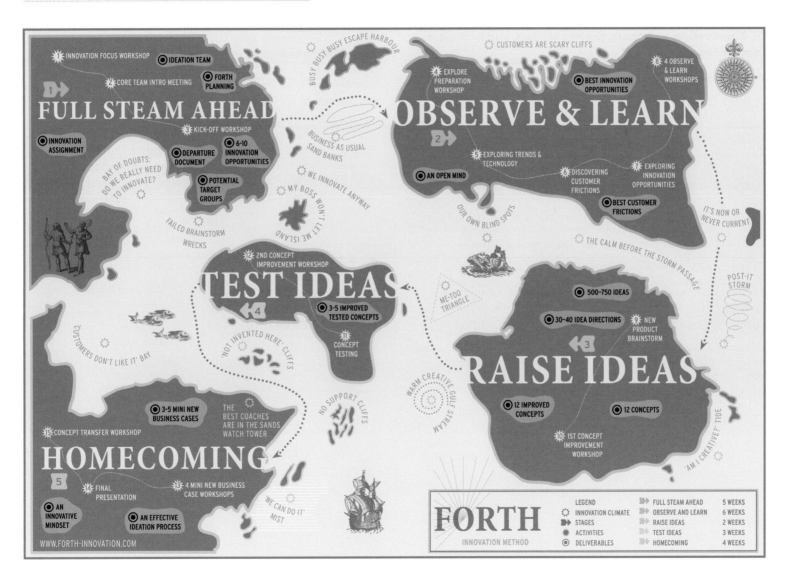

WHY DO A FORTH INNOVATION JOURNEY?

The world is changing fast. The Covid-19 years have disrupted sectors, businesses, and their business models, products, and services. Even when everybody is talking about being agile and having a purpose, that does not mean that organisations act alike. There are two modus operandi in companies. Operational excellence – meaning focus on exploitation, efficiency and stepwise growth by improvement – and innovation excellence, focussing on exploration and jump-wise growth by breakthrough. The first one secures survival today, and the other survival tomorrow. These modi operandi require a different approach and mindset: No-failing versus fast failing, certainty versus uncertainty, minimal budgets versus investing, tight planning and control versus iterative experimenting.

In our experience, most companies focus solely on operational excellence, which creates a huge risk because the culture and the people unlearn to cope with high uncertainties, take risks, and accept failure as valuable learning experiences. Covid-19 had a massive impact on some sectors, as we discussed extensively in Chapter 1. In the chart below, you see that airports and airlines' business models were hit hard when the number of flights collapsed. That is a huge challenge in itself. But most airports and airlines applied only operational excellence. Changing their mindset and speeding up innovating their business is sure to be a major turnaround, as we will notice in practice. That's when applying the FORTH innovation method makes real sense. We say, 'FORTH makes the old elephants dance again'.

CHART: EXPLORE VS EXPLOIT MODE (Source: Alex Osterwalder)

EXPLORE	⬅ ➡	EXPLOIT
Search and breakthrough	FOCUS	Efficiency and growth
High	UNCERTAINTY	Low
Venture-capital style risk-taking, expecting few outsized winners	FINANCIAL PHILOSOPHY	Safe haven with steady returns and dividends
Iterative experimentation, embracing speed, failure, learning, and rapid adaption	CULTURE & PROCESSES	Linear execution, embracing planning, precitability, and manimal failure
Explorers who excel in uncertainty, are strong at pattern recognition, and can navigate between big pictures and details	CULTURE & PROCESSES	Managers who are strong at organizing and planning and can design efficient processes to deliver on time and budget

ONLINE INNOVATION

% change compared with the same month of previous year (Source Eurocontrol)

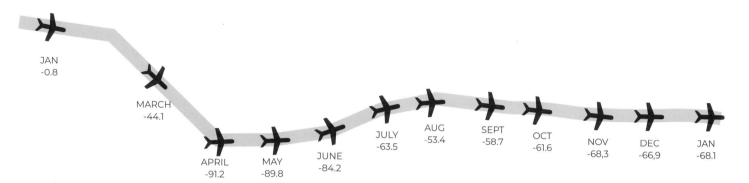

JAN
-0.8

MARCH
-44.1

APRIL
-91.2

MAY
-89.8

JUNE
-84.2

JULY
-63.5

AUG
-53.4

SEPT
-58.7

OCT
-61.6

NOV
-68,3

DEC
-66,9

JAN
-68.1

Gijs van Wulfen originated the FORTH methodology, having the operational-excellence-only in mind of all organisations whose markets get disrupted and suddenly need to innovate their offerings and organisation. With a clear structure and smooth process, FORTH secures the buy-in of all stakeholders while delivering three to five innovative mini new business cases and a team with an innovation excellence mindset (again).

The re-invention story of FORTH innovation facilitator Florian

As an innovation consultant and facilitator in the pre-Covid-19 era, I facilitated in-person workshops and training. When Covid-19 hit, all my orders for the whole year got cancelled in less than a week. I was devastated and did not know what to do, like probably a lot of you. For a few days, I just enjoyed 'nothing-to-do-anymore'. And at the same time, I was paralysed by the shock of not knowing what will happen next.

As a father of two little kids, being away from home made me feel missing out on them every day. And as an introverted person, the full-day in-person workshops are very exhausting to me. So, I thought that changing my business could be an opportunity. I love technology, so I spent the next two months experimenting with tools and methods around digital innovation workshops almost 24/7.

Less than three months later, I was back in business, with a clear focus on doing innovation online only, which gave me much more energy. My learning I love to share with you is to try to see opportunities in a crisis. Realise that are you able to change. And use your strengths and the ones of your organisation to pivot and find new ways of delivering value to customers.

THE FORTH POWER

Founder of the FORTH innovation method, Gijs van Wulfen, worked as a marketer in the food sector and later as a consultancy firm strategy consultant. He experienced all the frustrations at the fuzzy front end of innovation himself, being faced with undecisive leaders not knowing in which direction to lead their organisations. The main problem for why the start of innovation is so hard is not the creative process as such. No. It's the lack of buy-in and commitment of managers rejecting change. Design thinking alone would not solve the problem. For him, it was crystal clear that you have to combine design thinking with business thinking to secure that new innovative business cases will be adopted by the business environment and are transformed into real products, services, or business models. When he designed the FORTH innovation method in 2005 he wanted to:

▶ Take away the fear of making a big jump.
▶ Give the deciders and participants a secure and understandable path.
▶ Give the participants the feeling of making progress at any moment of the journey.
▶ Give the deciders opportunities to steer without interfering with the process dramatically.
▶ Reduce the risk of uncertainty for everyone.
▶ Get full buy-in and commitment of the deciders all along the total process.
▶ Increase the success rate of new concepts launched on the market.

Florian learned the hard way

I discovered the FORTH innovation method in 2016 when I became an independent innovation consultant. I was looking for something to structure innovation, I thought. But what I was looking for was something that unites the R&D and the business side.

Before becoming independent, I was engaged in product development projects and worked on ideas in the industry's fuzzy front end. I had to learn the hard way what it means if you do not get the buy-in and the deciders' commitment. My team and I had excellent new solutions that made so much sense (at least from my perspective), but they were all turned down.

Only later did I realise I was so ignorant, because I never asked the leaders of my company about their perspective and what they think, or what they were looking for. So there never was a link between my organisation's business needs and the creative process of finding new solutions. And that's how I have experienced personally that FORTH really helps you. Because you will share buy-in and commitment from the deciders through the whole journey leading to tangible innovative outcomes.

Integrating all these elements made FORTH a very structured, clear, and understandable innovation process, with a clear time frame delivering three to five innovative mini new business cases (MNBC). Each of the short 23 workshops of the online version of FORTH have tangible outcomes, which are the next workshop's input. That secures constant progress in small steps and prevents shortcuts that lead nowhere.

By drafting an innovation assignment at the beginning of the process, a clear and common understanding is generated as is the buy-in of the deciders. All decisions that will be made during the expedition are based on this assignment. It is the North Star of the FORTH Journey. The project sponsor and the rest of the steering committee join the so-called extended team, by which all deciders are involved in the process and contribute themselves. They also get a deep understanding of customer frictions and current innovation opportunities. They also raise ideas and give feedback throughout the whole process. By allowing them to fill in additional requirements for the MNBCs and being a godfather while the teams create the MNBCs, the risk of uncertainty will be reduced, and they can select the best ones, as all relevant information is available. That secures the commitment and increases the adoption rate of the delivered business cases in the regular product development stage-gated process.

The main-catch is the by-catch, and the by-catch is the main-catch

Kees van Zijderveld, when CEO of ESKA, an industrial firm producing solid cardboard, said to Gijs after finishing a FORTH innovation journey, 'Gijs; the main-catch of FORTH is the by-catch, and the by-catch is the main-catch'. Gijs asked, 'What do you mean Kees?' And he replied, 'We engaged on a FORTH innovation journey as our company needs to innovate drastically, as our main markets like books, office binders, and board games are on their decline. And FORTH delivered results as we "came home" with five solid new business cases, of which one could be implemented directly. But in the end, I consider this as a by-catch. What I even value more is that the ten men that enrolled as core-team all made a huge personal development. They learned how to explore, postponing their judgment. They talked to customers. They learned to ideate new ideas and to make concepts. They made new business cases. I have seen those men change during our FORTH innovation journey. You not only have an innovation programme, it's also a culture-change programme. And Gijs asked, 'Kees, if I would have come to you six months ago and told you I have this wonderful culture-change programme. Would you have

adopted it?' 'No, of course not', Kees answered. 'Culture-change programmes never deliver results....'

Who is the FORTH Innovation Process for?

With its structured framework and focus on all stakeholders' buy-in, FORTH is suitable for organisations that got stuck in operational excellence. Besides them, the methodology is also used very successfully by innovative companies that want to lead their markets, filling their innovation pipelines with new innovative offerings. We recommend FORTH for midsize and large organisations. It suits all areas and sectors. It has been successfully implemented in healthcare, fast-moving consumer goods, the construction sector, the chemical industry, the ICT sector, high-technology industry, the energy sector, the telecom sector, the financial sector, the non-profit sector, universities, and even governments.

FORTH is focused on 'making old elephants dance again'. That is why the process incorporates the buy-in of the decision-makers. That makes the process last for 12 weeks, which is longer than such startup methods as Lean-Startup or a Design-Sprint (up to five days). These methods are focused on a single idea or issue and require an innovative mindset from the start.

For what topics can the method be used?

On the one hand, we recommend FORTH for any kind of innovation. It does not matter if you are looking for a new service, product, process, customer experience, or business model. Or if it is for a tech, social, or frugal innovation. We even use FORTH to costovate organisations combining cost-saving while 'wowing' customers with new offerings. On the other hand, FORTH is a 12-week culture change program, where at the end of the journey, the innovation team has an open and innovative mindset and has improved their skills.

Initially, in 2005, FORTH was created to help organisations with new products and services. Over time it was also used to innovate business models and customer experiences. Nowadays, being used worldwide, it is also used to innovate internal processes and have a cultural impact.

The outcomes of a FORTH expedition.
Implementing a FORTH innovation journey will ultimately deliver for you and your organisation the following ten outcomes during the process:
1. A clear and shared understanding of the goal of the innovation journey with the innovation assignment.
2. Potential target groups identified.
3. Six to ten innovation opportunities with valuable insights.
4. An understanding of the most relevant customer frictions connecting to customers.
5. An inspired team with their blinders off.
6. Five hundred to a thousand ideas.
7. Twelve to fifteen tested and improved new concepts.
8. Three to five mini new business cases.
9. A final selection of mini new business cases adopted for development.
10. An open-minded team sparking a culture of innovation.

Taking FORTH online
The FORTH innovation method is a best practice innovation method and has been proven worldwide in in-person workshops. When Covid-19 forced almost the whole world into the first lockdown, a group of more than twenty FORTH facilitators decided, on Coenie Middel's initiative, a FORTH facilitator from South Africa supported by Gijs van Wulfen, to 'go online'. The case and innovation assignment we chose focussed on generating three to five innovative solutions that significantly reduce the estimated negative impact of Covid-19 on society by 50%. You can imagine that our first version of FORTH online was a rough and bumpy journey as we just copied exactly online what made the method so successful in-person. We made all the beginner's mistakes ourselves, and that's why we could write this book and finetune FORTH online as a smooth-running online methodology with 23 short online workshops in 12 weeks generating the same deliverables as the in-person version.

The advantages of an Online FORTH process
As FORTH focuses on midsize and large organisations, the participants are primarily in different countries. Online, it does not matter where you are. With a few mouse-clicks, the whole team is working together, saving over the entire journey many days of travel time and ten thousand euros for flights and accommodation, apart from the environmental benefits. Another advantage is that working online on collaboration platforms helps more introverted people. They can contribute their ideas and be heard without being pushed on stage or talked over on Miro (which we use for FORTH) by the extroverts by writing in bulk mode, using the anonymous voting function, and using the board's round-the-clock availability asynchronously. As everybody is working on the same board simultaneously and votes are done with a simple click, it saves a lot of time and speeds up the innovation process. Using asynchronous and synchronous work helps make the workshops shorter and populated with the most relevant issues. Everything that can be done alone could also be done asynchronously. But the limit of transferring tasks to asynchronous work is the engagement and commitment of the participants. That's why we start with a very low-impact part of asynchronous work and gradually increase it over the course of the FORTH journey.

The challenges of an online FORTH process
International teams can work across different time zones. So, the time slots might not be optimal for everyone. For one, it's early morning, and for another, it is already evening. But, on

the other hand, if people were to meet in person, we would need to consider a jet-lag, as well. In our online FORTH innovation project with Philip Morris International, we had a core team from Europe and an extended team member from the USA. He had to be up at 5 o'clock in the morning, which was not optimal for him.

As we described earlier, natural engagement online is lower than it is in-person because participants are in their environment and have their second and third screen. That's why the FORTH online workshops are created to be highly engaging, and rules are set to limit distraction.

Technical issues are the enormous risk of any online workshop, and so it is for an online project with FORTH. If the internet breaks down, the power goes off, or tools are not allowed to be used, it's over and done.

The biggest challenge is the lack of personal interaction, of course. The coffee-corner or water-cooler moments, or a little chat with your neighbour, that's not possible. We are all missing these moments.

The tools set-up for a FORTH online expedition
For the online-FORTH, we use the online collaboration platform, Miro. When we took the FORTH process online, we found this to be the best match. Miro and significant features like the mindmap and voting tools helped us make the online-FORTH process easy, fast, and straightforward. The FORTH process now has fully designed Miro templates and agendas for all of the 23 workshops. The templates are well designed, easy to understand, and follow the FORTH process.

For our facilitator agendas, we use SessionLab. That helped us to easily co-design the workshops and make changes in an instant. For videoconferencing, we prefer Zoom because it is

very stable, has good audio and video quality, allows break out rooms, and has good facilitator rights, like mute/unmute everybody and 'bring everybody back from break out rooms'. For customer feedback on the concepts, any kind of survey tools like Google Forms or Typeform can be used.

STEP 1 – FULL STEAM AHEAD

The first phase of the FORTH Journey is Full Steam Ahead. Here it is about getting ready for the journey. It has two parts. We meet with all relevant deciders before the real start of the online expedition to get a clear and shared understanding about the innovation assignment and stakeholder buy-in and to compose the team for the journey. In this pre-phase, it might happen that the journey fails to start because there is not sufficient buy-in from the decider side.

GOAL

an enthusiastic, multidisciplinary team ready for the innovation expedition

until week 1

DELIVERABLES

- Departure document with innovation assignment, innovation team and FORTH planning

- six to ten innovation opportunities

The second part of Full Steam Ahead is kicking off the journey in four short workshops. The main focus is on team alignment and identifying and choosing innovation opportunities to explore in the next phase.

Deliverables

There are two significant deliverables. The departure document consists of the innovation assignment, the innovation team, and the FORTH workshop planning. The departure document is like a project charter. The innovation assignment describes the goal (why they are innovating, what they are looking for, for whom, and where and when it should be on the market) and the success criteria that the new offerings need to be accepted and transferred into the internal innovation development process.

After drafting the innovation assignment, a project sponsor and a project leader are chosen. They are responsible for setting up the innovation team. In this stage, look for a diverse, multidisciplinary team in age, department, experience, sex, attitude, and personality. An ideal team consists of six to ten people. This core team is supplemented by the extended team, who are the members of a steering committee that in FORTH also takes part in this journey to get their buy-in.

Part of the departure document is the planning of the FORTH-journey. Because it is a journey of 12 weeks with 23 workshops and many people, it has to be planned properly. When everything is set, the journey can begin. Additionally, doing it online, we have to arrange some IT-related activities. What video conferencing tool will we use? Is it Miro compliant, or do we have to find alternatives? Does everybody have the right computer and equipment, like a camera, microphone, and stable internet connection available?

The second major deliverable of the phase Full Steam Ahead is six to ten innovation opportunities, depending on the core team's size because each core team member will pick one innovation opportunity to explore in the next phase: Observe and Learn. The deliverables are the end products of the following four workshops.

Workshop 1. Innovation Focus workshop

This is one of the most relevant workshops in the whole FORTH Journey. All relevant deciders are present. And the goal is to get a clear and common understanding of the innovation assignment and their buy-in.

From our experience, we recommend not more than eight relevant deciders for this online workshop, otherwise, it could get too messy. The workshop structure is straightforward. You bring all deciders to the Miro template you are using and ask them six questions.
1. Why do you want to innovate now?
2. What are you looking for?
3. Who is the target group?
4. Where – in which region – do we focus?
5. When do you want to introduce it?
6. What are the criteria the innovations have to meet?

Each question is answered on an online post-it by each decider, and most of the time, the answers will vary. Now it is the facilitator's task to draw a clear conclusion, and everybody agrees on it. This process is repeated for all questions, so in the end, we have answered all questions and have the buy-in from everyone on a clear, concise assignment. Facilitating and handling the deciders and drafting a conclusion that gets their buy-in within a minimal timeframe is demanding.

Workshop 2. Team Introduction workshop

The team kickoff workshop is the first time the core team meets. The purpose is to build trust within the team by getting to know each other better personally and professionally. Even before they start the journey, all team members get invited to a welcome whiteboard on Miro. With an introduction video, you help them get familiar with the tool before starting the workshop. We learned that people need to get familiar with the online tools, otherwise they cannot concentrate on the content. Start the workshop with personal connections, getting to know each other. Do some exercises to gain a feeling of trust with the new team and the facilitators.
In the in-person version, we always have a wonderful dinner together afterwards. And after a night in the bar together, the team has connected. Online, it is more difficult. We learned that getting the team to bond takes much longer online and is more difficult than in very structured and time-boxed workshops. That's why we integrated 'FORTH-Cafés', which are virtual meetings outside the workshops, with no agenda. Just time to get to know each other better and talk about whatever you like, without facilitation.

Workshop 3. Kickoff workshop

After the core team workshop, we facilitate the official Kickoff. In the beginning, the core team and the extended team get to know each other with some short networking in break out rooms. Then the project sponsor and project leader explain the background and the goal of the journey. They present their innovation assignment, and the project leader answers questions. In the end, they describe the online-FORTH process and the activities for the next 12 weeks.

Workshop 4. Innovation Opportunities

The goal of the innovation opportunities workshop is to select the most relevant innovation opportunities. It includes subjects, themes, technologies, trends, areas, or target groups that provide great opportunity to realise the innovation assignment. Before the workshop, the project sponsor and project leader, together with us as facilitators, agree on four major topics relevant to fulfil the innovation assignment. At the beginning of the workshop, we split the team into four groups, and all participants fill out a mind map on one of the four topics. In the second step, we ask them to generate innovation opportunities inspired by their mind map. Out of the huge amount of innovation opportunities, we let every group pick their favourite ten. The top 40 participants in the plenum choose the top six to ten innovation opportunities with anonymous voting in Miro that makes this decision process fast, simple, and democratic. The last step in this workshop is that core team members select and adopt one innovation opportunity to explore in the next phase: Observe and Learn.

STEP 2 – OBSERVE AND LEARN

Observe and Learn, with four workshops, is, in our experience, the most undervalued and underestimated phase of the process. Its purpose is to get the operational-excellence blinders off and get new insights on opportunities, new learnings on trends and technology, and understand customer needs and pain points. It is undervalued because most people like to skip or shorten it. They do not see the value before doing it. It is underestimated because new ideas are not coming from old information. New ideas are sparked by new insights and learnings outside your comfort zone and are inspired by understanding customers and their customer frictions.

You can tackle this issue in two ways: online, but also offline. The first option is a method. Use structured methods like FORTH or Design Sprint, where the steps are clear, and all are essential for an effective outcome. 'Trust the process' of proven best practices is here the most valuable reply. When you want solid outcomes, apply the process as it is meant to be. The second option is learning by doing. When deciders are so focused on their existing ideas or believe they know what their customers want, you could suggest a design sprint (see Chapter 9). You will get customer feedback on one solution in less than a week. And either they were right, or they were wrong. Both outcomes are huge learnings. When they were right, they got already one new product or service ideated and checked. And they implement FORTH for exploring more, or they are happy and focus on implanting one idea. When they fail, they learned the hard way they didn't understand their customers and started a FORTH with a thorough Observe and Learn phase.

'We know our customers and what their pain points are. Let's skip Observe and Learn and start directly generating new ideas'. CEO, We-Know-It-All-Corporation Ltd.

The major deliverables are the top innovation opportunities and top customer frictions. The top innovation opportunities are the most relevant insights that the team discovered during their two weeks. According to the innovation assignment, the top customer frictions are the most relevant customer pain points the team gathered during the customer interviews.

CHART: OBSERVE AND LEARN

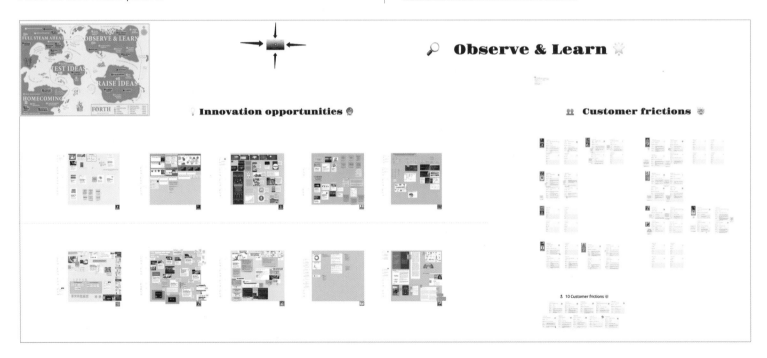

Workshop 5. Discovery Preparation workshop

Most participants are not used to collecting insights and doing customer interviews. This workshop is meant to help the team get started and understand what they need to do and where on the Miro board to document the information they gather. They get to learn the concept of customer frictions and explore how to identify them.

Workshop 6. Customer Frictions

The Customer frictions workshop aims to gain insights from customers by interviewing customers by the core team. We recommend that the interview be conducted by two people, and either record the interview or have all the other participants witness it, but with their own cameras and microphones turned off. That sounds like a waste of time, but it is not. Each team member has a different background, different personality, and different experience. We learned that they also hear and interpret things differently. We are looking for so-called customer frictions in the interviews, which, as described is a need or desire that is not fulfilled because of an obstacle.

Customer friction:

I am _____.

I need _____.

But _____.

GOAL

Get your blinders off,
get inspired
get deep understanding about
your customers

week 2-4

DELIVERABLES

🎁 Best customer frictions

🎁 Best innovation opportunities

Workshops 7 and 8. Observe and Learn workshops

The two Observe and Learn workshops are when each core team member shares his or her thoughts on the innovation opportunity with the total team. The big advantage online is that all information, all gathered insights, and all customer frictions are accessible at any time. We facilitate sharing workshops for two reasons: First, each core team member has his stage for a couple of minutes to present what he found out. That gives him the possibility to be visible to the participating deciders, and it also puts pressure on them to do their research and have something meaningful to present. The second reason is that the extended team understands the findings and insights and gets their blinders off too.

At the second Observe and Learn sharing workshop, we will also select the top customer frictions and highlight the top innovation opportunities according to the innovation assignment.

After gathering a lot of new insights, we continue with the next phase.

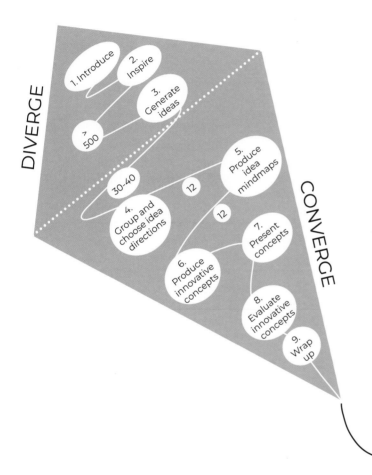

DIVERGE

CONVERGE

1. Introduce

2. Inspire

3. Generate ideas

> 500

30-40

12

5. Produce idea mindmaps

4. Group and choose idea directions

12

7. Present concepts

6. Produce innovative concepts

8. Evaluate innovative concepts

9. Wrap up

STRUCTURED BRAINSTORMING

STEP 3 – RAISE IDEAS

In Raise Ideas, we generate in six workshops as many ideas as possible, select the best ones, and draft and improve twelve to fifteen concrete concepts. The brainstorm has two parts. The diverging stage, where five hundred-plus ideas are generated, features two workshops. First of all, we transform an innovation assignment into an ideation assignment without restricting criteria and conditions. The second part, converging, focusses on selecting the best ideas and converting them into concept statements. This part contains four workshops. All selection decisions are based on fulfilling the innovation assignment.

ONLINE INNOVATION

Workshop 9. The Braindump

The ideation workshop's goal of Raising Ideas is to harvest all ideas that popped up in the minds of the participants during Observe and Learn. Before starting specific ideation methods to make participants think from a different perspective or focus on a specific problem, we apply a so-called braindump. We ask the participants to write down all ideas they have in their mind. For this goal, we open up an ideation-space-template on Miro already a few days before the actual start of Raise Ideas. While participants are still in the Observe and Learn mode, they can write down all the ideas they already have on the ideation space template, where a personal ideation spot is created for everyone. At the actual workshop, we also offer at the beginning a short moment to fill their personal ideation space to make sure everybody contributes. Then starts generating and sharing new ideas, building on the ideas of others. In groups in break out rooms, we ask one person to start reading out her ideas and have the others listening and creating new ideas. Afterwards, everybody has time to read in silence through the other groups' ideas to get even more inspiration.

Workshop 10. Ideation Workshop

After the braindump workshop, you sometimes get the feedback that people think it makes no sense to do another ideation workshop because there are already so many ideas. They are so ... wrong. But that is what you need. When participants have no more ideas in their minds, they are ready to generate more by applying design thinking techniques. In the ideation workshop, we use specific ideation methods to force the participants to take a different perspective or focus on a specific issue. We also use the technique together-alone (where everybody works on the same task but in silence on their own) intensively for this workshop. We form groups that generate together solutions on a specific topic or question. We designed on the Miro template specific spots for each ideation technique. So, in each group, everybody can see what the other group members are writing. That helps people elaborate on others' ideas and save time because we do not need to share ideas reading them out loud in the group.

We recommend that you start with customer frictions. In groups, participants are asked to generate ideas on how to solve specific relevant customer friction. Depending on the innovation assignment, the company, and the readiness of the participants, we use two to four other ideation methods like SCAMPER, What Would Apple Do?, Comic Book Hero, or Silly Things. For all the methods, we use the technique together-alone.

At the end of the ideation session, we have at least five hundred, and often more than a thousand ideas. The last point on the agenda is to give the participants homework for the next 48 hours. We ask them to select their two favourite ideas. Two out of a thousand? Without clustering, without affinity diagram? Yes, this has no benefit. That's why we give people time and space on their own to scan through all the ideas. They need to develop one evolutionary idea, meaning a quite feasible idea that sounds good, and one revolutionary idea, suggesting an excellent, attractive solution whose feasibility is relatively low. We differentiate because, otherwise, people like to pick only the feasible ones.

Workshop 11. Making Idea Directions

Did you ever experience that the level of detail of ideas varies a lot? The solution in the FORTH process is called the idea direction workshop. It comes right after every participant has chosen his two favourite ideas. The goal is to bring all ideas to a similar level of detail, a level where the idea is both focused and has the potential to fulfil the criteria innovation assignment. In this workshop, each participant creates an idea direction for their selected ideas. We give them a hint, 'What is the direction behind that idea?'.

Example of making idea directions

Assume you are in a FORTH innovation process creating new digital offerings in the fashion sector. Your two selected top ideas are, 'a web store' and 'a top 100 black dresses web store'. The first one is far too vague. The second idea is far too detailed, resulting in a small opportunity. The recommended idea direction for both could be, 'a top 100 fashion web store'. Now it has a focus and has the potential to fulfil the innovation assignment.

At the end of the idea direction workshop, 20 to 40 idea directions have been drafted, and you select, according to the innovation assignment, the best 12 to 15 idea directions.

Workshop 12. Concept-Making Workshop

In the concept-making workshop, we transform the idea directions into tangible concept-statements. But before we do this, we diverge again in the converging process, making mindmaps for every idea direction first. All participants have to answer for each of the chosen 12 to 15 idea directions four questions about 1. the target group, 2. the offering (product/service), 3. the business model, and 4. how to it in a mindmap. It has the advantage that we collect the whole group's knowledge and insights on all 12 to 15 idea directions. In this process, we work asynchronously in between the ideal direction and the concept making workshop.

As first step in the workshop, we create pairs. They decided on their own which mindmap they pick to work out as a concept statement. Normally, with 10 to 20 people in the workshop, every pair works out one or two concepts in around 30 minutes until all the mindmaps of the top idea directions are transformed into concepts. We use break out sessions with everybody working on the same board.

A concept consists of four parts:
1. The concept name.
2. The customer friction that the concept solves.
3. The offering with a description of the new solution, the benefits, and the business model.
4. A catchy slogan.

MAKING, RATING AND IMPROVING CONCEPTS

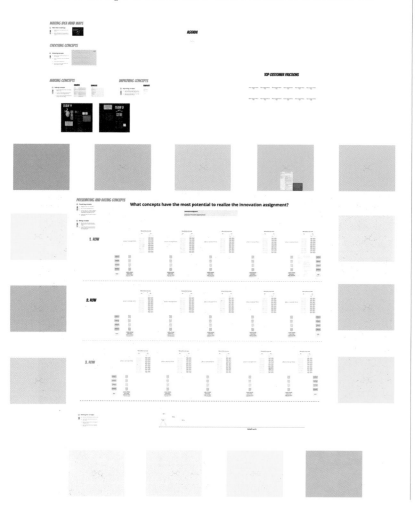

Workshop 13. Concept Presentation and Rating

Next, each concept statement is evaluated by all participants on the criteria of the innovation assignment. For this workshop, the extended team is also on board. Each concept is not pitched. It's just read out loud. Otherwise, the best sales pitch would win instead of the best concept. Then everybody rates the concept by writing a 'top' (what they like most) and a 'tip' (what they dislike), and they will rate it with the anonymous voting function in Miro on the main criteria of the innovation assignment. At the end of the workshop, we will have ranked all concepts, and everybody shares tips to make them better.

Workshop 14. Concept Improvement

The concepts are now improved based on the received feedback in a workshop. It could be done asynchronously. But our experience teaches us that it is more valuable for the participants when there is a fixed blocked time slot in their calendar instead of finding a common time slot with their partner on short-term notice. At the end of Raise Ideas, we have now generated 12 to 15 improved concepts ready to be tested by customers.

STEP 4 – TEST IDEAS

In Test Ideas, we test in four workshops all concepts with customers, improve them again according to the feedback and select the three to five best ones according to the innovation assignment.

Workshop 15. Customer Interviews or Surveys

We can get customer feedback either with online interviews of individual customers or send out a simple online survey to customers. We recommend to perform individual online interviews for business-to-business settings to get a good impression of how customers evaluate new ideas. It's qualitative market research, where understanding why people like or dislike the concept is more important than having a huge number of responses. We try to get each concept evaluated by ten people from the relevant target group for that specific concept.

Workshop 16. Presenting Customer Feedback

In this workshop, we share the feedback with the core team and the extended team. It helps everyone in the team to understand better how customers perceive the concepts. We get feedback on all concepts on the following seven aspects:

1. Is customer friction recognised?
2. Is the concept clear?
3. Is the concept attractive?
4. Does the concept match the brand name or company?
5. How does it rate overall on a 1 to 10 scale?
6. What do customers like about the concept?
7. What do customers dislike about the concept?

It's an exciting moment where there's often a clear distinction between the top concepts and the bad ones. Some participants see their darlings killed.

Workshop 17. Concept Improvement

Like in the first improvement workshop, workshop 14, the core team improves all concepts, now based on customers' feedback. We make pairs, where one person is the founder of the concept, and match her with another person who was not involved in drafting the original concept, bringing in fresh blood. At the end of this workshop, we have 12 to 15 improved, tested concepts ready for the innovation team's final assessment.

Workshop 18. Concept Assessment

This last workshop of the Test Ideas is a crucial one, as we make your final selection of three to five improved concepts that will be worked out as mini new business cases. Each concept is evaluated on both feasibility and attractiveness according to the innovation assignment. It's of the utmost importance that both the core and extended team fully understand the concepts. Therefore, between the improvement workshop and the assessment workshop, all participants get the task to reread all improved concepts independently. The first step in this workshop itself is answering the questions, so all participants have a clear understanding of all concepts.

CHART: CONCEPT ASSESSMENT

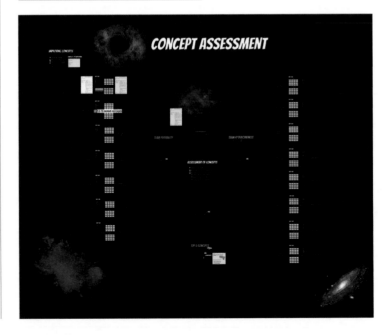

You will assess the concepts both on attractiveness and feasibility. Compose two teams: Team Attractiveness and Team Feasibility. The attractiveness team consists of participants from marketing, sales, finance, and the c-suite, of course. They rate all concepts on the attractiveness according to the innovation assignment. For the feasibility team, we invite people from R&D, production, ICT, buying, finance, and the c-suite. They rate all concept on feasibility. After both groups are done, combine their ratings in a feasibility/attractiveness matrix. So, it is simple to see which three to five concepts make sense according to the innovation assignment. The project sponsor and project leader may use their wildcard to select a concept they favour and deselect one from the original top three to five concepts.

STEP 5 – HOMECOMING

The last phase of the FORTH innovation process, Homecoming, transforms the top three to five concepts into mini new business cases (MNBC) in five workshops. A connecting design thinks of the last phases with business thinking again. The mini new business cases contain all information deciders need to decide which ones to adopt, develop, and introduce. Pre-defined pairs from the core team will each select a concept to work out as a business case. Extended team members will get the responsibility to be a godfather for at least one MNBC. They support their team with input and feedback during the three-week process. In these three weeks, we have three mini new business case workshops where the progress of the business cases is presented and assessed by the core team.

Deliverables
Coming home at the end of our online expedition creates three major deliverables:

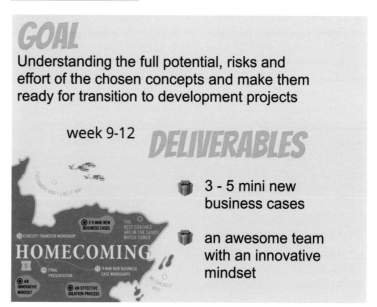

Three to five mini new business cases.

A management decision on which new business cases are to be adopted.

An open-minded innovation team, ready to be ambassadors to spark innovation in the rest of the organisation. FORTH lets old elephants dance again.

Workshop 19. Mini New Business Case Introduction
We start the MNBC introduction workshop by reflecting on the chosen concepts and explain what will happen in the next three weeks. Each pre-defined pair will choose one business case, and together, they explore all the elements of a

1. THIS IS THE CUSTOMER FRICTION	2. THIS IS OUR NEW CONCEPT	3. THIS IS THE BENEFIT FOR THE CUSTOMER	4. WE CAN PRODUCE IT
WHAT IS THE SITUATION? WHAT IS THE NEED? WHAT IS THE FRICTION?	TARGET GROUP DESCRIPTION OF THE NEW CONCEPT NEW TO US, NEW TO THE MARKET, NEW TO THE WORLD? NEW CONCEPT FOR AN EXISTING OR NEW MARKET?	WHY WILL THE CUSTOMER CHOOSE THIS CONCEPT? WHO ARE OUR COMPETITORS? WHAT'S OUR POSITIONING? HOW WAS OUR CONCEPT RATED IN TESTS?	FEASIBILITY POTENTIAL PARTNERS FOR CO-CREATION NEXT STEPS IN THE DEVELOPMENT PROCESS

CHART: 6 MINI NEW BUSINESS CASE SHEETS

good business case for innovation, which you can read in the chart with the six mini new business case sheets. We recommend to invite a business controller from the organisation, helping the teams with the right financial estimations and calculations. For this workshop we transfer our workspace from Miro to typical presentation software like Powerpoint or Keynote so the mini new business cases are drafted within the ICT environment of the organisation itself.

Workshops 20 to 22. MNBC Progress workshops
These three progress workshops serve three purposes.
1. Sharing the progress and content within the core team.
2. Receiving valuable feedback from other team members.
3. Learning how to present the MNBC in 20 minutes at the end presentation.

We have good experience with the possibility to engage people during and directly after each presentation. We ask them to already write their questions during the presentation so directly after the presentation the presenters can answer them directly. After that, we ask all participants to give one Top (compliment) and one Tip (advice) to the team.

Workshop 23. End Presentation workshop

For the final online workshop in the FORTH innovation all MNBCs are presented to the whole innovation team and top management. Most who have been on the online journey themselves as extended team members will decide which concepts will be transferred into the internal innovation funnel to be developed. The deciders have to commit themselves to make a decision right after the presentation in the workshop. And they can because they were able to define the requirements in the MNBCs and were godfathers of them. A decision in the workshop is relevant for two reasons. First of all, it prevents time from being wasted to start the development process. The second reason is to

ONLINE INNOVATION

5. THIS IS WHAT WE GET	6. WE WILL CONTINUE IN THIS WAY
POTENTIAL TURNOVER POTENTIAL MARGIN AND PROFITS FURTHER COSTS FOR DEVELOPMENT	WHY PROCEED? WHAT ARE THE UNCERTAINTIES? NEXT STEPS: TEAM PLANNING COSTS

honour the innovation team's work and end the online FORTH process.

The online MNBC presentations are, as practised, in 20-minute slots, with a Q&A session of five to ten minutes right after each presentation. You can benefit from having a break after every two presentations. After the last presentation, the top managers gathered to get in a break out room for 30 minutes to make their final selection. As a facilitator, we help them when needed to make sure there is a concrete result at the end. In the main meeting afterwards, the project sponsor explains and motivates their decision to the team. To make that last workshop a magical moment, we send all participants and decision-makers a physical snack box containing, for example, popcorn for the 'final presentation', and a bottle of champagne to celebrate the success of the online FORTH innovation journey.

KEY MESSAGES FROM THIS CHAPTER

▸ **An online FORTH innovation process makes sense for midsize and large (international) organisations with an ambitious innovation challenge.**

▸ **FORTH is used online (and in-person) to generate new products, services, business models, processes, and customer experiences.**

▸ **The FORTH-power makes this innovation method one of a kind, proving itself in an online setting as a best practice.**

▸ **The online framework of 23 short workshops, the clear process, and the ready-made online templates make it easy to use and easy to understand for all innovation team participants.**

▸ **Because you get new ideas only after getting new insights, the ideation phase is in the middle of a FORTH project after 'getting the blinders off' in Observe and Learn.**

▸ **FORTH online delivers concrete tangible outcomes with three to five mini new business cases.**

▸ **A FORTH online process sparks a culture for innovation, and lets old elephants dance again.**

Sources
https://ec.europa.eu/eurostat/documents/4187653/11571495/EU-TW-COMMER-CIAL-FLIGHT.jpg 24.02.2021

CONTENTS

CHAPTER 11

HYBRID INNOVATION THE BEST OF BOTH WORLDS

Working from home or from anywhere is here to stay, considering the enthusiasm. This means that online innovation is also here to stay and will accomplish spectacular growth. Soon we will move from 2D platforms for collaboration to 3D tools with AR/VR. At least that is our prediction. For now, both offline and online innovation have their merits. And whether we innovate online or in person, we have to compensate for the disadvantages of the option chosen. In this final chapter, we will merge both ways of innovating into one: hybrid innovation. And we will apply our hybrid innovation to the FORTH innovation methodology, giving new insights into which workshops and activities to do in person or online.

There is still a lot of potential to improve in the way we innovate.
The innovation process from idea to market itself is still full of pitfalls and inefficiencies. Stage-Gate founder, Robert Cooper, shows that for every seven new product ideas, about four enter development, one-and-a-half are launched, and only one succeeds[1]. A study by Stevens and Burley gives even more disastrous ratios. Their study shows it takes three thousand raw ideas to come up with one successful product[2]. This means that enormous amounts of enthusiasm, energy, time, and financial resources are spent in the innovation process without direct returns. Innovation, of course, is a learning process full of experimenting and trial and error, where you can't always expect to get things right the first time. You learn an awful lot from all the iterations in a new concept, which pays off in other projects or your daily business. But do you accept wasting more than 85% of your time and money on innovation. We see enormous potential for improvement.

Online innovation processes deliver excellent results, too.
Online innovation with collaboration whiteboards work; the practice has been proven. Of course, a lot of the innovations ideated last year have not been developed and launched yet. But taking into account the reviews of the users of online innovation processes, you can conclude that they work pretty well. Our practice is the FORTH innovation expedition we implemented completely online with Philip Morris in supporting them to ideate new smoke-free products. As you can read in the chart, Luca Rossi, their vice-president of product research and consumable development, states, 'the magic of the FORTH method online is that it lays out a structured roadmap, implementing 25 online workshops via Microsoft Teams and Miro with templates and tools with a very clear timeline that kept both the discipline and inspiration high.' He was not only very satisfied with the process itself but also with the results, stating 'besides delivering six disruptive new business cases with new-to-the-world technology applications, FORTH created a "from-idea-to-market" perspective among our R&D people, working together across departments in a completely new way.' The project was rated 8.4 on a scale of 10 by all the participants. When facilitating FORTH offline, we get evaluations with the same score between 8 and 9 on a 10-point scale. Other FORTH facilitators applying the methodology get the same results. So, after taking our offline innovation method online in 2020, we can conclude it works.

PHILIP MORRIS PRODUCTS S.A.

October 1st, 2020
Neuchatel Switzerland

Concerns: **Recommendation for the FORTH innovation method 100% online**

To whom it may concern,

Philip Morris International (PMI) is a leading international tobacco company, with a diverse workforce of around 73,500 people. At the moment more than 400 R&D scientists, engineers and technicians are working on smoke-free products.

We started a 100% online innovation process, in times of Corona, with the FORTH innovation methodology to create new disruptive technologies for one of our priority innovations in smoke-free products. The magic of the FORTH method online is that it lays out a structured roadmap, implementing 25 online workshops via Microsoft Teams and Miro with templates and tools with a very clear timeline that kept both the discipline and inspiration high.

We have successfully employed FORTH in our front-end discovery work at PMI. Besides delivering six disruptive new business cases with new-to-the world technology applications, FORTH created a 'from-idea-to-market' perspective among our R&D people, working together across departments in a completely new way.

I would recommend the FORTH method to anyone who is tasked with disruptive innovation.

Yours Sincerely

Luca Rossi

Vice President Product Research & Consumable Development

Philip Morris Products S.A.
Quai Jeanrenaud 3, 2000 Neuchâtel, Switzerland

Online is here to stay

Is working from home or being able to work from anywhere here to stay? The answer is a clear, YES. As you can see in the chart below, in polls among professionals on LinkedIn[3] an overwhelming 70% of more than 8,000 people answered yes. Seventy-seven percent feel more productive at home than in the office, and 74% said they feel more entrepreneurial than before. The Covid-19 crisis and consequent lockdowns have changed the way we work. Working remotely in teams will be a common good, as will be innovating 100% online.

Would you be open to working from home, permanently?

Yes	70 %
No	30%

8,388 votes

Do you feel you're more productive while working from home or less productive?

More productive	77%
Less productive	23%

11,187 votes

Has remote work brought out the'hustler' in you (more grit, initiative, creativity,...)? Are you feeling more 'entrepeneurial' than before?

Yes	74%
No	26%

4,681 votes

Four benefits of innovating online

As you read in previous chapters, innovating online gives us new insights into the way we can innovate in our organisations. And while practising it, we discovered four benefits of online innovation over offline innovation processes.

Information is always accessible. The online collaboration boards with all the insights, customer frictions, ideas, concepts, test results, and new business cases are always accessible for the whole team. It's convenient when you want to add something, check it, or change it.

It provides individual flexibility. Now that collaboration boards are online, people can work on them asynchronously instead of performing all activities in the workshop and the rest of the team, which gives you flexibility as a participant.

It's easy to apply. When you work together with others from all over the country, continent, or even all over the globe, innovating entirely online is an easy way to create together while being in different time zones.

It's easy to share. All the insights, customer frictions, ideas, concepts, test results, and new business cases are digital, which means it's very easy to share with someone else. As you saw in the phase of testing concepts with customers, this is quite handy using, for example, Google Forms, or when you want to share the process or the results with others within the organisation.

These online benefits make innovation easier and the innovation process more efficient.

New AR/VR tools will help create magical moments online.

Although online workshops have these advantages, the Achilles' heel is the participants' low engagement, making it hard to share emotions and get into a 'group flow' with a high energy wave of excitement in your team.

We are very glad that many new tools are emerging for virtual meetings, which are powered by augmented reality and/or virtual reality. In these virtual spaces designed as actual rooms, our lifelike avatar talks, moves, and interacts, mirroring in-person collaborative sessions. It looks very promising as it might increase our engagement and help us experience magical moments online together.

The AR/VR tool Spatial brings people together for hangouts, team planning, and brainstorms in 3D based on AR/VR technology headsets like Quest, Nreal, HoloLens, and Magic Leap. Spatial enables you to sit next to others from across the world. It feels like science fiction because your lifelike 3D avatar interacts like an in-person collaborative session. Your monitor and your hands are your mouse, expressing and sharing ideas with whiteboarding, notes, and photos. Spatial officially supports 30 participants in VR, with an additional 20 joining from the browser spectator mode. At the end of 2020, they introduced their Augmented Reality app for iOS and Android, which runs on almost any current generation of mobile devices. You hold up your phone, and you are an active part of any virtual meeting and see lifelike avatars of co-workers right in your living room.

MeetinVR is another app with great avatars and a great user interface inside and outside VR. Besides that, it has interactive elements that increase engagement in meetings. It's easy to pick up a pen and produce a writing surface of your own chosen size and colour, starting to brainstorm while holding it in your hand. Then you take the post-it or paper and quickly snap it to a wall. It increases engagement, and that's the Achilles' heel of online workshops now with online collaboration platforms in 2D.

VISPA also launched a tool for remote collaboration in 3D virtual spaces. The participants can move freely through a 3D environment and interact with all workshop elements they encounter, answer questions, generate ideas, vote the best one, and give feedback. The advantage is that VISPA creates interaction between people, which provides you with a real workshop feeling. After the real-time workshop, you can go back to the room, show it to other colleagues or stakeholders and elaborate on the original workshop outcomes.

Sparked by the Covid-19 crisis, a lot of VR apps became available. Next to the three mentioned, we found a long list of others, like Virtualist, Glue, FrameVR, BigScreen VR, Rumii, Mozilla Hubs, AltSpace, and Rec Room Immersed. We are pretty confident that further evolution of these AR/VR tools will help us create 'group flow' with a high energy wave of excitement in our online workshops in the near future.

The future of innovation projects is hybrid.
What will the future of innovation projects look like? Will we all go back to in-person workshops with the original 3M post-its because we miss personal contact with our team members and the excitement of group flow? Or will we keep innovating online from home or from anywhere behind our laptop or iPad without traveling?

In our vision, we combine the best of both 'the online and offline world', which leads to hybrid innovation projects. Working remotely in innovation teams will be the common good. So, innovating 100% online will be the starting point, as the benefits of innovating online are quite clear: it's easy, efficient, and flexible.

At this point, however, the lack of personal connection, missing joint experience of emotions, and low likelihood of getting into a group flow using online tools make us choose for some offline workshops for reasons of effectiveness. In choosing which activities and workshops to do online or offline we will match them with the benefits of each way of innovating in the next chart. Do we choose efficiency of online working or do we need offline workshops' effectiveness? That's the question.

Innovation project activities	Aligning people	Gathering information	Discovering customer insights	Sharing information	Ideating	Testing	Improving	Deciding
ONLINE efficiency								
OFFLINE effectiveness								

As you can see in this chart, we choose to gather information, share information, test concepts, and improve them online for sake of efficiency. To align people on the innovation team and to decide which concepts to develop we prefer the effectiveness of offline workshops. These two activities can be done, or should be done, both offline and online.

First of all, there's a very important activity of discovering customer insights. Because a great innovation is a new solution for relevant customer friction, this activity is crucial for every innovation project's success. Discovering customer insights always focuses on finding out WHY people prefer what they prefer and do what they do. When you have clients all over the world, it's efficient to do it online. When you have millions of customers like in consumer goods or services it's also efficient to do it online. But I have experienced myself many times that you get better insights offline while visiting customers live. Making real contact with them leads most of the time to a more open attitude, deeper conversations and, as a consequence, better customer insights. So, when you work in mass markets, consider doing both: visiting a small selection of customers live and interviewing a large selection of customers online.

Then we have the ideating of new ideas. We have great experience in facilitating ideation for more than 250 innovation projects offline. And our structured way of ideation leads to great results with often more than a thousand ideas in a workshop. In those ideation sessions, you can feel moments of great energy in the room when people share their ideas and build upon others' ideas. Interestingly enough, we also get in our online brainstorms more than a thousand ideas, as you can see in this chart. So, getting quality by quantity is possible both online and offline.

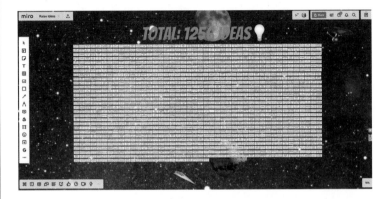

You can see, feel, and hear the team's enthusiasm, energy, and the WoW emotions driving the offline ideation process. The big difference with working online is that you can't experience this with the present collaboration whiteboards and video conferencing tools while ideating online.

Ideating with an innovation team of twenty or more people is an experience offline, often in a special venue in the middle of nowhere . It's a 'moment of togetherness' where people connect, share emotions, and celebrate together, which greatly impacts their relations, not only during the innovation project but also beyond that. An experience like it is not feasible yet online; we prefer to organise the ideating activity as a 'live' event.

Online ideation on collaboration whiteboards like Mural or Miro has five valuable extra benefits we experienced in our innovation projects:
1. As you ideate online in silence, the ideation process empowers more introverted and reflective personalities.
2. ll ideas are easy to read as they are typed instead of being handwritten on post-its.

3. The voting features of tools like Miro are much quicker than the alternative to mark the post-its you prefer with dots and counting all the dots by hand.
4. Since all ideas are digitally stored on the online white-board, you can easily access them later for review.
5. Sharing ideas with others within the organisation is very easy.

For reasons of togetherness, group flow, sharing positive emotions, we prefer ideating in a live event. But because online tools empower more reflective and introverted people and have excellent voting features, we suggest ideating in a 'live' set-up using online collaboration boards. Another advantage is that all ideas are digitised, making it easy to reflect on them later and share them within your organisation.

A Hybrid Innovation process in practice
To see how the hybrid model works in practice, we apply it to the FORTH innovation methodology, presented to you in Chapter 10. We use as a starting point the original set-up of the methodology, which, at its origin, was facilitated 100% offline.

As you know, the methodology, depicted as an innovation journey, consists of 15 workshops in five phases: Full Steam Ahead, Observe and Learn, Raise Ideas, and Test Ideas. We will discuss each workshop and its character to determine whether to facilitate it offline or online. In this way, you may learn the reasons behind it, and you will be able to apply it to the methodologies you use online yourself.

1. **Innovation Focus workshop**
In the innovation focus workshop, a small group of decision-makers discusses and determines the assignment for the innovation journey. They know each other very well and, for the sake of efficiency, this could very well take place **online**.

2. **Core Team Introduction Meeting**
The core team introduction meeting takes place the night before the kickoff. It's the moment when the members of the innovation team meet for the first time. Because the goal is to get better acquainted and build teams, it should come as no surprise that we prefer to facilitate this **offline**.

3. **Kickoff workshop**
At the kickoff workshop, the whole team meets for the first time. The innovation assignment is discussed and the team brainstorms innovation opportunities to be explored in the

next step, Observe and Learn. For team building and motivational reasons, it makes the most sense to facilitate this workshop **offline**.

4. Explore Preparation workshop

The Explore Preparation workshop is an instruction workshop with the core team to empower them to start discovering. For efficiency, you can do it **online**.

5. Exploring Trends and Technology

Exploring Trends and Technology is an individual activity for core team members. For efficiency, this can take place very well 100% **online**. You might invite subject matter experts as guest speakers in Observe and Learn workshops where the information is shared with the total team.

6. Discovering Customer Frictions

Discovering customer insights is a very important and inspiring activity of the core team. It can be facilitated in online personal interviews with customers or online group discussions with customers. Of course, it's efficient to facilitate it **online**. It might be wise to take it offline in some cases, which we will discuss later in this chapter.

7. Exploring Innovation Opportunities

Individually each core team member explores one innovation opportunity to learn the 'ins and outs', which could be well done **online**.

8. Four Observe and Learn workshops

In Observe and Learn workshops, the core team shares information on the opportunities, trends, technology, and customer insights with the total team. It works excellently to do this **online** and is efficient in this way, too.

9. New Product Brainstorm

As we call it these days, the new product brainstorm, or ideation workshop, is an offline two-day workshop and five shorter online three-hour workshops. You know it works either way. For togetherness, group flow, and sharing positive emotions we prefer ideating **offline**, using an online collaboration platform like Miro.

10. First Concept Improvement workshop

Based on the 'tops and tips' of the initial concepts, we improve all of them in this first concept improvement workshop with the core team for which an **online** setting would work great.

11. Concept Testing

In concept testing, we test the concept statements among potential target groups to see how they resonate and get input to make them better. Concept testing works fine **online**. However, when you are working business-to-business, you might also consider personal interviews offline to pay individual customers more regard if that resonates with them.

12. Second Concept Improvement workshop

Based on the customer feedback, the total team will improve all concepts and choose the final three to five improved concepts to be worked out as a mini new business case. For efficiency, an **online** workshop will do the job fine.

13. Four Mini New Business Case workshops

In pairs, the core team members transform the concept into a mini new business case. In four mini new business case workshops, they share their work in progress while getting 'tops and tips' from the other core team members. Doing this **online** works great.

14. End Presentation

Core team members are gathered to present the mini new business cases to the decision-making managers, deciding, on the spot, which of the business cases they will take into development in their regular R&D stage-gated process. Of course, for togetherness and sharing positive emotions at the end of a real innovation expedition, we prefer an **offline** event.

15. Concept Transfer workshop

After the FORTH project is officially finished, we facilitate another workshop to transfer the concept from the ideating FORTH team to the development team, which could be done **online** for the sake of efficiency.

In the following chart you will see the hybrid FORTH innovation process overview with all the workshops just described. It becomes instantly clear that in the 15-week journey, there are three touch-points with the total team in live workshops: at the kick-off, at the ideation workshop, and at the end presentation. All the other activities and workshops can be facilitated efficiently and effectively online.

CHART: THE HYBRID FORTH INNOVATION PROCESS
(NEXT PAGE)

Depending on your sector and your innovation assignment, discovering customer insights and concept testing might be taken 'live' to enhance the team's impact on the clients interviewed. This could be when you're innovating in a business-to-business setting supplying tools to Wind Energy Farms and you want to understand the user behaviour. Watching Wind turbines being repaired live would add substantial value to interviewing repair professionals online.

Innovating 100% online really works, we have experienced. And this experience we just shared with you. Hybrid innovation projects mixing online and offline events combine the best of both worlds and are effective and efficient. New VR/AR tools will enable us to interact better and experience more emotions online to increase our innovation effectiveness.

Whenever online, offline, or hybrid; we wish you wonderful innovation expeditions.

[1] Robert G. Cooper, Winning at New Products, Basic Books, New York, 2011, p. 18.
[2] Stevens, G.A. and Burley, J.,'3000 Raw Ideas = 1 Commercial Success!', (May/June 1997) research Technology Management, Vol. 40, #3, pp. 17-27.
[3] Ryan Holmes, December 2020, https://medium.com/the-helm/i-asked-1-7-million-people-about-remote-work-heres-what-they-said-6e1235c1e005

THE HYBRID FORTH INNOVATION PROCESS

| | ONLINE COLLABORATION BOARD | INNOVATION ASSIGNMENT IDEATION TEAM FORTH PLANNING INNOVATION OPPORTINUTIES |

ONLINE COLLABORATION BOARD

INNOVATION ASSIGNMENT
IDEATION TEAM
FORTH PLANNING
INNOVATION OPPORTINUTIES

ONLINE ACTIVITIES

ONLINE WORKSHOPS

1. innovation focus workshop

FULL STEAM AHEAD

PHASE

TEST IDEAS

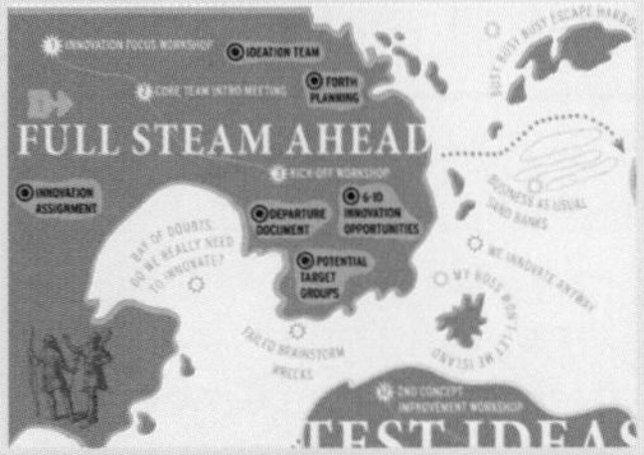

OFFLINE WORKSHOPS

2. core team meeting
3. kick-off workshop

The numbers of the workshops and activities match the numbers on the FORTH map.

ONLINE INNOVATION

INSPIRATION FROM THE INNOVATION OPPORTUNITIES CUSTOMER FRICTIONS	500-750+ IDEAS 30-40 IDEA DIRECTIONS 12-15 CONCEPTS 12-15 IMPROVED CONCEPTS	CONCEPT TESTING RESULTS 12-15 IMPROVED CONCEPTS 3-5 CONCEPTS CHOSEN	3-5 MINI NEW BUSINESS CASES IMPLEMENTATION PLAN

↑

5. Exploring trends & technology
6. Discovering customer frictions
7. Exploring innovation opportunities

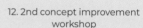 

11. concept testing

↑ ↑

4. exploration preparation workshop
8. 4 observe& learn workshops

10. 1st concept improvement workshop

12. 2nd concept improvement workshop

13. 4 mini new business case workshops
14. concept transfer workshop

↑ ↑ ↑ ↑

9. New product brainstorm

14. Final presentation

CONTENTS

TOOLKIT 25 ONLINE TOOLS FOR INNOVATION

This toolkit lays out 25 online tools for you to kick-start your innovation workshops and – projects 100% online. Section 1 covers 7 online collaboration platforms like Miro and Mural. Section 2 presents 6 video conferencing tools. Of course, we included Zoom, but we advise you to have a look at runner-up Butter too. Section 3 describes 4 tools for preparation and instruction, among which SessionLab to get your agenda straight and Loom to make great instruction videos. Section 4 introduces 5 tools for proto-typing and testing, including Marvel and Toonly. In section 5, you find 3 tools to make your online workshops more interactive, like Mentimeter and Tscheck.in. We assessed all tools. Their overall rating you find in the title of each tool. We rated our most favourite ones with five stars.

1. ONLINE COLLABORATION PLATFORMS

TOOL 1: MIRO
REVIEWED BY MARIA VITTORIA COLUCCI

OVERALL RATING

***** (5 out of 5 stars). Miro is a powerful - and flexible tool that facilitates me to apply all the innovation techniques for all my innovation workshops.

WEBSITE

www.miro.com

WHAT?

Miro is a cloud-based collaboration tool. It features a digital whiteboard on which you can go from ideation to execution on an infinite canvas. It's scalable, includes 100+ pre-built templates and works cross-device. Together with Mural, it's one of today's most popular and trusted tools to co-create online. There is a free version available with a limited set of boards.

WHY?

I love Miro because I can design my workshops' flow and interactions with participants functionally and engagingly. I can create spaces for individual workshop sections or subgroups to work together on different innovation method tasks. It has mindmaps, Kanban tables and hundreds of ready-to-use posts-its that you prepare for your participants to use. I can also upload slides, images, formats and use it as the only board to share. I can create my template to improve and reuse and to share with other co-facilitators. I also enjoy the timer, which everyone can see and hear, so I don't need to inform people about time left for the exercises. Participants don't need to have a Miro account and can access the board through a link. Miro has many useful features for online facili-tation, such as anonymous voting, writing post-its in bulk mode, and design tools to make the participant experience immersive and engaging.

EASE OF USE FOR NEW PARTICIPANTS

*** (3 out of 5 stars). 3 is an average value as people love it for the infinite possibilities it gives them, while others are frustrated not being able to write post-its or to use it smoothly. If your participants have never used it, you will need some time to teach them the basic features and let them get used to it. For this reason, I suggest you send the link to the board with some explanations a few days in advance and set aside some time at the beginning of the workshop to give some tips on how to use it and let people try it out.

EASE OF USE FOR FACILITATORS

**** (4 out of 5 stars). If you've never used it, you'll need some time to learn.

FIT TO METHOD

I find Miro super flexible; you can use it with all the methods mentioned in this book. All the FORTH templates are made in Miro and in Miroverse, the community templates gallery. You can also find here templates that fit some other innovation methods, like problem framing or design sprint.

FIT TO TECHNIQUES

In Miro, I apply 7 of the techniques for online innovation mentioned in the book: Asynchronous work; if the team has to work between the workshops, I leave frames and templates they need to use with clear instructions, then I can see if and when someone is working on it, so I can monitor the progress. Working together-alone, I prepare settings and post-its to let people brainwriting in silence. I always suggest using the Bulk mode to write ideas on post-its for two reasons: people won't struggle with post-its; they just have to write and are not influenced by others. Voting anonymous; I use this a lot, and when possible, I prepare the voting session in advance. Chat function; I use it mainly during the asynchronous work to give feedback and answer questions. Lightning Demo; I prepare the frame and spaces in advance.

KILLER FEATURE

With no doubt, the killer feature is the bulk mode. It allows participants to concentrate only on their ideas without worrying about selecting the arrow, moving the post-its, and change style and colour.

TECHNICAL REQUIREMENTS

Miro is browser-based. It works best with Google Chrome. It doesn't work well on Internet Explorer in my experience. There is also an app-version of Miro for desktop, and you can use it on your mobile.

DEVICE TYPE

Mobile.
Tablet.
Desktop.

AVOID IF

I avoid using Miro for short workshops when participants have never used it, and I'm not going to use it again with them. In that case, other tools are easier to use.

TOOL 2: MURAL
REVIEWED BY FLORIAN HAMEISTER

OVERALL RATING

***** (5 out of 5 stars). Mural is, for me, the best and most intuitive tool for remote facilitation at the moment; I love to work with it.

WEBSITE

www.mural.com

WHAT?

Mural is a cloud-based collaboration tool. It features a digital whiteboard on which you can go from ideation to execution on an almost infinite canvas. It's scalable, includes 100+ pre-built templates and works cross-device. Together with Miro, it's one of today's most popular and trusted tools to create together online.

I love Mural because it is so intuitive for me as a facilitator and also for my participants. The tool is designed for workshops, and I love the possibilities you have with designing your boards. I can really create an experience for my participants. With that, it is the perfect place for innovation processes with all their different stages that need space for insights, creativity and focus. You can design your process here. The participants can work all together at the same time or when it suits you, as on Miro.

EASE OF USE FOR NEW PARTICIPANTS

***** (5 out of 5 stars) It is very intuitive for first-time users.

EASE OF USE FOR FACILITATORS

***** (5 out of 5 stars) It gets a 5-star rating for facilitators because it has everything relevant for workshops. It's easy to use and gives me as a facilitator all the possibilities I need to make and facilitate an awesome workshop.

FIT TO METHOD

As Mural is a whiteboard, you can use it for all the methods mentioned, as it is super flexible. I am in favour of designing structured processes, and that works perfectly here.

FIT TO TECHNIQUES

With Mural, I apply the following 6 techniques for online innovation. Working synchronous-asynchronous with sharing the board link with exercises before and after the workshop. Working together-alone during the workshop and also using the voting anonymous for getting unbiased feedback. For preparation of ideation workshops, I use Lightning Demo. Mural boards, I like to design, so it fits the company and the innovation phase (virtual room design).

KILLER FEATURE

Its facilitation superpower is the feature that makes the difference. You can get all participants together and hold them together. These are features that help you run a productive workshop.

TECHNICAL REQUIREMENTS

Mural is browser-based and works best with Google Chrome. It also has an application for Mac and mobile.

DEVICE TYPE

Mobile (scan post-it, limited functions).
Tablet (scan post-it, limited functions).
Desktop (full function).

AVOID IF

As it is cloud-based, you might experience internet security arguments with Mural. I avoid Mural if the internet speed of my participants is slow, then it gets hard to use Mural.

TOOL 3: TRELLO
REVIEWED BY ANDREW CONSTABLE

OVERALL RATING

**** (4 out of 5 stars). A very versatile platform and easy to use.

WEBSITE

www.trello.com

WHAT?

Trello is a 'highly visual' work management app. It draws on the principles of Kanban, a method of visualising workflows, to provide an overview of a project from start to finish. This is done using Trello's boards, lists and cards. A board focuses on a specific project, like an innovation challenge. Each board contains lists that may, for example, indicate the steps of the method used. The cards within the lists hold information on a specific task.

WHY?

I like Trello as it's a visual way for teams to collaborate. Without a lot of effort, I can bring other people together to digitally work on various types of projects, among which innovation. In one glance, Trello tells me what's being worked on, who's working on what, and where something is in a process.

EASE OF USE FOR NEW PARTICIPANTS
**** (4 out of 5 stars).

EASE OF USE FOR FACILITATORS
**** (4 out of 5 stars).

FIT TO METHOD
Although Trello is not a whiteboard like Miro or Mural and is less flexible, I still use Trello for all the online innovation methods mentioned.

FIT TO TECHNIQUES
In Trello, I apply the following 3 techniques for online innovation: working synchronous-asynchronous. Working together-alone. Visualisation.

KILLER FEATURE
I guess that the killer feature of Trello is that people can use it in so many different ways, even to plan your marriage :-).

TECHNICAL REQUIREMENTS
On the desktop, Trello supports Chrome, Safari, Firefox and Edge browsers. The Trello app is available for IOS and Android. The Trello Desktop App is available for macOS and Windows.

DEVICE TYPE
Mobile.
Tablet.
Desktop.

AVOID IF
I tend to avoid Trello when you have a lot of convergence processes, moments of choice in your online innovation project. Other tools like Miro offer you a better anonymous voting tool.

TOOL 4: PADLET
REVIEWED BY FLORIAN HAMEISTER

OVERALL RATING
**** (4 out of 5 stars).

WEBSITE
www.padlet.com

WHAT?
Padlet is a website that provides users with a digital canvas. Users can post text, videos and images from a mobile device or a desktop. Multiple users can post at the same time. It is a great visual tool that could be used as an inspiration board for a brainstorm session or as a board for sharing pdf files, videos and other stuff you want to share. You can also adjust the look and feel if you want to change the design according to your branding or personal taste. For each board, you can create a unique URL and a password. You can also easily generate a QR-code with the URL to share with your team.

WHY?
I use Padlet, for example, to collect inspiration for an ideation session, like pictures, video's, favourite innovations, links to websites, et cetera. I also use it as a source for energisers and warm-ups. And it is also useful to share documents like pdfs and other files in an organised way when you want your team to have easy access.

EASE OF USE FOR NEW PARTICIPANTS
***** (5 out of 5 stars) It's very simple and intuitive.

EASE OF USE FOR FACILITATORS
**** (4 out of 5 stars) It's very simple and intuitive but also limited to innovation workshops.

FIT TO METHOD
Padlet fits any method where you need an inspiration board or where you need an organised easy overview of relevant content, like, for example, in a Design sprint or in the FORTH innovation method. It is less applicable for short sessions like the Lightning Decision Jam.

FIT TO TECHNIQUES
You could do synchronous and a-synchronous work with Padlet and also put Lightning Demo on it. I just use it for sharing and not as a tool to use in workshops themselves.

You are able to adjust the look and feel if you want to change the design according to your branding or personal taste.

TECHNICAL REQUIREMENTS

Padlet is available for IOS, Android, Mac and Windows.

DEVICE TYPE

Mobile.
Tablet.
Desktop.

AVOID IF

There is no specific reason to avoid Padlet.

TOOL 5: SLACK
REVIEWED BY ANDREW CONSTABLE

OVERALL RATING

*** (3 out of 5 stars). A good alternative to email and instant message, although it can be overkill for small projects.

WEBSITE

www.slack.com

WHAT?

Slack is a communication medium that is billed as an alternative to email. I use Slack across various options of communication such as channels, private groups and direct messaging. As this is similar to email, I share documents, files across teams and in a one-to-one format.
I add apps, for example, from Miro. Pushing activity from my Miro boards to Slack keeps everyone on my team aware of new comments, mentions, projects, or team activities.

WHY?

Innovation projects can become disjointed unless you ensure that you have a clear and concise communication channel. As an Innovation facilitator, I set up specific channels per project to keep everyone informed of the project updates.

EASE OF USE FOR NEW PARTICIPANTS

*** (3 out of 5 stars).

EASE OF USE FOR FACILITATORS

*** (3 out of 5 stars).

FIT TO METHOD

As Slack is a communication tool, I use Slack for all the innovation methods mentioned when keeping my project team updated.

FIT TO TECHNIQUES

I use this communication medium to share files, keep my team updated and provide asynchronous work opportunities.

KILLER FEATURE

I love the killer feature, which combines instant messaging and email, but all in one channel to promote a more effective communication medium in the project I am managing.

TECHNICAL REQUIREMENTS

Slack is available for IOS, Android, Mac and Windows.

DEVICE TYPE

Mobile.
Tablet.
Desktop.

AVOID IF

I tend to avoid Slack when the project environment is very small, and there are limited messages being sent between individuals in my project team.

TOOL 6: HOWSPACE
REVIEWED BY FLORIAN HAMEISTER

OVERALL RATING

**** (4 out of 5 stars). Howspace is an impressive tool with a lot of potential for remote workshops.

WEBSITE

www.howspace.com

Howspace is an AI-powered digital collaboration tool that has quite a lot of awesome features that help you to engage your participants before, during and after the online workshops.

WHY?

The social aspect of online innovation journeys is an Achilles heel. Using this tool can help to get people connected and engaged on a social level as well as on a professional level. I tested Howspace, and I believe in the power of the tool. Especially because it is so flexible and is the one spot where all participants can share their thoughts with the group in a very simple way. The AI helps you to get insights into chats, word clouds or polls. I personally do not use it at the moment, because it is quite expensive, and I also have the feeling that people are overwhelmed with so many tools.

EASE OF USE FOR NEW PARTICIPANTS

***** (5 out of 5 stars). It is very intuitive as it works as a platform.

EASE OF USE FOR FACILITATORS

**** (4 out of 5 stars). As a facilitator, you need to dig into the tool a little bit to understand how it all works. The AI-support is something that really helps us as facilitators.

FIT TO METHOD

It is not for a specific method; it is more for social connection and learning. That takes part in all methods.

FIT TO TECHNIQUES

Working a-synchronous and synchronous. Working together alone and voting anonymous. Use break out rooms. Lightning demos. Using questionnaires and polls. Use the chat function. Design a virtual room.

KILLER FEATURE

For me, the killer feature is AI that helps to analyse and summarise the answers and comments in no time. It's great that Howspace operates like a website. Everybody knows how to use it.

TECHNICAL REQUIREMENTS

Howspace is browser based.

DEVICE TYPE

Mobile.
Tablet.
Desktop.

AVOID IF

Avoid Howspace when you want to use it for small groups and for one-time usage, from the facilitator side. It is quite costly too.

TOOL 7: KLAXOON
REVIEWED BY FLORIAN HAMEISTER

OVERALL RATING

*** (3 out of 5 stars). It's a cool idea to have an all-in-one tool, but for me personally not very user-friendly.

WEBSITE

www.klaxoon.com

WHAT?

Klaxoon claims to be the full suite of collaborative tools for efficient teamwork. Besides a whiteboard, it has a video conference tool and engagement tools like surveys, questions, quizzes, adventures and mission features.

WHY?

It combines video conferencing, documentation, surveys as well as a whiteboard in one platform. I like the concept behind it. But for me, as an innovation facilitator, it is too complicated. It is the opposite of Mural. It wants to cover everything, and that makes the user experience not really intuitive.

EASE OF USE FOR NEW PARTICIPANTS

*** (3 out of 5 stars). I think the whiteboard is not as simple and easy as Mural or Miro.

*** (3 out of 5 stars). I tried to understand it, but I lost interest very quickly because the user experience was not good.

FIT TO METHOD

As Klaxoon has also a good whiteboard, you can use it for all the methods mentioned, as it is super flexible.

FIT TO TECHNIQUES

Working a-synchronous and synchronous. Working together alone and voting anonymous. Lightning demos. Using questionnaires and polls. Design a virtual room.

KILLER FEATURE

What is really great is that you can change your whiteboard into columns or lists and back via a button. With a lot of filter options, you can export very easy all needed information in the wanted format.

TECHNICAL REQUIREMENTS

It is browser-based.

DEVICE TYPE

Mobile.

Tablet.

Desktop.

AVOID IF

Avoid it as a facilitator for one-time-use only because it is quite complex.

2. VIDEOCONFERENCING TOOLS

TOOL 8: ZOOM
REVIEWED BY ANDREW CONSTABLE

OVERALL RATING

***** (5 out of 5 stars). One of the best, great for facilitators due to breakout rooms.

WEBSITE

www.zoom.us

WHAT?

Zoom is a cloud-based videoconferencing tool that allows you to set up virtual video and audio conferencing. I tend to use the chat option as well as screen-sharing, breakout rooms and other collaborative capabilities. For more interaction, there is the option to do an online poll which I find very good to use. Zoom has the gallery view mode that allows you to see every person on the call at once, which, as a facilitator, allows me to manage the session better.

WHY?

A big part of Zoom's appeal to me is its simplicity. It's easy to get started, the app is lightweight, and the interface is relatively intuitive to use.

EASE OF USE FOR NEW PARTICIPANTS

***** (5 out of 5 stars).

EASE OF USE FOR FACILITATORS

***** (5 out of 5 stars).

FIT TO METHOD

As Zoom is a video conferencing tool, I use it with all the innovation methods mentioned for communication and collaboration.

I use it across these techniques: working synchronous-a-synchronous and working together-alone during the video-conference by muting yourself and using the chat function. Working in break out rooms.

I love the killer feature of break out rooms, which are great for collaboration in smaller teams.

Zoom works on Windows, Mac, iOS and Android. You can use the app or use it via a web browser.

Mobile.

Tablet.

Desktop.

I tend to avoid only when the security restrictions of your organisation don't allow using Zoom. Otherwise, it's my go-to video conferencing tool.

TOOL 9: MICROSOFT TEAMS
REVIEWED BY MARIA VITTORIA COLUCCI

*** (3 out of 5 stars). The user experience of Microsoft Teams is limited as you can only see 9 participants (50 with the extended view, which is not stable).

www.microsoft.com/en-ww/microsoft-teams

Microsoft Teams is a unified communication and collaboration platform combining videoconferencing, chat, and content sharing. The service integrates with the Microsoft 365 suite and has end-to-end security standards. This made Teams very popular in companies and preferred over other

cloud-based or open-source video conferencing tools. In my experience, big companies often ask to use it. There is a free version in which video calls last up to 60 minutes. The gallery view is limited to 9 people. The others being in small circles at the bottom of the screen. This means that you and the rest of the people don't see each other. There's also an extended gallery mode, but in my experience, there is significantly more delay in videos when using this model.

It is the most popular platform in companies, and participants probably already use it in their day-by-day work. You can use channels and calendar to share with the team.

**** (4 out of 5 stars) Usually, you use Microsoft Teams as the company already uses it, so project teams know how to use it.

*** (3 out of 5 stars) I assessed it with 3 because when you're using Teams with a team working in a company, either you ask for an internal account or you have some limitations, for example, accessing the channels or getting notifications.

Teams is a video conferencing tool, so you can use it with all the innovation methods mentioned.

On Teams, I've applied the following four techniques for online innovation: a-synchronous work, using the channel feature. Working together-alone, asking participants to mute themselves. The chat function and the reactions to communicate. Break out rooms. You can title each room and send people randomly or not, broadcast messages, while you cannot switch participants among rooms once you've set. And this limits you a bit as a facilitator. The Teams chat remains available also after the meeting is finished. So, if you need to pick information or feedback, you will find it easily.

The availability of channels to communicate with the team on different topics, to share documents and to have continuous conversations during the asynchronous work are the killer features. As it's integrated with the company email, people get notifications; you can call them during instant meetings, as they're always on.

TECHNICAL REQUIREMENTS
Microsoft Teams is browser based and works on desktop and mobile devices.

DEVICE TYPE
Mobile.
Tablet.
Desktop.

AVOID IF
I usually use it when the company asks for it. I prefer not to use it if I need more flexibility, to change settings easily during the workshop or to have engaging interaction between participants.

TOOL 10: BUTTER
BY FLORIAN HAMEISTER

OVERALL RATING
***** (5 out of 5 stars). Butter focuses on remote workshops and really understands what is needed. I love it.

WEBSITE
www.butter.io

WHAT?
Butter is an all-in-one platform with all the tools you need to host interactive workshops and training sessions.

WHY?
Butter is my new favourite video conferencing tool for workshops. It is easy to use. It combines a videoconference tool with an agenda planner, polls, questions, Miro-integration and good interaction tools, cool music and a fun design that makes videoconferencing an experience.

EASE OF USE FOR NEW PARTICIPANTS
***** (5 out of 5 stars) Butter creates an awesome user experience.

EASE OF USE FOR FACILITATORS
***** (5 out of 5 stars) It focuses on facilitators. With all the features, it helps me to make awesome workshops and helps me to focus on facilitation.

FIT TO METHOD
Butter is a video conferencing tool, so you can use it with all the innovation methods mentioned.

FIT TO TECHNIQUES
You can apply the following techniques for online innovation: working together-alone during the videoconference by muting yourself. Using the chat function and doing polls. Butter also provides break out rooms.

KILLER FEATURE
My killer feature is that I can design workshops up-front with agendas, polls, breakout sessions, timer, et cetera in one tool. Templates I can use over and over again.

TECHNICAL REQUIREMENTS
It is browser based, and we recommend using Chrome.

DEVICE TYPE
Mobile.
Tablet.
Desktop.

AVOID IF
There are some incompatibilities of Butter with browsers like Explorer or Edge. In some cases, participants are not able to connect their video and audio.

TOOL 11: JITSI MEET
REVIEWED BY MARIA VITTORIA COLUCCI

OVERALL RATING
*** (3 out of 5 stars). My overall rating is only 3 as Jitsi has no

break out rooms, and the layout is not very engaging.

WEBSITE
www.jitsi.org/jitsi-meet

WHAT?
Jitsi Meet is a free, open-source, time-free system for making video calls. It does not require registration or the installation of any software. You can use it from your browser, giving it the necessary permissions to manage your computer's microphone and webcam.

WHY?
It's super easy; it allows you to make video calls at the touch of a button, literally.

EASE OF USE FOR NEW PARTICIPANTS
***** (5 out of 5 stars). Jitsi is easy to use for participants.

EASE OF USE FOR FACILITATORS
***** (5 out of 5 stars). Jitsi scores a 5 as it is extremely easy. With 2 clicks, without a download, you can start a meeting as a facilitator.

FIT TO METHOD
Jitsi Meet is a video conferencing tool, so you can use it with many methods. I don't use it working with companies as it's not known by them, and there can be security restrictions. Jitsi doesn't provide break out rooms, so I won't suggest it for large groups.

FIT TO TECHNIQUES
On Jitsi Meet, I've applied two techniques for online innovation: work together-alone during the videoconference by muting the group. Using the chat function, reactions are unfortunately limited to raising your hand.

KILLER FEATURE
You can directly embed a YouTube video in Jitsi Meet and show it to all participants. If you connect it with your YouTube account, you can do live streaming.

TECHNICAL REQUIREMENTS
You need a browser or the Jitsi legacy desktop app. There are some incompatibilities with Google Chrome on some versions of Windows. I recommend using Mozilla Firefox.

DEVICE TYPE
Mobile.
Tablet.
Desktop.

AVOID IF
I avoid Jitsi Meet when I work with companies and with large groups as break out rooms is not provided.

TOOL 12: WONDER.ME
REVIEWED BY FLORIAN HAMEISTER

OVERALL RATING
**** (4 out of 5 stars). Wonder.me is simple to use, and the background can be personalised. That helps to create an atmosphere on the workshop topic. For personal interaction Wonder.me is nice.

WEBSITE
www.wonder.me

WHAT?
Wonder.me is a virtual space where people can meet and talk. Participants can see who is speaking to whom. They can move their avatars around with their mouse. To join a conversation, they move closer; to leave it, they move away.

WHY?
It is not only a videoconferencing tool, Wonder.me enhances the social interaction because simple one-one - and small group talks are possible. I like to use it for workshops where you do a lot of work in smaller groups. I also use it in longer projects to host informal meetings.

EASE OF USE FOR NEW PARTICIPANTS
***** (5 out of 5 stars) It is very easy to use.

EASE OF USE FOR FACILITATORS
**** (4 out of 5 stars) It is simple to set up, but as a facilitator, it can be challenging to get all people together.

It is a video conferencing tool, so you can use it with almost all the innovation methods.

FIT TO TECHNIQUES

You can apply the following techniques for online innovation: working together-alone during the videoconference by muting yourself. Using the chat function. Break out rooms.

KILLER FEATURE

I love that participants can form easy, intuitive groups on their own.

TECHNICAL REQUIREMENTS

It is browser based.

DEVICE TYPE

Mobile (only audio).
Tablet (only audio).
Desktop.

AVOID IF

I avoid Wonder.me when I have workshops with very structured processes and when people need to be focus on adding content in another digital tool, because in Wonder.me it is easy to start moving around and get distracted.

TOOL 13: GOOGLE MEET
REVIEWED BY ANDREW CONSTABLE

OVERALL RATING

**** (4 out of 5 stars). Simple to use, part of the google suite of apps. The only drawback is the lack of breakout rooms.

WEBSITE

www.meet.google.com

WHAT?

Google Meet is primarily designed as a way to host video meetings. However, I like the ability to enable the camera and microphone independently, so you can just use it for audio calls if you wish, which is great for low bandwidth connec-tions, which I have experienced myself.

WHY?

Google Meet allows me to connect with innovation project team members and customers so I can chat over video and text. As it's integrated into the Google platform, this is a seamless task and can be used across different platforms, which makes it much easier for me when running a workshop or meeting.

EASE OF USE FOR NEW PARTICIPANTS

***** (5 out of 5 stars).

EASE OF USE FOR FACILITATORS

**** (4 out of 5 stars).

FIT TO METHOD

As Google Meet is a communications platform, I use it for all the methods mentioned as it allows for screen share, and the chat function is useful during sessions with my teams.

FIT TO TECHNIQUES

I use Google Meet across the following techniques. The chat function to prevent interruptions in the session. Make videos to show results. Working together - alone, as you can mute yourself and the rest of the meeting when using this platform which is great to stop interference.

KILLER FEATURE

The integrations with the Google platform and 3rd party apps via the app store are great for me and my team's needs.

TECHNICAL REQUIREMENTS

Google Meet is available on the web and on phones and tablets for Android and iOS.

DEVICE TYPE

Mobile.
Tablet.
Desktop.

AVOID IF

I tend to avoid Google Meet when you want to use breakout rooms during your session as currently, as of 2021, there is no function for this.

3. TOOLS FOR PREPARATION & INSTRUCTION

TOOL 14: SESSIONLAB
REVIEWED BY MARIA VITTORIA COLUCCI

OVERALL RATING
***** (5 out of 5 stars). With SessionLab, I create my session templates, simulate different time boxes, share with co-facilitators and review and change after the session.

WEBSITE
 www.sessionlab.com

WHAT?
SessionLab is an online workshop planning platform that allows me to set my agenda, break my content into chunks and outline a session, and organising it into various time blocks. You have different colours for activity types, like ice-breakers, activities, debriefings, and you can add your own categories and colours. It has an inspiring library of activities to integrate into your session and allows you to collaborate with co-facilitators.

WHY?
SessionLab is easy to use. It helps me to plan my workshops with more time awareness, and, especially online, where timeboxes are very short, it's incredibly valuable. When I co-design with colleagues, we share the first draft agenda and ask each other to contribute by changing parts, timebox or adding notes. I have my own templates customised with my logo, and I reuse them, adapt and update. I also look for other facilitators templates to get inspiration. Simply drag and drop exercises and modules in a session plan.

EASE OF USE FOR NEW PARTICIPANTS
Participants don't use it; they receive the easy-to-read agendas. The different parts are outlined with different colours, so they have a broad vision at a glance.

EASE OF USE FOR FACILITATORS
***** (5 out of 5 stars).

FIT TO METHOD
I use it for every method for which you need to make a detailed session plan and planning like the FORTH innovation method, a Design Sprint and a Lean Sprint. You can decide which level of detail to share with participants.

FIT TO TECHNIQUES
It is for session preparation, so it doesn't relate to a specific facilitation technique.

KILLER FEATURE
I like to drag around modules and exercises, while the timing always stays correct. Co-create workshops with my colleagues. It's also of great value for me.

TECHNICAL REQUIREMENTS
It is browser based.

DEVICE TYPE
Tablet.
Desktop.

AVOID IF
I'm using it almost always. However, when I have to run a short workshop where the structure is very simple and straightforward, I skip it.

TOOL 15: BOARDLE
REVIEWED BY MARIA VITTORIA COLUCCI

OVERALL RATING
***** (5 out of 5 stars). I get lots of inspiration as Boardle puts together, all in one, the best of Miro, Mural, Klaxoon templates for the main innovation methods.

WEBSITE
www.boardle.io

WHAT?
Boardle is a tool offering more than 200 templates for remote

workshops, a list of worldwide remote facilitators, and a community to exchange ideas and practices with worldwide facilitators.

I enjoy Boardle as a fantastic source of inspiration for my boards. I can find templates already made by other facilitators and save time. In addition, I have access to an international community of facilitators to share ideas, experiences and thoughts.

EASE OF USE FOR NEW PARTICIPANTS

***** (5 out of 5 stars).

EASE OF USE FOR FACILITATORS

***** (5 out of 5 stars).

FIT TO METHOD

Boardle offers ready-made templates for Problem Framing, Prototyping and Pretotyping, Lighting Decision Jam, Design Sprints, as well as templates for brainstorming and creative Icebreakers that you can use in all online innovation methods.

FIT TO TECHNIQUES

Boardle collects templates from boards such as Miro, Mural, Klaxoon, so I've applied all the techniques from those tools, like working asynchronous and synchronous. Working together alone and voting anonymous. Lightning demos. Using questionnaires and polls. Design a virtual room.

KILLER FEATURE

Boards are organised by methodology, technique, and tools. I love to search and get inspired.

TECHNICAL REQUIREMENTS

It is browser based.

DEVICE TYPE

Desktop.

AVOID IF

There's no reason to avoid it unless you think you don't need or want to inspire others ...

TOOL 16: LOOM
REVIEWED BY FLORIAN HAMEISTER

OVERALL RATING

***** (5 out of 5 stars). With just one click, I can record my screen and make instructions. On click more, and I can share the link with my participants. That saves me so much time. I love Loom.

WEBSITE

www.loom.com

WHAT?

Loom is a video messaging tool that helps you get your message across through instantly shareable videos. With Loom, you can record your camera, microphone, and desktop simultaneously.

WHY?

I use Loom extensively for quick explanatory videos, for example, when you want to explain a feature of an online tool while showing how it works on screen. I use Loom too for instructions on exercise participants have to do at home as preparation for a session. For me, it is easier to make a short video showing them the needed context instead of writing it.

EASE OF USE FOR NEW PARTICIPANTS

***** (5 out of 5 stars). Participants just need to watch the video.

EASE OF USE FOR FACILITATORS

**** (4 out of 5 stars). Once installed, it is pretty easy to start a recording.

FIT TO METHOD

Loom can be used for any method where you want to clarify or explain things with a video rather than in text.

FIT TO TECHNIQUES

Record videos to explain tasks or to instruct participants. Working synchronous and a-synchronous.
Set up templates to be filled by participants.

What I love about Loom most is that it's just one click away from being able to record your screen and your face at the same time. Sending the link for the video directly afterwards to the participants is fast and helpful.

TECHNICAL REQUIREMENTS

Mac, Windows, iOS and most web browsers (not on Internet Explorer).

DEVICE TYPE

Mobile.
Tablet.
Desktop.

AVOID IF

You may avoid Loom when you prefer to explain things in writing.

TOOL 17: CALENDLY
REVIEWED BY ANDREW CONSTABLE

OVERALL RATING

***** (5 out of 5 stars). So much easier than going back and forth to arrange the timings of a meeting.

WEBSITE

www.calendly.com

WHAT?

Calendly is an app that offers me a versatile set of features that allow me to schedule one-on-one appointments, group events and team meetings. There is a free version available which I use.

WHY?

My goal is to eliminate the problematic back-and-forth when trying to nail downtimes for a workshop. Rather than email chains and phone tag, I can send my availability with a link, even if the people booking time with you don't use Calendly. It's really a time-saver for me.

EASE OF USE FOR NEW PARTICIPANTS

***** (5 out of 5 stars).

EASE OF USE FOR FACILITATORS

***** (5 out of 5 stars).

FIT TO METHOD

I use Calendly for all methods where you are working with teams and have to schedule workshops.

FIT TO TECHNIQUES

Not relevant.

KILLER FEATURE

Calendly has calendar integrations with Google Calendar, Office 365, Outlook and iCloud Calendar. So I am never double booked. It's one of the best apps I use.

TECHNICAL REQUIREMENTS

No specific requirements.

DEVICE TYPE

Mobile.
Tablet.
Desktop.

AVOID IF

Avoid it when you're still a fan of paper planners and calendars, which I am not. I would recommend you move your manual process to this great app.

4. TOOLS FOR PROTOTYPING & TESTING

TOOL 18: MARVEL
REVIEWED BY RODY VONK

OVERALL RATING
***** (5 out of 5 stars). Your first prototype doesn't have to be perfect at all. Create the first draft quickly so you can learn from user feedback as soon as possible. I definitely recommend Marvel for this purpose when you prototype apps.

WEBSITE
www.marvelapp.com

WHAT?
Marvel helps you transform your pen and paper ideas into an interactive iPhone or Android prototype. Quickly snap your sketches to simulate your app idea. I really like it since you don't need to build a full technical backbone for an app in order to test your very first draft of your idea while giving testers an interactive experience.

WHY?
It is very easy to use and makes it simple to get your ideas out of your head and into a format that you can easily share with people. Marvel saves time and helps you refine and iterate your ideas quickly. I find this tool a great example of how easy you can combine good old sketches with smart technology.

EASE OF USE FOR NEW PARTICIPANTS
As Marvel is a prototyping tool, not a tool for participants in an online workshop, the star rating doesn't apply.

EASE OF USE FOR FACILITATORS
As Marvel is a prototyping tool, not a facilitator's tool, the star rating doesn't apply.

FIT TO METHOD
I find Marvel very useful in any method that aims for building pretotypes and testing simple first drafts quickly, like the FORTH innovation method. Design Sprint. Lean Sprint. Lean Startup. Pretotyping.

FIT TO TECHNIQUES
Creating a prototype with this tool can be helpful when you want to use questionnaires/surveys to gain insights about a digital solution like an app. I would combine the two. Create a questionnaire with what you want to learn from testers with a tool like Google Forms while your target audience is using your prototype created in Marvel.

KILLER FEATURE
I think it is so smart that within Marvel, you can create hyperlinks over sketches! It really gives you the experience as if you were using a real app.

TECHNICAL REQUIREMENTS
iPhone, iPad, Apple Watch, Apple TV and Android.

DEVICE TYPE
Mobile.
Tablet.

AVOID IF
I would not use Marvel when you are in a further stage of the innovation process where you need prototypes that should almost look like the end solution. There are other tools out there that will serve you better at that point.

TOOL 19: TOONLY
REVIEWED BY RODY VONK

OVERALL RATING
**** (4 out of 5 stars). The drag-and-drop functionality combined with the library of backgrounds and characters to easily create animated video's is what I love about Toonly. I would have given it 5 stars if there was a free trial version available.

www.toonly.com
WHAT?

Toonly is an animated explainer video creator that you can use to create simple videos to provide instruction on how to do something, marketing for a product or service, and more.

WHY?

Animated videos are more engaging and are perceived as being more valuable than text. I recommend using Toonly since it so is easy to use. It offers a library of scenes, backgrounds and figures. Literally, with one click, you select the movement you want for a specific character.

EASE OF USE FOR NEW PARTICIPANTS

As Toonly is not a tool for participants in an online workshop, the star rating doesn't apply.

EASE OF USE FOR FACILITATORS

Toonly is not a facilitator's tool, so the star rating doesn't apply.

FIT TO METHOD

This app is great for making a video presentation of a solution to get feedback. This is done in, for example, the FORTH innovation method, Design Sprint, Lean Sprint and Lean Startup. It is also a helpful tool for pretotyping.

FIT TO TECHNIQUES

From a facilitator's point of view, I like to use Toonly recording videos to explain tasks or to instruct participants to gain understanding in an engaging way.

KILLER FEATURE

There are tons of images and audio to choose from, so nothing feels canned or regurgitated.

TECHNICAL REQUIREMENTS

Desktop Windows or Mac.

DEVICE TYPE

Desktop.

AVOID IF

In all its simpleness, Toonly has a limited selection of scenes, backgrounds and characters (but everything has its price, and Toonly doesn't cost you a fortune). If you need specific scenes, backgrounds or objects, you can import them, but you may need to hire an expert to create the illustrations for you or find suitable ones in stock libraries.

TOOL 20: SPEECHELO
REVIEWED BY RODY VONK

OVERALL RATING

**** (4 out of 5 stars). Speechelo is a very user-friendly tool; I think some of the available voices sound a bit robotic, and the range of available voices in the standard version isn't large enough. Despite this, it works great!

WEBSITE

www.speechelo.com

WHAT?

Speechelo instantly transforms text into a video voiceover using AI technology. By simply typing or copying and pasting written text, the tool creates a realistic-sounding voiceover in seconds. What I like is that you can choose from different languages, so even if you are not a native speaker, you can create great voiceovers in the languages offered in Speechelo.

WHY?

Speechelo provides a voiceover service for individuals that do not feel comfortable recording their own voice, have maybe a poor microphone or when English is not your first language. For me, using a tool like this saves a lot of time since I don't have to record voiceovers myself for explanatory videos, for example.

EASE OF USE FOR NEW PARTICIPANTS

As Speechelo is not a tool for facilitation, the rating does not apply.

EASE OF USE FOR FACILITATORS

**** (4 out of 5 stars) Although Speechelo isn't a tool to use while facilitating, I find it very handy creating videos to explain certain process steps or templates you want participants to execute or use.

FIT TO METHOD

Speechelo can be used to communicate a message to stakeholders and customers. It is particularly well suited when using methods such as Design Sprints, FORTH, Pretotyping and Lean Startup methods to outline a concept, for example, when prototyping a solution.

FIT TO TECHNIQUES

I apply a tool like Speechelo for the following techniques for online: record videos to explain tasks or to instruct participants to aid understanding. Make videos to show results so people can see this asynchronous. Visualisation to provide structure to get a common understanding. Lightning Demos to aid the creative process.

KILLER FEATURE

It only takes 3 clicks to complete a voiceover of your video. To me, a tool like this should be as simple as possible, and this tool is!

TECHNICAL REQUIREMENTS

As Speechelo is web-based, it can be used with all browsers.

DEVICE TYPE

Mobile.
Tablet.
Desktop.

AVOID IF

I would not use Speechelo when you wish to record more authentic videos. Your own voice does still sound more human than an AI voice, but that is probably just a matter of time.

TOOL 21: CANVA
REVIEWED BY ANDREW CONSTABLE

OVERALL RATING

***** (5 out of 5 stars). Easy to use, my go-to design platform.

WEBSITE

www.canva.com

WHAT?

I use Canva as a design platform to create graphics, presentations, posters and other visual content in an easy-to-use format.

WHY?

I love Canva, as it allows me to create graphical presentations and other formats that can be used by innovation teams to communicate the message to customers or stakeholders. Due to its online nature, I have used this in a simultaneous manner with participants to allow greater visibility when creating graphical artefacts.

EASE OF USE FOR NEW PARTICIPANTS

***** (5 out of 5 stars)

EASE OF USE FOR FACILITATORS

**** (4 out of 5 stars)

FIT TO METHOD

As Canva is a graphical tool, I use it to create designs that can be used in customer experience decks, Design Sprints, FORTH and Pretotying, plus many more.

FIT TO TECHNIQUES

In Canva, I use it to apply the following 6 techniques for online innovation: working synchronous-asynchronous. Working together-alone. Lightning Demo. Visualisation. Set up templates to be filled by participants.

KILLER FEATURE

Canva has designs for every situation, ease of use and photo editing; it's one of my favourite go-to apps.

Canva is a browser-based platform that can be used across Mac, Windows, IOS and Android.

Mobile.

Tablet.

Desktop.

I tend to avoid Canva when I am in a low bandwidth area or country due to the high-performance requirements.

TOOL 22: GOOGLE FORMS
REVIEWED BY MARIA VITTORIA COLUCCI

**** (4 out of 5 stars). I use Google Forms to make personalised surveys in an easy and flexible way, even if some features are limited for non-Google-users.

www.docs.google.com/forms

I use Google Forms for conducting online surveys, getting feedback from testing and pretotyping. All the information gathered with the survey is automatically recorded in an Excel spreadsheet in real-time.

I like it as It's very easy to use. You can insert different types of questions, open multiple-answer fields, numerical fields, et cetera, and design an attractive graphic template. Then I have all the answers in a spreadsheet to elaborate and analyse them.

***** (5 out of 5 stars).

**** (4 out of 5 stars).

You can use it in all innovation methods that require gaining insights from customers.

I've used it in 2 techniques for online innovation: use a questionnaire/survey to gain insight in a quantitative form and feedback online from customers. Working synchronous-asynchronous, where participants can fill the forms asynchronous and then discuss the results synchronously.

Google Forms can also handle photos, videos and files, which you can include in your form, and it lets respondents upload files in their responses too.

You need to have a Google account to set up the questionnaire; in some cases, respondents must have a Google account too.

Tablet.

Desktop.

I avoid it when the security restriction of the organisations does not allow employees to connect to a Gmail account. For quick answers and polls, you also have easier tools.

5. TOOLS TO MAKE WORKSHOPS INTERACTIVE

TOOL 23: MENTIMETER
REVIEWED BY MARIA VITTORIA COLUCCI

***** (5 out of 5 stars). Mentimeter is great for my audience engagement, both synchronous, as it is super easy and smart and asynchronous. I display the results in many appealing ways.

WEBSITE

www.mentimeter.com

WHAT?

I use Mentimeter to create live polls, quizzes, word clouds, Q&As to get real-time input and to engage my team. I create my poll then share a QR code or a link with the team. and as they answer, I can visualise and share the results with them in different formats as tag clouds, charts, matrixes.

WHY?

I use it to add interactivity and keep the audience engaged since online feeling more distant than being in the same physical room. It's extremely easy to use. During a meeting, I share the QR code, and participants can answer in a few seconds with their phones. I share the screen to show the results in real-time.

EASE OF USE FOR NEW PARTICIPANTS

***** (5 out of 5 stars).

EASE OF USE FOR FACILITATORS

***** (5 out of 5 stars).

FIT TO METHOD

I use it with any method to make my sessions more engaging.

FIT TO TECHNIQUES

I use Mentimeter to apply the following techniques for online innovation: Working synchronous-asynchronous as you can use it during the workshop or send the link or QR code and ask to answer, using polls and questionnaires.

KILLER FEATURE

It has a smooth mobile integration through the use of QR-codes, and it gives a surprise effect to your audience.

TECHNICAL REQUIREMENTS

Mentimeter recommends using a desktop computer for the presenter and handheld devices for the voters. For the presenter, most web browsers will work. The audience might use Android, Windows Phone, iOS, or Chromebook.

DEVICE TYPE

Mobile.
Tablet.
Desktop.

AVOID IF

Be careful when you want to integrate it with PowerPoint, as it doesn't work properly.

TOOL 24: TSCHECK.IN
REVIEWED BY RODY VONK

OVERALL RATING

**** (4 out of 5 stars). What I like about Tscheck.in is that its functionality is limited to what it was meant to do: provide you with check-in - and check-out questions for your sessions. It would have been nice if the tool contained more questions or if you could add your own.

WEBSITE

www.tscheck.in

WHAT?

Tscheck.in is a website with a database of checking-in and checking-out questions that appear on your screen randomly. I like this tool because of its simplicity. It is no more than a question on your screen.

WHY?

Use tscheck.in starting or ending a workshop. By asking questions unrelated to the topic you are working on, you improve the connection between participants, which makes your online workshop more personal. Having these questions at hand in an online tool is what makes it so helpful for me as a facilitator.

EASE OF USE FOR NEW PARTICIPANTS

***** (5 out of 5 stars). Participants have to do nothing on their computer. They only have to answer the question on the screen (which can sometimes be a bit hard, to be honest...).

EASE OF USE FOR FACILITATORS

***** (5 out of 5 stars). Also, here a 5 star rating, since as a facilitator, you only have to go to the website and click on a button to go to the next question. It is as simple as that!

FIT TO METHOD

You can use it for any session for every method.

FIT TO TECHNIQUES

It's for synchronous work, not related to a specific technique.

KILLER FEATURE

The killer feature is the tool itself since it is as simple as showing a question on the screen, nothing more.

TECHNICAL REQUIREMENTS

You can use it on any platform.

DEVICE TYPE

Mobile.
Tablet.
Desktop.

AVOID IF

When you are running a short session (about 60 to 90 minutes) where you need to get to specific objectives, you may run out of time if you are asking participants to answer questions that are not related to the topic of your session.

TOOL 25: KAHOOT
REVIEWED BY RODY VONK

OVERALL RATING

***** (5 out of 5 stars). I like the combination of game-based learning and the (new) feature to import your slides which makes Kahoot a powerful tool for creating engagement with your audience while presenting your content, all with one tool.

WEBSITE

www.kahoot.com

WHAT?

If you want - just like me - to make your online workshops more interactive, use Kahoot. It is an online game-based system to help educate participants using quiz-based learning. It allows me to create a fun and social learning experience for participants. At the time of writing, Kahoot was announcing the option to create full presentations with slides or even import your slides from other software to build interactive presentations on one platform.

WHY?

I like to use it for fun and to create interactivity and engagement, but a Kahoot quiz can also be a great way to check the knowledge of participants before you start your workshop to help you to avoid making it too simplistic or too complicated for your audience.

EASE OF USE FOR NEW PARTICIPANTS

***** (5 out of 5 stars). Kahoot gets 5 stars since it is very easy to join by just entering a code. In a quiz, participants just have to click on the colour-coded answer on their mobile device.

EASE OF USE FOR FACILITATORS

**** (4 out of 5 stars) For facilitators, it requires some effort to prepare polls and quizzes. It is quite simple to do, but you will need some preparation time.

I use Kahoot for any moment in a session or workshop (which can be part of any method) that I want to make more engaging.

Since the tool is for participants to interact live, use Kahoot for synchronous work. The usage is not related to a specific technique.

What I really like is the ability to search for user-made Kahoots. I find it very inspiring to see what others have created.

It works on most devices, thanks to being cloud-based. You can create your Kahoot on a desktop computer or laptop; participants can use their smartphone for answering questions.

Mobile.
Tablet.
Desktop.

Kahoot is simple to use. In online sessions, though, it requires that participants use 2 devices or 2 screens on a device (one for seeing the questions and another one for clicking on the answer of their choice). For less tech-savvy people, this may be a bit complicated.

CONTENTS

OVERVIEW 10 ONLINE INNOVATION METHODS

You find an overview of 10 innovation methods you can use for your online innovation workshops – sprints or – projects. Each method was explained in depth in chapters 7-10. Section 1 covers 3 innovation methods for short online workshops like Problem Framing, the Customer Experience Deck, and the Lightning Decision Jam. Section 2 presents 2 methods for online innovation sprints of a week or less, like Prototyping and the Design Sprint. Section 3 describes 5 methods for online innovation projects in which we feature the FORTH innovation method, Lean Startup, the Business Model Canvas methodology, the Purpose Launchpad, the Circular Design Process.

1. 3 INNOVATION METHODS FOR SHORT ONLINE WORKSHOPS

METHOD 1: PROBLEM FRAMING

WEBSITE

www.designsprint.academy/about-problem-framing

WHAT?

Problem Framing is a design thinking method to define the actual and most relevant problem. More on Problem Framing you find in chapter 7.

WHY?

You use it because most of the time, the so-called problem is not the actual problem, or it is not well precise enough described.

HOW?

You start with the problem discovery to find out what problems there are and categorise them. Afterwards, you focus on understanding the context of the relevant problem and the relevant user. Then the experience of the most

relevant user will be defined. And finally, the problem statement will be drafted.

WHICH TECHNIQUES?

In a Problem Framing process, all of the online innovation techniques besides the lightning demos can be applied.

WHICH TOOLS?

You can use whiteboards like Miro, Mural or Klaxoon and videoconference tools like Zoom, MS Teams or Butter to stay visually connected. For check-in and check-out in the sessions, Tscheck.in works fine.

DURATION?

90 minutes - 6 hours.

RESULTS?

The outcome is a clearly defined problem statement at the end of the problem space, which is the ideal start for the HMW (how-might-we) question and the ideation phase.

PITFALL?

The pitfall is that everyone is thinking already in solutions.

TIP?

Most of the time, the real problem hides behind the stated problem, so take your time to find the real problem.

METHOD 2: THE CUSTOMER EXPERIENCE DECK

WEBSITE

www.ridersandelephants.com/thecustomerexperiencedeck

WHAT?

The Customer Experience Deck (CXD) was created in 2019 by Jeremy Dean to "help teams build a shared understanding about their customers." It's a simple nine-step process to build a shared vision of who your customers are and to start innovating their customer experience. More on CXD, you find in chapter 7.

WHY?

You apply it to create a shared understanding of the client's needs and get insights on the critical elements of the desired customer experience and how you can work together to shape it. You can integrate it in other more structured methodologies as the FORTH innovation method in the Observe & Learn phase before the Customer Friction interview. Or in the Business Model Canvas in the customer relationship section.

It is a process of 9 micro-steps that lead a group, after identifying a customer segment they want to work with, to understand the customers' desired and undesired feelings.
In the first seven steps, participants individually address how we want our customers to feel and not feel. Then, they share the results with the group and vote for the top 5.
In the last two steps, they start working together, identifying ways to detect the feelings, understand the causes, and take actions.

The techniques you can apply for a CXD workshop are working together-alone choosing the feelings. Voting anonymous for the top 5. Use Bulk mode to write ideas on post-its in the action phase. Using the chat function. Working in Break Out Rooms to discuss the outputs.

For a CXD workshop, you can use any online collaboration platform, although we would prefer Miro or Mural to structure the online process. It will help if you use a video conferencing tool with break out rooms. We've used Zoom but also Microsoft Teams or Butter to get a good experience. For example, all the other tools for preparation & instruction, SessionLab to create and share the program and the tools to make sessions interactive are of great value for a CXD session.

A CXD workshop can take from 2 to 3 hours, depending on the size of the group.

The outputs are the top five desired and not desired customer feelings shared by the group. Plus, a canvas is drafted with actions to create this experience. It can be a great starting point for developing innovation based on the client's needs.

CXD is a method of gaining insights into your customers, but on its own, it is unlikely to trigger a process of innovation.

Collect customer experiences directly, using CXD to conduct interviews or focus groups with potential clients so that the output will be much more meaningful.

METHOD 3: THE LIGHTNING DECISION JAM

www.ajsmart.com/ldj

The Lightning Decision Jam (LDJ) is an exercise to generate solutions for a problem with a product or service, try to come up with new product features, or solve a problem within a team or process, any problem you can imagine. It helps to identify problems and to decide on the first steps to take to solve them. Whether you work in a 5-person company or a multinational, this exercise is useful in any workshop where you want to put an end to useless, unstructured discussions. More on LDJ, you find in chapter 8.

Use the Lightning Decision Jam to quickly identify problems the participants have on their minds and define the most important problem to solve quickly.
The highly structured process is aimed at coming up with a

lot of solutions fast (very creative ones or those that may have been overlooked). The process also helps find the best solution based on how much impact the participants think a solution will have and the effort they expect it to take to implement it. After identifying the best solution, the workshop ends with a shortlist of clear actions to test the solution, with names of those responsible for taking those steps and a timeline for executing them.

HOW?

Without discussion, all participants take a couple of minutes - in silence - to write down the problems and challenges they can think of. After that, everyone votes individually for the most important challenges they think should be solved. The problem with the most votes will be used to generate solutions in silent brainstorm. By doing this in silence, discussions are avoided, and everyone can contribute. Go for quantity over quality. Solutions can be judged and refined later. Again, by voting, the solutions are prioritised. Based on how much impact a solution is expected to have and the effort it would take to realise it, the solutions are compared. This determines which solutions should be tried out first. Then a list of actions is made with a timeline to start testing the solutions chosen.

WHICH TECHNIQUES?

The technique 'working together alone' is key in this process, just like 'voting anonymous'. This is key to prevent discussions from happening. The 'bulk mode' in the tool Miro helps participants write ideas quickly without being distracted by what other participants are writing.

WHICH TOOLS?

Microsoft Teams, Zoom or Butter for videoconferencing (no breakout rooms needed) can be used. Use Miro or Mural for writing post-its. Slack is helpful for follow-up with the team involved in the execution phase of solutions.

DURATION?

60 to 90 minutes.

RESULTS?

There are 4 outputs. 1. An overview of prioritised problems and actionable solutions from a team/colleagues in a short period of time. 2. Decisions made on which solution(s) to test first. 3. Actionable steps to start testing the chosen solutions. 4. A list of next best solutions to try if the top prioritised solution doesn't work in the test phase.

PITFALL?

The effectiveness of the LDJ is based on no discussion. As a facilitator, it can be challenging to keep the team from preventing to discuss.

TIP?

Manage expectations beforehand and explain why there is no room for discussion. Be strict on the timings per step in the LDJ to keep the speed up (and prevent discussions).

2. 2 METHODS FOR ONLINE INNOVATION SPRINTS

METHOD 4: PRETOTYPING

WEBSITE

www.pretotyping.org

WHAT?

Pretotype is a neologism created by Alberto Savoia to indicate, in the process of innovation, the realisation of a fake product-service we want to realise that simulates (pretend) and precedes the real one. The aim is to validate quickly and economically whether the idea we have had is worth pursuing. There are different types of pretotyping techniques, depending on the product, service, or target audience. More on Pretotyping, you find in chapter 7.

WHY?

To quote the inventor of Pretotyping: "to make sure you are building the right it before you build it right." It aims to see if the market is interested in a product or service before investing too much time and resources in developing an innovative idea.

HOW?

There are five steps in Pretotyping:
1. Isolate the key assumption and define what the premises of the new idea are.
2. Draft a concrete, verifiable market engagement hypothesis by clear and quantifiable assumptions
 3. HypoZoom: think about how you might test locally, quickly, and inexpensively while staying true.
4. Choose a type of pretotype, plan it, test it. In this phase, we choose the best technique to validate the data and build the pretotype, costs, and time.
5. Analyse the data, make tweaks, repeat the process.

WHICH TECHNIQUES?

In the pretotype method, you can use all the techniques suited to work and co-create together. Visualisation techniques are more critical than others to figure out how the product/service will appear.

WHICH TOOLS?

In online prototyping, you can use all the prototyping and testing tools mentioned above, plus Invision, Proto.io, YouTube. Besides, you can use online collaboration boards, such as Miro, Mural, for their flexibility.

DURATION?

Pretotyping is used to obtain the rapid validation of one's hypotheses. The benchmark for pretotyping and getting high-quality data is the "Hour-To-Data," which gives a good idea of the time frame.

RESULTS?

The pretotyping outputs are significant YODA, Your Own Data, that validate or not the market engagement hypothesis. You can interpret this data based on a meter divided into five success categories from very unlikely (10%) - to very likely (90% success).

PITFALL?

It is a quick and easy method, and the risk is to trivialise it. Be careful in choosing the right market on which to test the pretotype and in analysing the data!

TIP?

Start testing immediately; do not make the phase of choosing and implementing the pretotype last too long. Share the data analysis and interpretation with two people you trust who are not yet as in love with the innovative idea as you are. It will help you to be less biased.

METHOD 5: THE DESIGN SPRINT

WEBSITE

www.gv.com/sprint/

WHAT?

The sprint is a five-day process for answering critical business questions through design, prototyping, and customers' testing ideas. More on the Design Sprint you find in chapter 9.

WHY?

Working together in a sprint, you can shortcut the endless debate cycle and compress months into a single week.

HOW?

A Design Sprint is a time-constrained, five-phase process that uses design thinking with the aim of reducing the risk when bringing a new product, service or feature to the market.

WHICH TECHNIQUES?

In a Design Sprint, we combine design thinking and rapid prototyping. We use most of the ten online innovation techniques throughout the 5-day process.

WHICH TOOLS?

In the design sprint, we use Miro or Mural as our digital whiteboard. We use Zoom or Google Meet for video conferencing and integrate other tools for booking the sessions and recording notes.

DURATION?

The Design Sprint can be run between 3 to 5 days, depending on the variation used. In this book, we explain the 5-day-process.

RESULTS?

The outputs of a Design Sprint are a validated prototype following customer useability tests.

PITFALL?

The pitfall is cutting out the steps in the recipe. Only experienced sprinters should change this; otherwise, there is a risk of losing the process's effectiveness.

TIP?

Look to have a second facilitator in the sessions who understands the process. They can help with running the sessions and running the technical elements.

3. 5 METHODS FOR ONLINE INNOVATION PROJECTS

METHOD 6: THE FORTH INNOVATION METHOD

WEBSITE

www.forth-innovation.com

WHAT?

The FORTH innovation methodology was introduced in 2005 by its founder and author of this book, Gijs van Wulfen. It is a structured methodology to start innovation from challenge to new business cases with a diverse internal group of participants. It's applied worldwide in every sector you can imagine with great success. It was brought online in 2020 very successfully. The online FORTH process consists of a series of 23 short workshops in 12 weeks. With FORTH, you can generate 100% online new evolutionary – and/or revolutionary products, services, business models, experiences, and processes. More on the FORTH innovation method you find in chapter 10.

WHY?

FORTH has been scientifically proven to more than double the output of your innovation stage-gate process. The internal support for the new business cases generated is huge as both the innovation team as the senior managers are taking part in the online expedition.

HOW?

FORTH is an acronym and stands for Full steam ahead, Observe and Learn, Raise ideas, Test ideas and Homecoming. In Full Steam Ahead, you draft together with your management the innovation assignment, select the team and kick-off the project. In Observe & Learn, you discover innovation opportunities and identify customer insights online. On the island of Raise Ideas, you create more than 1000 ideas on a collaboration platform like Miro and work out the best 15 into new concepts. On Test Ideas, you get feedback on all concepts from customers, improve them online and select the top 5 improved concepts. They will be worked out online as mini new business cases for decision making by your top management.

In an online FORTH innovation project, all 10 of the online innovation techniques are applied, which is one reason why the methodology gets great results digitally.

We like to work with Miro as our preferred online collaboration platform in FORTH, although some FORTH facilitators also get great results with Trello. We use as a video conferencing tool Zoom, of course, but also Microsoft Teams or Webex. And we are fans of Butter. All the other tools for preparation & instruction, prototyping & testing and the tools to make sessions interactive are of great value to the FORTH innovation process.

A full FORTH innovation project of 23 shorter workshops would take you around 12 weeks.

The outputs of the FORTH innovation process are 3-5 mini new business cases for your innovation challenge, which will have great support among both the participants of the expedition as the top managers. Next to that, a very positive side-effect of a FORTH expedition is that the journey is so immersive that it will change their mindset into an innovative one. FORTH is known for its ability to kick-start a culture for innovation in organisations applying the method.

With 23 short workshops in 12 weeks, the FORTH methodology is an intensive process that requires dedication and time. Although all the workshops are planned, there is also some asynchronous work to be done. And the main pitfall is that

the participants are completely booked with back-to-back meetings that there hardly is any time left, except at night....

FORTH is "the royal way" to start innovation online. Apply it when innovation is relevant, and a big jump has to be made by your organisation.

METHOD 7: LEAN STARTUP

www.theleanstartup.com

Lean Startup is a methodology for developing businesses and products. The Lean Startup method was first proposed in 2008 by Eric Ries, using his personal experiences adapting lean management and customer development principles to high-tech startups. The method combines experimentation, iterative product releases, and validated learning. The Lean Startup method seeks to increase value-producing practices during the earliest phases of a company to have a better chance of success. It emphasises customer feedback over intuition and flexibility over planning. More on Lean Startup, you find in chapter 7.

The Lean Startup methodology aims to shorten product development cycles and rapidly discover if a proposed business model is viable.

Unlike typical yearlong product development cycles, Lean Startup eliminates wasted time and resources by developing the product iteratively and incrementally. Developing a minimum viable product (MVP), the "version of a new product which allows a team to collect the maximum amount of validated learning about customers with the least effort", plays a crucial role in Lean Startup.

In an online Lean Startup project, all 10 of the online innovation techniques could be applied, depending on your preferred tools.

For a Lean Startup innovation project, you can use any online collaboration platform, although we would prefer Miro or Mural. We use the videoconferencing tool Zoom, but also Microsoft Teams or Webex. And we are fans of Butter. All the other tools for preparation & instruction, prototyping & testing and the tools to make sessions interactive are of great value to a Lean Startup process.

"The Lean Startup method is not about cost; it's about speed" — Eric Ries. But how long it takes from idea to successful business will vary greatly among sectors.

A tested and validated MVP (minimum viable product) and business model would be the methodology's first deliverable.

In Lean Startup, you test hypotheses and then pivot your idea accordingly. But when you try as many directions as possible and see what holds, it might create chaos that is very hard to deal with: for you, for the development team, for management, and eventually for even for your customers.

At the core of Lean Startup is making your assumptions explicit and adding a second tip is to talk to your potential users as soon as possible to get real customer insights of real users.

METHOD 8: THE BUSINESS MODEL CANVAS

www.strategyzer.com/Canvas/business-model-Canvas

Alexander Osterwalder developed the Business Model Canvas in the 2000s. It is a methodology to innovate the business model of a product, service or organisation. More on the Business Model Canvas, you find in chapter 7.

The Business model Canvas helps you create innovative business models to develop new ideas or new markets.

There are five steps to define a new business model:
1. Mobilise; where you prepare, create awareness, and the momentum. Define the team.
2. Understand; where you research and analyse elements needed for the business model design.
3. Design; where you transform the ideas into a prototype or, better, a pretotype to validate your ideas.
4. Implement, where you put into practice what you've designed.
5. Manage; where you adapt and modify the business model in response to market reaction.

In an online Business Model Canvas, you can apply all 10 of the online innovation techniques.

You can use any online collaboration platform. Besides, on Boardle, you can find a Mural template of the canvas ready to use. It will help if you have a video conferencing tool with break out rooms, like Zoom, Microsoft Teams or Butter, to get a fresh experience. All the other tools for preparation & instruction, SessionLab to share the program, and the tools to make sessions interactive are of great value.

There's no fixed duration. It may take you a few hours, to a few days, to a few weeks, when you iterate the process.

The business model outputs are the clear and shared definition in a canvas of the nine essential elements of the new business model, plus pretotypes or prototypes to be tested, and clear and defined actions on how to proceed.

PITFALL?

It is a very well-known and articulated method. The main pitfalls could be limiting yourself to a Business Model Canvas that remains unrealised or making the structured analysis phase last too long.

TIP?

Draft the canvas with a reasonably well-diversified team. Use an iterative process: realise it completely and then repeat the process.

METHOD 9: THE PURPOSE LAUNCHPAD

WEBSITE

www.purposelaunchpad.com

WHAT?

Purpose Launchpad is an open methodology and a mindset to generate and evolve early-stage initiatives into purpose-driven organisations to make a massive impact. It was developed by Francisco Palao, with the input of +150 contributors around the world. More on Purpose Launchpad you find in chapter 7.

WHY?

Purpose Launchpad was designed to help you build purpose-driven organisations and evolve your mindset to become explorers who will discover the right path to create a new organisation, business, product, or service that will positively impact the world.

HOW?

The Purpose Launchpad has eight key areas. The way you develop these key areas is by making some progress in the first area (Purpose) and then making some more progress in the following area (Customer). The iterative process has a

specific order (Purpose, People, Customer, Abundance, Sustainability, Processes, Product and Metrics) since the eight areas are connected in a way that a certain area always needs some previous evolution of the other ones. Purpose Launchpad is a meta-methodology, using other methodologies like Design Thinking, Business Model Canvas and Lean Startup.

WHICH TECHNIQUES?

In an online Purpose Launchpad, all 10 of the online innovation techniques could be applied.

WHICH TOOLS?

Purpose Launchpad is a meta-methodology; many of the online tools presented in this book could be applied.

DURATION?

Purpose launchpad is an ongoing process. The heart of Purpose Launchpad is a sprint, a time-box of one, two or more weeks (depending on the level of evolution of the initiative) during which the team makes real progress evolving along the Purpose Launchpad Axes.

RESULTS?

The iterative process on each of the eight key areas has three evolution levels (Exploration, Evaluation and Impact). On a polar graph, you can spot the evolution status of all the Purpose Launchpad Axes.

PITFALL?

The pitfall might be that it's an iterative, ongoing process, which, of course, might stop at some point in time without urgency or priority.

TIP?

While implementing the Purpose Launchpad, you not only evolve your initiative alone but also your team's people. And that's the most powerful evolution.

METHOD 10: THE CIRCULAR DESIGN PROCESS

www.circulardesignguide.com

WHAT?

The Circular Design Process is a design thinking process specialising in creating circular designed products, services, and business models, originated by IDEO and the Ellen Macarthur Foundation. More on the Circular Design Process, you find in chapter 7.

WHY?

The economy has reached a point where we have to think differently. The circular design process gives you all tools on hand that help you innovate new products and services that are more sustainable and lead us in the direction of a circular economy.

HOW?

The process provides well-known methods modified for a circular design for all four stages (Understand, Define, Make and Release) and are ready for use.

WHICH TECHNIQUES?

In an online Circular Design Process, all 10 of the online innovation techniques could be applied.

WHICH TOOLS?

Digital whiteboards (Miro, Mural, Klaxoon) work fine. And to get connected Zoom, Microsoft Teams or Butter make sense. Loom and SessionLab help you prepare the sessions, and with Canva and Google Forms, you can prepare prototypes for simple tests.

DURATION?

It may last from a couple of days to a month.

RESULTS?

The output is circular products, services and business models.

PITFALL?

The Circular Design Process helps you get in the right circular direction, but the mindset and the focus of the participants have to be already on sustainability.

TIP?

There are a lot of great methods in the guide. Take your time and pick the ones that suit your process best. Make sure you, as a facilitator, understand the why? And for what? of each method.

ABOUT THE AUTHORS

Gijs van Wulfen

Gijs (Dutch; 1960) is a worldwide authority in innovation and design thinking. He worked as a marketer in the fast-moving consumer goods industry, and as a strategy consultant before founding the FORTH innovation method in 2005. FORTH is a scientifically proven methodology for the start of innovation, which is implemented on six continents. In 2020 the methodology was taken 100% online with great success.

His third book on innovation, 'The Innovation Maze', was crowned as Management Book of the Year. As a LinkedIn Influencer, he has 330,000 followers.

From Crete, the island where he lives, he inspires people all over the world to be amazing innovators in a practical way with his keynotes, books, webinars, Clubhouse audio-events, and YouTube videos. Recently Gijs is one of the authors of the Future-Fit Manifesto, the successor of the Agile Manifesto of 20 years ago.

www.gijsvanwulfen.com
gijs@gijsvanwulfen.com

Maria Vittoria Colucci

Maria Vittoria is Italian, living in Milan. In her job, she supports leaders and organisations to innovate and to build a culture for innovation. Her expertise is in innovation methods and remote facilitation, as well as in cultural and leadership innovation.

She is a business economist who started her career as a marketing consultant, then became fascinated by design thinking and human experience (HX). Having graduated in Economics, earning an MBA, becoming a FORTH Innovation Master facilitator, Executive Counsellor, and Coach, she likes to combine and merge knowledge and practices to promote innovation, change, and well-being.

She's been working for more than 25 years in management consulting companies with major clients across different industries. In 2015 she co-founded Evidentia B-Corp, a consulting agency based in Milan (www.evidentia.it). She co-edited the Italian version of the book 'The Innovation Expedition' of Gijs van Wulfen.

In the 100% online switch she is working to give a human touch to the online experience.

https://www.linkedin.com/in/mariavittoriaco-lucci/
mariavittoria.colucci@evidentia.it